A SERIOUS DISAPPOINTMENT

A SERIOUS DISAPPOINTMENT

The Battle of Aubers Ridge, 1915
and the subsequent munitions scandal

by

ADRIAN BRISTOW

LEO COOPER
LONDON

First published in Great Britain in hardback in 1995 by
LEO COOPER
190 Shaftesbury Avenue, London WC2H 8JL
an imprint of
Pen & Sword Books Ltd,
47 Church Street,
Barnsley, South Yorkshire S70 2AS

A CIP record for this book is available from the British Library

ISBN 0 85052 462 8

Typeset by Phoenix Typesetting, Ilkley, West Yorkshire
Printed by Redwood Books Ltd., Trowbridge, Wilsthire

To the memory of Private J. H. Bristow

(1896–1986)

4th Battalion Royal Sussex Regiment

'Such an offensive, before an adequate supply of guns and high-explosive shell can be provided, would only result in heavy casualties and the capture of another turnip field.'

LORD KITCHENER, June, 1915
on a future offensive in France

Contents

Sources

It is curious that no detailed narrative of this one-day offensive has been written other than the account contained in the Official History. Little is known or remembered about the actual battle; its name awakes no melancholy echoes like Loos, the Somme or Ypres, echoes that still go ringing down through the generations. I think there are probably three main reasons:

It was brief. Although the offensive was planned to last for several days, severe losses forced Haig to abandon it after one day. It was quickly followed a week later by the resumed offensive at Festubert and the military establishment gratefully allowed an unmitigated disaster to slide, if not into oblivion, at least into obscurity.

Aubers Ridge formed part of a major allied offensive in which the French were by far the dominant partner. It was therefore unlike Neuve Chapelle, for example, which was an independent attack undertaken solely by the British Expeditionary Force (BEF).

The offensive was launched right at the end of the Second Battle of Ypres and soon after the landings at Gallipoli on which, not unnaturally, the newspapers had been concentrating. It thus received very little immediate press coverage – though the aftermath of the battle did.

Eventually the failed offensive was officially designated as the Battle of Aubers, but to all those who were involved it was always known as 'Aubers Ridge'. Because it took place near Neuve Chapelle and was followed soon afterwards by the attack at Festubert, it has been variously and confusingly referred to on maps and in accounts as the Battle of Neuve Chapelle, the Battle of Festubert and the Battle of Fromelles. The Germans have always called it *Das Gefecht bei Fromelles* – the Fight at Fromelles – possibly because their troops were more strenuously involved in beating off the northern part of the two-pronged attack than they were in dealing with the assault by I Corps and the Indian Corps to the south.

British Sources

Like all writers on the battles of the Great War, I am indebted to the Official History, edited by Sir James Edmonds. The two chapters on Aubers Ridge contain a straightforward account of the battle, though some phases of the fighting are dealt with in much more detail than others. The only other account of the battle is contained in Alan Clark's interesting book *The Donkeys*. Here it forms part of his study of the British offensives in 1915, excluding Festubert; his theme is the destruction of the original divisions of the BEF and the competence, or otherwise, of the senior Army Commanders. I hope I have built further upon his consideration of this particular battle.

For my book I have consulted a number of divisional and regimental histories. The history of the 8th Division and that of the Indian Corps in France (see Select Bibliography) proved most useful; strangely, there appears to be no history of the 1st Division. I have examined the war diaries of all those battalions involved in the action, and specimens of the diaries, which may be unfamiliar to the general reader, are included in the appendices. I have also found a number of eyewitness accounts contained in letters, books and diaries, and I have drawn freely upon these.

German Sources

Unfortunately, the archives of the Imperial German Army were almost completely destroyed in 1945. However, I have consulted the fairly detailed histories of the 55th and 57th Regiments of the 14th Division which were published in 1928 and 1936 respectively. Luckily the archives of the Bavarian Army survived more or less intact at Munich and I have been able to draw upon the battalion war diaries of the 16th Reserve Infantry Regiment (6th Bavarian Reserve Division) and on the regimental history.

My warmest thanks are due to Dr Fleischer of the Bundesarchiv–Militärarchiv at Freiburg and to Dr A. Fuchs, Archivdirector of the Bayerisches Hauptstaatsarchiv-Kriegsarchiv at Munich, for their help in providing photocopies of relevant material.

Acknowledgments

I am indebted to the following for permission to quote extracts from copyright material:

Constable & Co. Ltd for *1914* by Sir John French and *With the Indians in France* by General Sir James Willcocks; A.P. Watt Ltd on behalf of the Trustees of the Robert Graves Copyright Trust for *Goodbye To All That* by Robert Graves; Messrs Peters, Fraser and Dunlop for 'Trench Nomenclature' by Edmund Blunden; the Peter Liddle Collection; Times Newspapers Ltd for extracts from the issues for 12 and 14 May, 1915; Mrs Elizabeth M. Roy for extracts from the papers of her late husband, Captain W.H. Roy; Mr D. Anderton for extracts from the papers of his father, Private E.H. Anderton; the Society of Authors as the literary representatives of the Estate of John Masefield for *The Old Front Line*; Herbert Jenkins Ltd for *Before the Charge* by Patrick MacGill; H.F. & G. Witherby Ltd for *Roundabout* by Viscount Buckmaster; Hart-Davis, MacGibbon Ltd for *Goughie* by Anthony Farrar-Hockley.

I should also like to thank the Trustees of the Royal Sussex Regiment Museum Trust and the County Archivist of the West Sussex Record Office for permission to quote from the War Diaries of the 2nd Bn and the 1/5th Bn Royal Sussex Regiment (West Sussex Record Office RSR MS 2/57 and MS 4/64 respectively); the Trustees of the Gurkha Museum Trust for permission to include the War Diary of the 2/2nd Gurkhas for 9 May, 1915; the Regimental Museum Staff of the Duke of Edinburgh's Royal Regiment (Berkshire and Wiltshire), the Black Watch and the Worcestershire Regiment and the Sherwood Foresters. Every effort has been made to contact the copyright holders of all the passages quoted in the book.

Finally, I should like to thank the staff of the Imperial War Museum and Peter Liddle of the Peter Liddle Collection for their generous assistance.

Genesis

I grew up in the 'thirties in that part of south-east London bordering the Thames which embraces Woolwich, Plumstead and Shooters Hill. Woolwich has a certain historic importance. Its Royal Dockyard, established by the Tudors, was the first and, for centuries, the principal dockyard in the country. The *Great Harry* was built there in 1562 and the *Royal George* in 1751, but shipbuilding ceased in 1869 and the Dockyard became a military store depot. A little way downstream from the Dockyard lay the vast expanse of the Royal Arsenal. The Arsenal grew gradually from Elizabethan times, developed rapidly in the early nineteenth century and reached its peak in terms of output and employees during the Great War. Guns, shells, torpedoes, small-arms ammunition and wagons were produced in huge quantities in its workshops to fuel the fighting on the Western Front.

I slowly became aware that I was living in a military centre of some distinction. Woolwich was the headquarters of the Royal Regiment of Artillery and the town was dominated by its vast barracks, parade ground, playing fields and hospital. The RA possessed its own garrison church, theatre, museum (the famous Rotunda) and a variety of the specialist buildings needed for men, horses and guns, spilling out across Woolwich Common. Woolwich also contained the Royal Military Academy, cousin to that at Sandhurst, responsible for the training of engineering and artillery officers.

Until I was five we lived near the Academy in Herbert Road and it was not until many years later (I am embarrassed to say how many) that I realized it had been named after Sidney Herbert, Secretary for War during the Crimean War and champion of Florence Nightingale. Many of the streets in the town were named after the military heroes of the Napoleonic and Crimean Wars, so as a child I walked unthinkingly along Wellington Street, Hill Street, Nightingale Place, Beresford Square and Raglan, Cambridge, and Paget Roads. Other roads were given specific military titles: Ordnance Road, Academy Road and Artillery Place. In fact, a street map of Woolwich is a useful primer of military history.

One of our favourite walks for several years was along Herbert Road, past the Royal Military Academy with its long, castellated façade, complete with miniature White Tower, and on to Woolwich Common. A little farther on appeared the immense sweep of the parade ground with the artillery barracks stretching endlessly along one side into the middle distance. On the right stood St George's Garrison Church, where the names of those of the regiment who had won the Victoria Cross were recorded on the walls of the apse. On fine Sunday mornings my father often took me down to the barracks to watch the march past after the church parade. This free spectacle was a popular diversion in the district at weekends. But for me the most enjoyable spectacle, the highlight of my year, was the Military Tattoo held in the Stadium on Woolwich Common. It was reckoned to be second only to the Aldershot Tattoo itself. I found the noise, colour and action all profoundly exciting, especially the grand finale. As darkness fell the Tattoo would culminate in the staging of some particular incident or assault from an eighteenth or nineteenth century battle.

If these were special occasions, I could hardly fail to be aware of the military activity all around me. The town was full of khaki, especially at weekends. During the day there were squads drilling on the parade ground, squads being marched off across the Common and squads moving at the double across the playing fields. To add further colour, convalescent patients from the Herbert Hospital, the military hospital built in 1861, dawdled round the streets in their hospital blues, white shirts and red ties.

Against this background, my childhood memories are suffused by talk of the army and the Great War of 1914–18 – and its legacies. These were not far to seek. Even as a small boy I was conscious of the number of men one saw who had been blinded in the war, of men with one leg or no legs, of crutches and wheelchairs, and of empty sleeves tucked into jacket pockets. In Beresford Square and Powis Street I often saw small groups of shabby ex-servicemen, medals pinned to their jackets or cast-off overcoats, drifting along the gutter, playing popular tunes of the day and the old songs of the trenches.

Domestic influences were powerful and insistent. My father was born and brought up in East Grinstead in Sussex and he had joined the Territorials in 1913. Most of his friends in the town did the same. When war was declared in August, 1914, he was mustered into the 4th Battalion (TF) of the Royal Sussex Regiment. I remember him telling me that he found virtually all his friends had been drafted into the 2nd Battalion with the regulars. They found themselves in France with the 2nd Brigade of the 1st Division and took part in the Battle of Aubers Ridge on 9 May, 1915, accompanied by the 5th Battalion (TF). The 2nd Battalion, especially, suffered grievous losses. Hardly any of my father's friends survived this battle; none survived the war. The casualties suffered by the 2nd and 5th Battalions led to Sunday, 9 May being commemorated by the Regiment as a Day of Remembrance for all those who were killed during the 1914–1918 War.

Meanwhile my father went with the 4th Battalion to Gallipoli as part of the 53rd (Welsh) Division and landed at Suvla Bay. Like thousands of others he was struck down with dysentery and was evacuated to Malta, where he spent some months convalescing. Later he rejoined the Battalion in Egypt and was attached to the 160th Brigade Light Trench Mortar Battery. The 53rd Division, now part of Allenby's army, advanced against the Turks from El Arish (First and Second Battles of Gaza) to Beersheba and on to Jerusalem and Jericho. After Allenby's victory the 1/4th Royal Sussex embarked for France in June, 1918. Fortunately, my father was not among them; he was transferred to the 1/7th Royal Welsh Fusiliers* who needed trained and experienced soldiers. Thus he missed the last offensives on the Western Front and eventually returned home in 1919 without a scratch, and still a private.

When my father met relatives or friends who had been in the war the air became heavy with reminiscence. I used to sit in a corner, pretending to read, as stories of adventure in the trenches and experiences in France and the Holy Land were recalled and told yet again. Foreign countries and their inhabitants were paraded and summarily dismissed, while bewildering slang and bits of Hindustani embroidered tall tales of army days and army ways. Eventually I was ordered upstairs and fell asleep amid a welter of confused pictures of army life in which bully-beef, barbed wire,

*The Regiment was styled Royal Welch Fusiliers from 1727 to 1881, Royal Welsh Fusiliers from 1881 to 1920, and thereafter reverted to Royal Welch Fusiliers. During the period covered by this book they should therefore be styled the Royal Welsh Fusiliers.

Gurkhas, duds, condensed milk, trench mortars, plum and apple, Aussies, the Mount of Olives, gyppos, Turks and *estaminets* were inextricably mixed. Other images were generated by turning the leaves of my father's photograph album and poring over pictures, already yellowing and indistinct, of him and his friends in the war in the desert.

In due course all these curious strands of my childhood slowly came together to give me a lasting interest in military history and in the Great War in particular. The scale of the carnage on the Western Front, the courage and endurance of the troops in conditions of unbelievable horror and desolation haunted my imagination and filled me, like so many others, with a variety of emotions that do not dim with time. For many years my interest in the Great War lay dormant. Yet, buried at the back of my mind, was my father's comment about the fate of his friends in the 2nd Battalion of the Royal Sussex in the fields below Aubers Ridge on Sunday, 9 May, 1915.

What follows is the story of that one-day battle and its place in the three British offensives undertaken in the first half of 1915 to seize Aubers Ridge: Neuve Chapelle, Aubers Ridge and Festubert. I have tried in my book to deal with the problem of the shortage of shells which plagued our early offensives on the Western Front. I have also sought to trace the sequence of events stemming from the fiasco at Aubers Ridge, which led to the fall of the Asquith Government and to the setting-up of a Ministry of Munitions under Lloyd George. If particular stress is occasionally laid in the narrative on the part played by certain battalions in the series of attacks, this is simply a reflection of the information available in official, regimental and personal records. It is in no sense an attempt to ignore the bravery and determination shown by the other battalions of the 1st, 8th and Meerut Divisions.

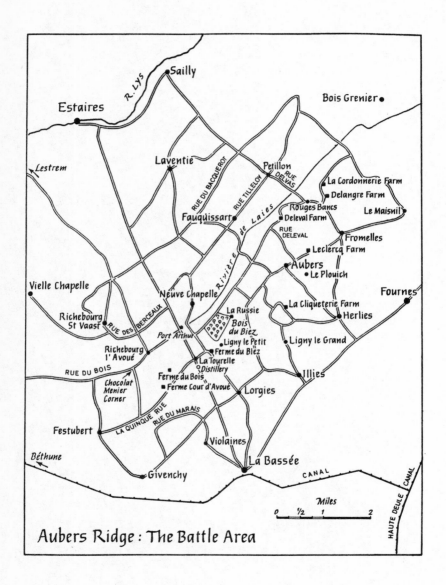

Aubers Ridge : The Battle Area

CHAPTER ONE

Aubers Ridge

In fact, it is hardly a ridge at all. It is nothing like the great ridge at Vimy a few miles to the south which, like some vast swell, builds up from the west and comes crashing steeply down upon the plain of Douai three hundred feet below. As you drive from Béthune across flat farmland towards the villages of Aubers and Fromelles lying upon the ridge, it seems only a slight rise, an insignificant swelling of the ground in the middle distance.

The ridge is at most only about seventy feet high but it is of immense tactical value. This is better appreciated if you travel from the east, from Lille, across a low plateau of farmland. As you reach Aubers and Fromelles the road quite suddenly dips and the ground slopes away to the fields below. There before you lie the battlefields of 1915, Neuve Chapelle, Aubers Ridge and Festubert, bounded in the north by the River Lys and by the La Bassée Canal in the south.

Below you, about a mile from the bottom of the slope, were the British and German trenches running parallel to each other across a no-man's-land some one hundred to three hundred yards wide. The fields across which the two armies built their trench systems are muddy and waterlogged from autumn until spring. The tiny Rivière des Laies wanders through where the old front lines once ran. This waterway, known variously as the Rivière des Layes, the Layes Brook, or the River Layes is actually a man-made drainage channel, wide and deep. In fact, the whole battlefield is seamed by dykes and streams and the fields are surrounded by deep drainage ditches. Only isolated farms and occasional clumps of trees relieve the monotony of a dull and featureless landscape.

The Indian Corps spent the winter of 1914 here. Sir James Willcocks, its commander, who was not a man given to flights of fancy, strikes a note of almost poetic distaste in his description of the landscape where so many of his men were to perish:

A dismal dead plain, dotted with farmhouses and here and there clumps of trees. The uninteresting roads only metalled in the centre; ditches and drains in every direction; observation beyond a very limited distance impossible, and for months the morning mists enveloped everything in a thick haze well into midday; canals, crossed here and there by bridges, added to the difficulties of communication . . . This monotonous land boasted no hills and valleys, not even a mound; it was just a flat dreary expanse in winter and studded with green leaves and some wild flowers in summer.

In August, 1914, a massive German army invaded Belgium and Northern France. In a campaign designed to last six weeks, it sought to achieve a spectacular victory over the French by sweeping round Paris and enveloping their armies in eastern France. Once the French armies had been destroyed, the Germans intended to turn their attention to Russia, France's ally in the East.

A British Expeditionary Force (BEF) of six divisions, under the command of Sir John French, was rapidly assembled and transported to North-West France where it took up its pre-arranged position on the left of the French army. Attacked by overwhelming German forces, the BEF was forced to retreat from its exposed position near the Belgian frontier and, with the French army, fell back on Paris. Yet the great encircling movement failed and the enemy's advance was halted in early September by the French at the Battle of the Marne. Outmanoeuvred by General Joffre, the Germans were forced to retreat to the line of the Aisne, where they established strong defensive positions along the ridge beyond the river. Our battered divisions, now reinforced but barely recovered from the rigours of their retreat from Mons to south of the Marne, followed the Germans and attacked their positions on the Aisne, only to be beaten back.

As other German army corps began to press westwards the Allies sought to outflank them to the north. The BEF was transferred back from the Aisne to Flanders in order to shorten its supply lines and to protect the Channel ports. The Germans now launched a series of violent attacks in an attempt to break through to the coast.

During the autumn, large armies wheeled and manoeuvred, attacked and counter-attacked across Northern France and Flanders. For the British it culminated in a collision between the BEF, seeking to advance east from Ypres, and the vastly superior German Fourth Army striking westwards.

Meanwhile, to the south, the Germans had captured Lille and were striving hard to extend their salient beyond La Bassée. (This small sector, part of what later became known as the Western Front, is the battlefield with which we are concerned in this book.) This area became the focus of fierce fighting in October as the Germans swept down from Aubers Ridge, only to meet determined resistance from the British. In desperate fighting their leading units were pushed back up the Ridge by the 9th Brigade (3rd Division), which captured the villages of Aubers and Herlies, together with part of the Ridge, on 17 October. However, they were not in sufficient strength to hold on to their gains. The Germans counter-attacked and in a few days had retaken the villages and forced our troops back down the ridge on to the muddy plain below. They also captured the village of Neuve Chapelle, which became the rather exposed tip of a large salient when the fighting finally died down and the exhausted combatants on both sides dug in for the winter.

This happened all along the rim of the vast bulge that the Germans had created in Northern France. By December the light field defences of the autumn had been transformed into parallel lines of primitive trenches stretching for some 475 miles from Dixmude on the Channel coast to the Swiss border. The mobile war had ground to a halt.

It is generally agreed that the BEF was the best-trained and most effective army we had ever sent abroad to fight. Of course it was ludicrously small by comparison with the enormous conscript armies of the continental powers. The contribution of the BEF at Ypres was crucial but the French at this time had about 100 divisions in the field against our seven. We had never contemplated raising an army on this scale, although we were prepared to assist our allies in campaigns in Europe. Our small regular army was designed for policing our vast colonial empire; it was accustomed to taking on and demolishing hordes of ill-armed natives and suffering only slight casualties. Its limitations were cruelly exposed in the Boer War of 1899–1902, where more men died of sickness than in battle and where barbed wire and an entrenched enemy were encountered for the first time. The cavalry, however, under Sir

John French, with Haig as his Chief of Staff, emerged with credit and with an air of conscious superiority that was to cost us dear in the next war.

But some hard lessons had been learned and during the next decade, especially during Lord Haldane's tenure as Secretary of State for War, various reforms were introduced by the 1906 Liberal Government. The standard of marksmanship among the infantry was raised, medical services improved, and the Officers' Training Corps started; above all, Haldane was the originator and organizer of the BEF. He even tried to introduce a General Staff on the German model (he once described Germany, unhappily for him, as 'his spiritual home'); though this was strongly opposed by Kitchener, it resulted in the formation of the Imperial General Staff.

Our army, the infantry, cavalry and artillery that went to France, had been trained for open warfare, for a war of fire and movement. When the great battles in North-West France subsided into trench warfare towards the end of 1914 the BEF and its senior commanders found themselves quite unprepared in every way for the highly unusual situation they faced – that of endless miles of continuous trenches.

The British troops settled down for the winter in their, by later standards, makeshift trenches to await the spring. The divisions of the BEF had suffered terrible losses in the first three months of campaigning and many of the original regular battalions had been virtually destroyed. They desperately needed reinforcements, rest and an opportunity to rebuild before they could contemplate taking the offensive. Instead, the troops now had to endure one of the most severe winters in living memory under arduous and dispiriting conditions.

Fighting, however, had not quite finished for the year. The French launched two offensives in late December, one in Champagne and one north of Arras. Both were disastrous failures, incurring heavy losses, although the French did manage to capture part of the Notre Dame de Lorette spur that marks the northern end of Vimy Ridge.

The sector we are concerned with, Aubers Ridge, became one of the key sectors on the Western Front during 1915. The enemy salient around Neuve Chapelle protected the important communication centres of La Bassée, Lille and Douai and the rail network which supplied the German divisions in the region. While our troops languished behind inadequate breastworks in the muddy

4

fields between the Lys and Rivière des Laies, the Germans established their defensive line in front of Aubers Ridge, based on Neuve Chapelle and running from Bois Grenier in the north to La Bassée. From the Ridge they were able to maintain excellent observation over the British trenches and rear areas, and they were prepared to defy any attempt to dislodge them from it. This skilled appreciation of ground and the ability to develop it for defence was an outstanding feature of German tactics. When, early in 1915, they were forced on to a strategic defensive on the Western Front in order to launch a large-scale attack on Russia in the east, they utilized the low hills, ridges and slopes of Flanders and North-West France to great effect. Thus the French, unwilling to yield another square metre of their country to the invader, and the British, following suit for reasons more political than military, usually found themselves occupying unfavourable terrain overlooked by the enemy.

Yet morale remained encouragingly high. By the end of December Sir John French had received considerable reinforcements from home and abroad and he was able to reorganize the BEF into two armies. His two corps commanders, Generals Haig and Smith-Dorrien, were given army commands. Haig took charge of the First Army, occupying the Aubers Ridge sector from Cuinchy to Bois Grenier, while Smith-Dorrien was appointed to the Second Army holding the Ypres Salient.

The three men, of course, had known each other for years. French and Haig were old comrades; Haig had been Sir John's Chief of Staff in South Africa where French had made his reputation with the cavalry. Haig had cause to be grateful to French who, despite his faults, was a kind and generous man and well-disposed towards him. A couple of years after the Boer War French was commanding the Cavalry Brigade at Aldershot, again with Haig as his Brigade Major. Sir John had been embarrassed for money since the end of the war and he was happy to accept a loan of £2000 from his subordinate. It seems that the loan was never repaid. In private, Haig was contemptuous of French's military ability and he confided his misgivings to King George V. He despised French's 'excitable demeanour', so different from his own stern and sober manner; he compared it to the opening of a soda bottle – all froth and bubble. He was also appalled by his chief's womanizing, for Sir John was what the Americans once called 'a sporting man'. Actually, it is quite refreshing to find a serious womanizer among the rumoured sexual ambiguity surrounding several senior army officers of the period. Haig, as befitted a Lowland Presbyterian Scot, disapproved strongly of illicit relations with women, as he did of risqué stories in the mess and naughty army songs. Throughout much of 1915 French was to be engaged in a passionate affair, and equally indiscreet correspondence, with a diplomat's wife called Winifred Bennett. They made an ill-assorted couple because Mrs Bennett was almost a foot taller than her short, short-tempered lover.

Sir John's violent temper was an unfortunate trait he shared with Smith-Dorrien, a most capable commander whom French had never forgiven for ignoring his orders during the retreat from Mons and saving the BEF by turning and fighting a brave delaying action at Le Cateau. A few months later he was to dismiss Smith-Dorrien, summarily and unfairly, towards the end of the Second Battle of Ypres.

With the dawn of a new year the allied commanders pondered their plans for 1915. At the beginning of February Joffre was ready to unveil his grand design. He planned three large-scale offensives for 1915, which involved his armies advancing as follows:

from Verdun–Nancy northwards to the Rhine

from Rheims northwards against the Mézières–Hirson railway and then, in due course, to swing eastwards through the gap between the Ardennes and the Dutch border

(and this is the offensive which concerns us here) after storming Vimy Ridge, to move eastwards against the German communication centres in the Noyon salient.

Meanwhile the Germans were content to maintain a defensive posture in the west while they sought to crush the Russian armies in the east. In February the Germans, under Hindenburg and Ludendorff, inflicted a heavy defeat on the Russians at the Battle of the Masurian Lakes and liberated East Prussia. But this victory was counter-balanced by successful Russian attacks in the Carpathian mountains against the other partner in the Central Powers, Austria–Hungary. The new supreme German Commander, General Erich von Falkenhayn, therefore decided on a major offensive in the east in the spring with two aims: to relieve the pressure on his ally's front and to deal the Russians such a blow that they would be unable to intervene effectively in the war for some time. He would then be able to turn the whole might of his military machine against the Allies in the west.

Following the success of his defences against the French attacks in December, Falkenhayn decided he could safely withdraw 100,000 men from the Western Front to form eight divisions of a new army for his Russian offensive. He achieved this by removing units from certain parts of his front line and by reducing the number of battalions in some divisions from twelve to nine. His decision was to be justified by the failure of two major attacks by the French in early 1915. Although it was not traditional campaigning weather, in February and March the French Fourth Army lost 50,000 men in penetrating 500 yards into the German lines in Champagne. Then in April they sacrificed 64,000 men in a pointless assault against the St Mihiel salient. This was the result of Joffre's policy of 'nibbling away'. 'I just keep nibbling away,' he used to say, but his attacks were proving expensive bites. *Punch* joked that the Germans had found a new popular song called, 'Stop your nibbling, Joffre'.

As for the British, Falkenhayn felt he had little to fear from the reinforced remnants of their 'contemptible little army'. He wrote: 'The English troops, in spite of undeniable bravery and endurance on the part of the men, have proved so clumsy in action that they offer no prospect of accomplishing anything decisive against the German Army in the immediate future'. This was a realistic assessment, although one would like to know what he meant by calling our regulars 'clumsy in action'. The Germans believed that the British Army had neither the will nor the resources to mount an offensive after its terrible losses of men and materials in the battles of 1914. The General Staff assumed that we would do no more than stand on the defensive and simply occupy a section of the front. They had therefore taken little trouble to build up effective defences to protect their positions in front of the Ridge.

The Allied commanders, particularly Joffre and the ebullient and enthusiastic Foch, the commander of the Northern Army Group, seized upon this reduction in the German troops in France. They saw an opportunity to mount an all-out offensive and, despite their heavy losses in the battles of 1914 and early 1915, they felt confident of smashing through the vast German salient and gaining a comprehensive and decisive victory.

There was also the matter of Russia. The Allies felt strongly that, in view of the great sacrifices Russia had made early in the war to help her allies, and was still making, they were morally bound to attack in the west in an attempt to weaken the coming German offensive against her.

In discussing the French attitude to the offensive, it cannot be stressed too strongly that they were consumed, not only by a steadfast refusal to yield more French soil, but also by a burning desire to drive the invader out of their country. It is, perhaps, difficult to appreciate the French High Command's mood at this time and their high confidence, given the appalling losses, especially among the officers, in the ill-conceived Battle of the Frontiers and in their other battles, defensive and otherwise. Yet they still possessed an enormous army, and their belief in the spirit of the offensive and in the élan of their infantry remained undimmed. They felt certain that, given their numerous divisions and the weight of artillery they could bring to bear on the chosen sector, there was no reason why the German defences could not be penetrated on a wide front and rolled up.

The sector which offered the most obvious opportunities of diverting the enemy's attention seemed to be the plain of Douai, already selected by Joffre as the northern prong of his triple offensive. This area contained the important railway junctions of Valenciennes and Douai through which passed a network of lines supplying three German armies. If these communications could be cut by an advance eastwards across the Artois plateau, then the enemy's position from Lille to Soissons would become untenable and the Germans would have to retreat.

It was suggested that the most appropriate British contribution to Joffre's plan would be a part in a combined Anglo–French attack in the La Bassée area planned for March. But at once problems arose. Joffre insisted he could not go ahead unless the British relieved the French IX Corps holding the sector north of Ypres. Sir John French declined to do this on the grounds that he did not have enough men. Piqued, Joffre postponed his northern offensive and intimated that the British should mount an offensive on their own. This attitude was not calculated to please Sir John who, following brushes early on in the war with General Lanrezac and Joffre, was not exactly enamoured of his allies. Red-faced, white-haired, stocky and choleric, he was the epitome of *le rosbif*; he hardly spoke or understood a word of French and he considered the French devious, unreliable and chauvinistic. The French High Command thought highly of him, too.

8

So Sir John, already irritated by continual carping by the French High Command about the British not pulling their weight, decided to go ahead on his own. For his attack he chose the salient of Neuve Chapelle in front of Aubers Ridge and on 15 February invited Haig, commander of the First Army, to draft a scheme for an offensive with Aubers Ridge as its objective. As Haig explained to the Commander of IV Corps, General Sir Henry Rawlinson, on 2 March:

Our objective [is] not merely the capture of Neuve Chapelle. Our existing line [is] just as satisfactory for us as if we were in Neuve Chapelle. I aim at getting to the line . . . of the La Bassée road to Lille and thus cut off the enemy's front. It seems to me desirable to make our plan in the chance of surprising the enemy and with the definite objective of advancing rapidly (and without any check) in the hope of starting a general advance.

By 'general advance' Haig meant that he hoped to create a breach through which he could release the cavalry massed in his rear. His cherished cavalry had not exactly distinguished itself during the battles of the Marne and the Aisne. Neither he, his cavalry commanders, nor his commander-in-chief had yet realized the impotence of cavalry against machine guns. Because of the destructive power of the machine-gun nests which the Germans were now siting some distance behind their trenches, even if the enemy's front line were breached, the cavalry were no longer able to break out and fulfil their classic role of exploitation in open country in the rear of the enemy.

The Battle of Neuve Chapelle should be seen as the first of a trilogy of battles fought in early 1915 to capture Aubers Ridge; the battle of Aubers Ridge is the second and the battle of Festubert is the third. The Ridge was not to be taken until almost the end of the war, when it was at last secured by the 47th (London) Division early in October, 1918. Although we are primarily concerned with the battle of Aubers Ridge, it is necessary to deal briefly with Neuve Chapelle for two reasons. It was the first occasion on which Haig had been entrusted with the conduct of a set-piece battle as Army Commander. It was also the first time in the war that the British had attacked a trench system proper and the methods and tactics used by Haig were to set the pattern, not only for Aubers Ridge, but for further offensives until late 1917.

Haig's plan of attack was prepared with meticulous attention to detail and contained a valuable element of surprise. After a brief but intensive bombardment (or as intensive as his limited artillery and ammunition allowed) lasting thirty-five minutes, fourteen battalions were to assault the thinly-held and sketchily-defended German front line on a front of 2000 yards. The enemy line was manned by only six companies with twelve machine guns. Two developments deserve notice. Because of the flat and open nature of the ground and the narrowness of no-man's-land, it was difficult to provide cover for the troops preparing for the assault. It was therefore decided to build shallow trenches with sandbag breastworks behind the front line. These were called 'forming up' or assembly trenches and were a prominent feature during the battle of Aubers Ridge. Later in the war, in attacks when no-man's-land was several hundred yards wide, these trenches were dug well in advance of the front line and were called 'jumping off' trenches.

There was another development. Up till now the primary function of the Royal Flying Corps had been reconnaissance. Now, in addition to its reconnaissance role, it was to patrol the skies over the battle. Two flights of No.3 Squadron were briefed for this purpose.

At 7.30 am on 10 March the barrage opened. The enemy was taken by surprise. Thanks to our overwhelming superiority in numbers, our troops burst through the German trenches in the centre of the sector and captured the village of Neuve Chapelle. However, problems arose on the flanks where uncut wire, heavy machine-gun fire and indecision held up the advance. Confusion and congestion then developed in the rear as Haig tried to bring up his reserves through what was admittedly a narrow sector of attack. Communications broke down and all these factors combined to rob the attack of its momentum. The Germans had several hours in which to bring up reinforcements and to strengthen their brittle second line, mainly with cleverly sited machine-gun posts. The delay proved disastrous for the British.

Haig gave the order to press home the attack, using a chilling phrase that was to become not unusual among army commanders on the Western Front, 'regardless of loss'. In the next three days our troops both repeated their attacks on the enemy lines and defended their own exposed positions against heavy German counter-attacks. With his troops exhausted and artillery ammunition running low, Haig finally gave the order on 13 March to break off the battle. The British had gained some 1000 yards on a front of 3000 yards at a cost of 583 officers and 12,309 other ranks.

Haig commented: 'So many good fellows no more; but it can't be done without incurring loss.' No successful commander shrinks from incurring necessary casualties in battle, but to order repeated frontal attacks against an entrenched enemy, when previous attacks have already failed, is both unjustified and a criminal waste of lives. Haig, a man set firmly in the mould of the Field Service Regulations of 1909 and convinced of the correctness of his views on matters military, was already showing signs of the obstinacy that would cost his divisions dear.

Rawlinson, an infantryman among cavalrymen, commanded IV Corps during the battle and was obviously uneasy about the tactics of his chief. He wrote shortly afterwards:

> I think D.H. would have been better advised to content himself with the capture of the village instead of going on with the attack on 11th, 12th and 13th for the purpose of trying to get the cavalry through. I advised him to do this in the first instance but he and Sir John were so obsessed with the cavalry idea that he would not listen. Had he been content with the village we should have gained just as much ground and reduced our casualties by three-quarters.

Despite its unhappy outcome, Neuve Chapelle was seen by French, Haig and First Army staff as an encouraging beginning, full, like our future offensives, of 'might have beens'. With the element of surprise and with vastly superior numbers they had broken clean through part of the German defences on the first day. Surely it was only inexperience in the handling of reserves, the lack of artillery and the need to conserve ammunition that had prevented the massed cavalry being sent pell-mell through the gap against the German rear areas? As Haig wrote to Rothschild:

> I think the main lesson of Neuve Chapelle is that, given sufficient ammunition and suitable guns, we can break through the enemy's line whenever we like!

So more men, more guns and more shells used on a broader front would lead inevitably to a breach in the German defences, which neither their reserves nor their artillery could seal. Sir Douglas Haig, imperturbable as ever and with his confidence undimmed, looked forward with relish to his next opportunity.

CHAPTER TWO

The Shell Shortage

More guns, more shells! The severely limited bombardment at Neuve Chapelle underlines the problems faced by the BEF in France and Flanders from the autumn of 1914. It cannot be emphasized too strongly that all the British offensives in 1915 were bedevilled by a lack of shells to feed the guns. This crucial shortage hung like some dark cloud over our planning and circumscribed our attacks. We were also short of guns, particularly heavy calibre weapons, but it was the shell shortage that caused a constant flow of telegrams, letters and reports from Sir John French to his chief, Lord Kitchener, at the War Office during the early months of the war.

It was not simply our offensives that were threatened by the shortage. Throughout the winter of 1914/15 our troops in their trenches were exposed to regular and considerable shelling. This obviously varied in intensity and duration according to the nature of the sector – there were some quiet parts of the line – but the plight of our men was aggravated by our inability to reply to the enemy in kind. Batteries were rationed to so many rounds per gun per day. For example, on the Second Army's front, after the Battle of Ypres, the allowance of 18pdr ammunition was reduced to two rounds per gun per day, which was also the ration for the 4.5-inch howitzers along the whole front. As for the troops, some idea of how the shell shortage affected them is revealed by Lieut-Colonel D.H. Drake-Brockman (whom we shall meet later during the battle for Aubers Ridge). He was in the trenches below the Ridge with the 39th Garhwal Rifles. He wrote:

If one telephoned up to the gunner officer for a little ammunition to be expended on some bomb gun or *minenwerfer* that was annoying us, the reply generally received was, 'Sorry, but I have used my allowance!' This was, at that time, eighteen rounds daily per battery.

Others were even worse off; some RHA batteries were being rationed to sixty shells per battery per week!

It was not simply the shortage of shells and guns that was a problem; the artillery arm was hopelessly unprepared for trench warfare. In most books about the battles on the Western Front attention is naturally concentrated upon the activities of the infantry since it was their task to break the enemy's front, occupy his positions and destroy his forces. The artillery, being very much a junior and less attractive partner, usually receives a cursory, if honourable, mention for its supporting role during the early years of the war in providing the preliminary bombardment. Its role, however, was to increase rapidly and become a dominant one. So in this narrative, the artillery and its problems will be given more prominence than usual, underlining the later description of the Great War as 'the artillery war'.

On the outbreak of war the field artillery of the BEF consisted of the Royal Field Artillery (RFA) which served the infantry, and the Royal Horse Artillery (RHA) which supported the cavalry. The standard pieces of the former were the quick-firing 18pdr and the 4.5-inch howitzer. The 18pdr (3.3-inch) had been developed after the South African War and became the backbone of the RFA. The RHA was equipped with the quick-firing 13pdr (3-inch), a lighter version of the 18pdr. These guns had naturally been designed for open warfare and they fired the shrapnel shells which had proved so successful in South Africa in flushing out and harrying the wily Boer. The effectiveness of shrapnel loomed large in the military mind; by comparison, high explosive (HE) shells were regarded as being very much at the experimental stage, with recurring problems over developing effective fuses and finding a suitable explosive to put in the shells. Lyddite eventually solved this problem.

Our howitzers were intended for heavy support and for destructive fire against strongpoints, fortifications and trenches. The difference between a gun and a howitzer is that the latter can be elevated more than 45°. A gun fires a shell at high velocity with a fairly flat trajectory. Compared with a gun of the same calibre, a howitzer fires a heavier shell at a lower velocity and with its high trajectory thus has a shorter range. It had not been necessary in the past, in our small, victorious Victorian wars, to call upon anything heavier than a 6-inch howitzer. So we transported a motley collection of heavy artillery to France with nothing beyond the 60pdrs apart from one recently completed 9.2-inch and some obsolescent 6-inch howitzers. There was also a small number of obsolete 4.7-inch and 5-inch howitzers. Unfortunately, there was little ammunition available for these and 70 per cent of that was shrapnel.

We shall usually be dealing with the artillery in terms of its basic organizational unit, the battery. This consisted of six guns (heavy batteries had four guns) and it was commanded by a major and had a complement of four officers and about 193 other ranks. Three batteries were grouped together to form a brigade and a division's field artillery at this time contained three brigades (54 guns), one howitzer brigade (18 guns) and one heavy battery (4 guns). In February, 1915, the heavy batteries were to be withdrawn into the heavy artillery reserve (HAR).

The Royal Artillery had been immediately plunged into the heavy fighting of the late summer and autumn of 1914 culminating in the savage First Battle of Ypres. No one could have foreseen the tremendous consumption of shells or the growing demand for HE shells, accelerated by the special needs of trench warfare. Sir John French quickly realized the seriousness of the problem and from the outset did his utmost to improve the supply of ammunition for his batteries. Even as early as September, 1914, he was writing to the Master-General of Ordnance (Major-General Sir Stanley von Donop) for an increasing percentage of HE shells for his howitzers and field guns, stressing that his reserves were low and his expenditure rapidly increasing. The unimaginative, bureaucratic and obstructive von Donop declined to do anything about it and sent a classic holding reply: 'the nature of the operations may again alter as they have in the past'. Meanwhile, Sir John's concern grew about the ammunition supply for his 18pdrs, where he was already using twice the number of shells per gun that the War Office was sending.

The shell situation was to develop into a running battle between the Commander-in-Chief, Sir John French, and the War Office, represented by Kitchener and von Donop. It reached an early climax during the Battle of Ypres where the BEF found itself fighting for its very existence against a German army possessing a huge number of heavy guns and an apparently limitless supply of shells. After a series of protests French managed to persuade von Donop to release ammunition he was holding for batteries not yet sent overseas. Kitchener added a footnote: 'You will of course see that economy is practised.' Kitchener was well known in the army for exercising a control over expenditure that bordered on the parsimonious. In private he was sceptical about the effectiveness of the unheard-of quantities of ammunition, by pre-war standards, that French appeared to be firing off along the Western Front.

There is a story told of how Kitchener, shortly after the Battle of Neuve Chapelle, strode into a Cabinet meeting and exclaimed in a voice thick with emotion:

'Oh, it is terrible – terrible!'
'Were the casualties very heavy?' members enquired anxiously.
'I'm not thinking for the moment of the casualties,' replied Kitchener, 'but of all the shells that were wasted.'

This military conflict between French and Kitchener now began to run parallel with political in-fighting involving Lloyd George, then Chancellor of the Exchequer, and the War Office. Lloyd George had made little secret of his contempt for the efforts (if 'effort' is the right word) of the War Office and the Ordnance Department to increase the production of shells to match the reality of demand on the Western Front. Jealous of their control over the management of munitions, they had refused the help offered by industrialists and had fought stubbornly, and fairly successfully, to prevent control passing to those politicians who were indignant about the situation and determined to do something about it. The Prime Minister was made aware of the munitions crisis and in October he set up a Cabinet Committee on Munitions (the 'Shells Committee'), despite the opposition of Kitchener, to look at the whole question of armaments with a view to increasing production and speeding up deliveries. Lloyd George contrived to have Kitchener appointed Chairman of this Committee, which also included Churchill and several other powerful figures, and it met for the first time on 12 October.

With Lloyd George and Churchill pushing Kitchener, the Committee did some useful work, although it was more concerned with gun production than with shells. It ordered rifles from the USA and increased orders already placed for 18pdrs, but it met with passive resistance from von Donop when it tried to boost armament production by mobilizing those firms in the engineering industry outside the charmed circle of approved War Office contractors.

Eighty per cent of munitions for the artillery was traditionally provided by the Royal Ordnance Factories, while the balance was provided by private armament manufacturers, such as Vickers Armstrong and Cammell Laird, known as the War Office List companies. Given that all its own armament factories were fully extended, the War Office seemed either unwilling, on specious technical grounds, or quite unable to organize a rapid increase in the number of factories making munitions, despite the nation's great manufacturing potential. The problem was exacerbated by the fact that during the rush to the Colours in the early days of the war the Army had happily accepted thousands of skilled engineering workers. The government had now begun the embarrassing and difficult task of discovering where they were and returning them to civilian production.

The last meeting of the Shells Committee was held on 1 January, 1915. Its work was virtually ended by Kitchener who said he could no longer find the time to attend. Kitchener found the idea of dealing with problems by setting up committees foreign to his nature. He was not a committee man nor did he believe in conducting either war or government by committee. He was accustomed to command, to give orders which would be obeyed without question. Dealing with silver-tongued politicians and knowledgeable industrialists was not his forte, although he proved quite adept at fighting his own corner.

It is perhaps difficult today to appreciate the tremendous reputation and influence enjoyed in 1914/15 by Kitchener, England's greatest soldier of the period. He was the most powerful figure in the Cabinet after the Prime Minister, and by far the most feared. He did not interfere with the work of other people or other departments and he would brook no interference with what he saw as his own responsibilities as Secretary of State for War. There was now no instrument for spurring the War Office into action. But Lloyd George was not so easily brushed aside. In the last few months he had learned much about the machinations of the War Office, about von Donop and something of the shell situation. He bided his time.

While these meetings were taking place, Sir John French continued to press for more shells and he peppered the War Office with telegrams and letters. He became steadily more frustrated at his lack of success. At last on 31 December he wrote to Kitchener at the War Office:

The present supply of artillery ammunition has been found to be so inadequate as to make offensive operations, even on a small scale, quite out of the question. Recent experience has shown that the ammunition available sufficed for scarcely one hour's bombardment of a small portion of the enemy's line, and that even this operation leaves no ammunition to repel a counter-attack or to give the assaulting columns sufficient support. Owing to the nature of the operations in which we are, and shall continue to be, engaged the supply of artillery ammunition is the governing factor . . . It is on the supply of ammunition for artillery that the future operations of the British Army will depend.

French went on to suggest his requirements, both for defence and for attack, and he stated that for his principal guns he needed the following:

50 rounds per gun per day for the 18pdrs
40 rounds per gun per day for the 4.5-inch howitzers
25 rounds per gun per day for the 4.7-inch howitzers

And this at a time when shells for his guns were being severely rationed! Little did he imagine that demand would soon reach 100 rounds per day for his field guns.

What he subsequently received – i.e. the number of rounds per gun actually supplied to him each month – is as follows:

	Month	18pdr	4.5-inch	4.7-inch
1914	Nov.	9.9	6.8	10.8
	Dec.	6.0	4.6	7.6
1915	Jan.	4.9	4.2	7.6
	Feb.	5.3	6.5	5.3
	Mar.	8.6	6.5	5.3
	Apr.	10.6	8.2	4.2
	May	11.0	6.1	4.3

His letter resulted in a reply from Kitchener on 9 January which stated baldly:

It is impossible at the present time to maintain a sufficient supply of gun ammunition on the scale which you consider necessary for offensive operations. Every effort is being made in all parts of the world to obtain an unlimited supply of ammunition, but, as you are well aware, the result is still far from being sufficient to maintain the large number of guns which you now have under your command adequately supplied with ammunition for offensive purposes.

French was not so easily deterred. During January and February he continued sending telegrams to the Master-General of Ordnance demanding more shells, asking for deliveries to be speeded up and complaining that he was not receiving the quantity of shells the War Office had promised him. At this time it was not so much future offensives that concerned French but the plight of his troops in the front-line trenches. None of these communications, like those sent in the previous autumn, went further than von Donop and Kitchener. Although Chairman of the Shells Committee, Kitchener had never shown it the contents of the various reports, memos and demands he had received from the Commander-in-Chief, nor had he revealed French's mounting concern at the shell shortage to the Cabinet.

Lloyd George now tried again to break the stranglehold so far exerted by the War Office over the production of munitions. Early in March, with the help of Balfour, the Conservative leader, who was a friend of his despite their pre-war political conflicts, he put up a scheme to Asquith which envisaged a strong committee to organize our industrial capacity to increase the output of armaments. He followed this a few days later by introducing a Bill to take the necessary powers. As this did not have the galvanizing effect upon the War Office he wanted, Lloyd George made another approach to the Prime Minister. After further discussions, on 8 April Asquith set up a special Cabinet Committee called the Munitions of War Committee. He appointed Lloyd George as its chairman with the brief of mobilizing our national resources; von Donop was Kitchener's representative on it. From the outset Kitchener sought to restrict the new committee's activities and during its brief life the War Office undermined its attempts to organize a rapid increase in the supply of armaments. Kitchener displayed a marked reluctance to provide the committee with information and he and von Donop refused to allow it to take responsibility for munition manufacture.

This then was the rather shabby background to the shell situation before the Battle of Neuve Chapelle, briefly described in the last chapter. Matters did not improve after it. While Asquith was spending the rest of March dealing with the establishment of an effective munitions committee, immediately after the battle French resumed his attack on the War Office. He fired off the first of several telegrams to Kitchener:

> Cessation of the forward movement is necessitated today by the fatigue of the troops, and above all by the want of ammunition. If we are to obtain results of value, we must have all possible support in men and ammunition from home.

On 16 March came the threat:

> The supply has fallen short, especially in 18-pounder and 4.5-inch, of what I was led to expect and I am, therefore, compelled to abandon further offensive operations until sufficient reserves are accumulated.

Two days later Sir John sent a letter to Kitchener in which he emphasized yet again that the efforts to supply him with adequate quantities of ammunition had been 'consistently disappointing':

> If the supply of ammunition cannot be maintained on a considerably increased scale it follows that the offensive efforts of the Army must be spasmodic and separated by considerable intervals of time . . . The weather and the state of the ground have no longer to be reckoned with as limiting the scope of our operations. The object of His Majesty's Government cannot be attained unless the supply of artillery ammunition can be increased sufficiently to enable the Army to engage in sustained offensive operations.

Kitchener was by no means unsympathetic to this plea but he was unable to help as he now found himself involved in finding men, guns and ammunition for the Gallipoli operation. A few days later the War Office was less sympathetic when it complained, rather tactlessly, about the number of shells Sir John's artillery had used at Neuve Chapelle and again urged economy in the future. French swallowed hard and tartly replied:

Our losses and the amount of ground gained are the best indication as to whether the expenditure of artillery ammunition was on an unnecessarily extravagant scale.

He hoped that he would not be embarrassed by lack of shells in his next offensive which was to be mounted in partnership with the French Tenth Army.

CHAPTER THREE

Haig's First Army

I am a courtier grave and serious
W.S. Gilbert, *The Gondoliers*

Soon after the battle of Neuve Chapelle had ended discussions were resumed between the French and British General Headquarters about a major combined offensive in Artois. There was now a much more cordial atmosphere. The British had impressed the French with their success at Neuve Chapelle by actually breaking through the enemy lines. Joffre even sent his corps commanders to see Haig to find out what lessons could be drawn from the action. Haig had worked hard at his French and was reasonably fluent, in contrast to his monolingual Commander-in-Chief, and he impressed the French with his determination – the firm chin, the steady blue eyes – and by his willingness to co-operate in a joint offensive. On 24 March Joffre formally asked if the British would be prepared to join in his postponed offensive in late April or early May. Joffre was in buoyant mood; he spoke optimistically about breaching the German line and rolling up their defences. He even went so far as to talk of reaching Namur and ending the war in three months. Sir John French discussed the offensive with Haig and told him to prepare for a First Army attack south of Neuve Chapelle. He then replied to Joffre agreeing to his proposal.

Shortly afterwards, on 6 April, Joffre sent him plans for a joint Franco-British offensive with the plain of Douai and Aubers Ridge as the objectives. Joffre planned to attack and seize the crest of Vimy Ridge between Farbus and Souchez, using his Tenth Army commanded by General d'Urbal. This force would consist of fourteen infantry divisions, some 220 heavy guns and over 720 field guns and howitzers. Once in possession of Vimy Ridge, which offered superb observation over the industrial area of Lens and the plain of Douai, he could then plan his next advance to the line of Cambrai–Douai.

This was to be the main offensive, but there were also to be two subsidiary attacks to the north. The aim of the first was to capture the eastern spur of Notre Dame de Lorette, which lay on the left flank of the main assault and was a prerequisite for a successful advance. This was to be launched on the day before the main assault. The second attack was to be delivered by IX Corps on the day after the main assault when the result of that attack was known. The idea was to widen the gap in the enemy line and generally support the left flank of the main attack. Joffre suggested that the attack of the British First Army on Aubers Ridge should take place after the main assault and on the same day as the French IX Corps subsidiary attacks. Its purpose was twofold: to widen still further the assumed breach in the enemy line on the left and to stop his reserves north of the La Bassée Canal being sent south to reinforce German resistance along Vimy Ridge. Joffre left Sir John French and Foch to prepare detailed plans for the offensives.

Three days later Sir John confirmed to Foch that his First Army would attack as agreed, but with a major alteration to his plan. After discussions with his senior staff, he decided that, instead of a single thrust south of Neuve Chapelle, he would break through the German front by means of a pincer attack north and south of Neuve Chapelle, though the main weight of the offensive would still be in the southern sector. He would seize Aubers Ridge and cut the vital La Bassée–Lille road, thus taking out the enemy salient at Neuve Chapelle. He told Foch that he would commit ten divisions (he had eight with another two due to arrive shortly) and about 100 heavy and 500 field guns to the offensive and, in addition, he would have five cavalry divisions standing by in reserve.

At this point let us examine the composition, condition and situation of Haig's First Army in April, 1915, as it prepared for its next attempt to capture Aubers Ridge. It consisted of I Corps, comprising the 1st, 2nd and 47th Divisions, IV Corps, with the 7th, 8th and 49th Divisions, plus the Indian Corps containing the Lahore and Meerut Divisions. These were mostly regular divisions, except for the 47th and 49th which were Territorial formations. French had also promised him the 50th (Northumbrian) and 51st (Highland) Divisions, which were due to arrive later on, although when they reached the front they were held in the general reserve.

I Corps was commanded by an old friend of Haig from his Staff

College days, Lieut-General Sir C.C. Monro. When Monro took over the 2nd Division, Haig noted in his Private Papers that 'he proved himself to be a good regimental officer and an excellent commander of the Hythe School of Musketry but some years with the Territorials had resulted in his becoming rather fat. He lacks practical experience in commanding a division.' Monro soon proved his worth as a level-headed and determined leader and was promoted to command I Corps. The Indian Corps was commanded by General Sir James Willcocks, a rather portly figure described as a 'stately old gentleman, very remote from the rough and tumble of trench life. He was known throughout the Corps as "James-by-the-Grace-of-God", but to the irreverent the order was reversed.' His chief pleasure was big-game shooting, which he had little opportunity to enjoy around Béthune.

.IV Corps was in the hands of Lieut-General Sir Henry Rawlinson Bt, 'Rawly' to his friends or 'Rawly the fox' to those less favourably disposed towards him. One of the ablest and most perceptive of Haig's army commanders, the articulate, sociable, intelligent Rawlinson was an infantryman with a different background from his army commander. He was a protégé of Lord Roberts, liked by Lord Kitchener and generally considered fortunate because of his background and connections. Widely travelled, physically vigorous, he threw himself wholeheartedly into whatever he did. His relationship with his chief was never easy, mainly because of his close friendship with Sir Henry Wilson, an intriguer and smooth-tongued operator who was distrusted and detested by Haig. Their relationship was further clouded by an incident during the Battle of Neuve Chapelle*, repercussions from which tended to rumble on for some time. Rawlinson remained a loyal and energetic subordinate despite disagreeing from time to time with his chief's tactics, but he was unable to conceal his distrust of Haig's obsession with the role of the cavalry and his pursuit of the breakthrough regardless of loss. As a corps commander he was, like Haig, meticulous in his planning and attention to detail. He cultivated a professional reserve, which gained him the reputation of being rather hard and cold, but in battle his optimism, cheerfulness and encouragement inspired confidence.

All the regular divisions had been in constant hard fighting since August, 1914, and had suffered severe casualties. It is a truism to say that the original BEF was largely destroyed by the end of the

*See p.176

First Battle of Ypres; swiftly the effects were far-reaching and swiftly apparent. The divisions had been reinforced and brought up to strength but many of the battalions had lost most of their original officers and senior NCOs and had incurred grievous losses among their trained and experienced troops.

It is instructive to examine what Haig's individual divisions had suffered by April, 1915. In I Corps the 1st and 2nd Divisions had not been significantly engaged during the retreat from Mons but they had lost 3500 men during the Battle of the Aisne. Both divisions suffered tremendous casualties at Ypres. For example, the 2nd Battalion of the Welsh Regiment in the 3rd Brigade had by this time lost its full fighting strength four times over. In IV Corps the 7th Division's casualties in three weeks' fighting at Ypres amounted to 356 officers (out of 400) and 9664 other ranks (out of 12,000). Reinforced, or re-created might be a more accurate term, it again suffered heavily at Neuve Chapelle, losing 138 officers and 2653 men. As for the 8th Division, its component battalions had to be brought home from various stations abroad before they could be organized for embarkation to France. The Division eventually crossed the Channel in early November and moved up to the Ypres Salient. It played a major part at Neuve Chapelle, where its casualties totalled 218 officers and 4616 other ranks.

But these divisions of the old regular army, although still brave and effective, were no longer quite of the same calibre as a fighting force in April, 1915, as they had been in 1914. Having suffered tremendous losses in the first months of the war, their offensive power had been somewhat diluted by the quality of the replacements. These consisted first of reservists, then of half-trained special reservists of pre-war enlistment, followed by re-enlisted men past military age and, finally, of men recruited since the outbreak of war with perhaps three or four months' training. Yet by the end of 1914 nearly all the reservists and special reservists had been used up. With a number of exceptions, the regular battalions were now scarcely better trained than the Territorial battalions they tended to look down upon as 'Saturday night soldiers'. In fact, as was to be demonstrated later, some of the Territorial battalions showed a dash and enthusiasm in attack which the regulars could no longer match.

One feels particular sympathy for the Lahore and Meerut Divisions of the Indian Corps. During the crisis in the autumn of 1914 the Indian Army was the only reservoir of regular troops available and these two divisions were hurriedly transported to France.

They arrived just as the war of movement was crystallizing into trench warfare and they helped to reinforce and shore up a sorely-pressed BEF. They spent the harsh winter of 1914/15 in unfamiliar and miserable conditions in waterlogged trenches in the Bois Grenier – La Bassée sector. In addition to the privations and discomfort of the line, they were exposed, like all troops on the Western Front, to enemy shelling with HE. Their previous experience in battle had been limited in the main to enduring sporadic rifle-fire from tribesmen on the North-West Frontier. It had not prepared them for the shattering effect of heavy shells falling on them as they crouched behind inadequate breastworks. This shelling caused an intermittent but depressing trickle of casualties among the Indian and British troops in the line and added up to a significant monthly total. In March at the Battle of Neuve Chapelle the Lahore Division had lost eight-five officers and 1609 other ranks and, as we shall see, had then been ordered north to the relief of the hard-pressed troops at the Second Battle of Ypres, where it suffered further casualties in the Battle of St Julien. The other division in the Corps, the Meerut, had suffered even more heavily at Neuve Chapelle, losing 103 officers and 2250 other ranks.

Thus, by April, 1915, Willcocks's Corps had lost virtually all its British officers. This was a serious and debilitating loss, for the Indians looked upon these officers as advisers and father-figures, and it contributed to a marked loss of morale. Not only were there not enough of them per battalion to begin with but they proved particularly difficult to replace. All too often they were followed by newcomers, who had little or no experience of the races they were to command in action. As for the Indian troops, the drafts sent from India as reinforcements were found to be of poor quality, even the reservists, and this further affected their efficiency. Recruiting in India was hampered by an unnecessary degree of secrecy about the activities and experiences of the Indian Corps on the Western Front and the replacements tended to come from all over the subcontinent, thus diluting the class regiments. (A class regiment was one composed of men of one race, such as the Garhwalis, for example.) There is no doubt that the morale of the two divisions suffered.

The rifle strength of the average Indian battalion was 750 men and Willcocks admitted in private that it was becoming difficult to maintain his battalions at their previous high standard of effectiveness. Considerations of morale apart, the Indian Corps was now seriously under strength; in fact, its two divisions were 5400 rifles short of the strength of a British Army Corps. Fortunately, there were close ties between the Indian troops and the British battalions which formed part of the Indian Corps Brigades. In the difficult conditions of 1915 it was the turn of the British to provide support, although for different reasons.

Willcocks had set up his Corps Headquarters at Lestrem, south-west of Estaires. Those British troops who had occasion to pass through the district were struck by the colourful and unusual spectacle that presented itself. The area was filled with a multitude of tents populated by Indians, both infantry and cavalry, of various races in a variety of headgear. Colonel W.N. Nicholson, a senior staff officer of the 51st Highland Division, spent a few days there at the end of April. He described Lestrem as:

A peaceful little town with grey-stone houses, orchards in full bloom, a small *place* in the one cobbled street, a church with two shells through the steeple – a memento that the Germans had occupied this neighbourhood before they retired beyond the Lys River. In the centre was the château, with its moat. A Sikh sentry stood at the great gate, a troop of Indian cavalry came clattering down the street, Indian troops were camped in the fields all around. An unforgettable contrast of peace and war.

In the account of the battle we shall be dealing primarily, not with divisions and brigades, but with battalions. A British battalion was commanded by a lieutenant-colonel and at full strength consisted of thirty-six officers and 1000 men, though its actual fighting strength was about 800 rifles. It was very much a close family unit, particularly in peacetime. It was made up of four companies, each containing four platoons of fifty riflemen each, though very few platoons put that number in the field at the start of an action. With various administrative and specialist troops added, a company amounted to some 240 men, normally commanded by a captain. At this stage in the war the company was the basic unit of attack, though later on, in early 1917, it tended to be superseded in this role by the platoon. A platoon was led by a lieutenant, assisted by a sergeant, and it was further broken down into four sections of twelve men, each in charge of a corporal. Four battalions formed a brigade, commanded by a brigadier-general, and three brigades made up a division under a major-general. With its artillery and other services, a division totalled some 20,000 men, of whom about 10,000 were riflemen (see Appendix 6).

At this early stage, indeed for most of the war, the mode of attack employed by a battalion was naturally based on pre-war methods and training. It was quite simple in concept. According to the Field Service Regulations of 1909 an assault would be delivered in lines, each line pressing the one in front and filling the gaps as men fell. In this way rifle fire was maximized. It was the function of the rifle to beat down the enemy's fire and prepare for the *coup de grâce* – a bayonet charge which would carry the enemy defences. As a battalion usually attacked on a frontage of about four hundred yards, this meant that two companies would climb out of their trenches shortly before zero-hour, pass through gaps made in their wire (if any), and form up for the attack side by side under cover of an artillery bombardment designed to smash the enemy front line and keep his troops under cover. Each company had two platoons in the first line and two in the second, extended at intervals of one man every two yards. When the bombardment lifted the first wave went forward four platoons abreast, followed by a similar second wave at a distance ranging from twenty-five to fifty yards or more, according to circumstances. A third company was available in support, with the fourth standing by in reserve. Sometimes both these companies would maintain the momentum of the assault by attacking together.

The First Army had spent a dispiriting winter occupying trenches in the waterlogged fields between Bois Grenier and Givenchy. These trenches were not the trenches of popular imagination. Most readers today have a mental picture, derived from photographs taken later in the war or from the cinema or television, of troops in steel helmets standing in deep trenches, complete with parapet, parados (the parapet which protects the backs of the defenders), firestep and duckboards. Tarpaulins cover the entrances to well-protected dug-outs. In 1915 such trenches simply did not exist.

Because the water-table in this area was only some eighteen inches below the surface, the trench could be no more than a shallow ditch protected by a breastwork made of sandbags raised above ground level. So the 'trenches' were basically breastworks which varied considerably in thickness and height. Sandbags were the most common material employed because they were simple to use, easy to repair and safer under shellfire. Earth for the sandbags was usually taken from in front of the parapet. Shelter for the troops,

28

from both the weather and shellfire, was in most cases a hole or ledge scraped out of the trench wall. Officers were housed in a primitive sandbagged shelter ('dug-out' is a misnomer), but there was little in the way of overhead cover for anyone.

In front of Aubers Ridge these shallow trenches became badly flooded during the severe winter of 1914/15. Men were manning and supplying the trenches knee-deep in water with which the hand pumps were unable to cope. The German breastworks opposite were equally affected and on several occasions men on both sides were to be seen standing miserably outside the breastworks trying to dry off while what proved to be vain attempts were made to reduce the water level in their trenches. It was something of a relief, therefore, when, in January, 1915, orders were issued to erect breastworks six feet high and eight feet thick on top of the ground about a hundred yards behind the front line. Six feet behind the front wall was a similar wall, the parados, with the inner faces of both walls revetted with sandbags. As the trench warfare dragged interminably on, breastworks were to become even thicker and stronger with more sophisticated protection provided for the men in the line.

To minimize the effect of the shelling and to prevent enfilade fire, both the British and German front lines below the Ridge were constructed with traverses (sandbag walls built out at right angles to the trench wall) at intervals along the trench, thus forming a series of bays. About two hundred yards behind the front line was a support line and about four hundred yards behind that lay the reserve line. These three lines were connected by a series of narrow communication trenches. Up and down these, where there was barely room for heavily laden troops to pass each other, all reliefs, walking wounded, runners and stretcher-bearers had to travel. All food and drink and military stores of every kind, including coils of barbed-wire, boxes of bombs and small-arms ammunition, duck-boards, corrugated iron and timber, had to be carried up to the front line, usually under cover of darkness. Mud frequently made these trenches virtually impassable to laden men who had to make their way across the open as best they could.

Even at this stage in the war the German trenches and trench system were considered much superior to ours. The reason is not far to seek; it sprang from a fundamental difference in attitudes between the two sides. The Germans, after making vast inroads into France, had gone on the defensive. Occupying favourable positions, from the end of 1914 onwards they had plenty of time to construct formidable defences: villages became fortresses, farms formed natural strongpoints, dug-outs became deeper and more heavily protected, belts of wire wider and blockhouses more numerous. They waited within their fortifications and invited attack.

The British and French, on the other hand, regarded the trenches and the whole trench system as quite a temporary arrangement, which would be abandoned in due course after their major offensives led to the return of a war of movement. Essentially the Allies were looking to advance and to the liberation of French soil from the invader. So they saw no need to provide sheltered accommodation which might blunt the aggressive edge of their troops. As a result, this meant that our infantry, in George Coppard's words, 'led a mean and impoverished existence in lousy scratch holes'.

The savage defensive battles of 1914, followed by the crystallization of the fighting into trench warfare, had soon revealed that our troops, who had been trained for a war of movement, were ill-equipped for this new kind of warfare. Apart from a rifle and bayonet, they had little else. There was a lack of flares, periscopes and wire-cutters, while even picks and spades were scarce. Steel helmets, or 'tin hats', were not issued until early 1916, so our men did their spells in the front line or carried out an attack wearing the regulation army cap. Moreover, the army was woefully short of the two weapons which were to become all-important in trench fighting: hand grenades and trench mortars.

Hand grenades had not been seriously used by the army since the Crimean War and we now found ourselves with ineffective grenades of outdated design. The BEF began the war with a small stock of the No.1 grenade, which had been introduced in 1908. It looked rather like a policeman's truncheon and consisted of a brass tube, filled with explosive and carrying a serrated cast-iron ring to produce fragments, mounted on a 16-inch cane handle. It was fitted with cloth streamers to ensure it landed head-first to set off the detonator. However, in action in the trenches it became a menace to thrower and neighbours alike, when, as frequently happened, the bomber swung his arm back and hit the rear wall of the trench. Its place was taken by several improvisations. Among these was the 'hairbrush' bomb, another percussion bomb which was nothing more than a slab of gun-cotton wrapped round a detonator and a handful of six-inch nails and secured by wire to a piece of wood shaped like a hairbrush. More popular and slightly more sophisticated was the 'jam-tin' bomb. This consisted of two gun-cotton primers in an empty jam tin, packed round with pieces of metal and stone. A safety fuse was inserted in the primers, which were lit with an ordinary match. An official development on the jam-tin bomb swiftly followed. This was the 'Double Cylinder', again a time-fused bomb, consisting of an inner cylinder containing the explosive charge and an outer one containing shrapnel. There was also the famous 'Pitcher' grenade. There were so many accidents with this one, caused by premature explosions, that bombers using it were called 'The Suicide Club'.

In his book *The First Hundred Thousand*, about the training of one of Kitchener's new battalions, Ian Hay gives a light-hearted survey of the bombs available in 1915:

> The jam-tin variety [he wrote] appeals more particularly to the sportsman, as the element of chance enters largely into its successful use. It is timed to explode about ten seconds after the lighting of the fuse. It is therefore unwise to throw it too soon, as there will be ample time for your opponent to pick it up and throw it back. On the other hand, it is unwise to hold on too long, as the fuse is uncertain in its action, and is given to short cuts.

Bold and athletic men were usually chosen for training as bombers. They were formed into bombing sections of nine men, consisting of two bombers, two bomb carriers, two bayonet men and two spare men, with an NCO in charge. The party worked its way up a trench from bay to bay by lobbing grenades over the traverses with the bayonet men dashing round to finish off the enemy. The process would then be repeated; it was not a job for the faint-hearted. The bomb was to become the most effective trench warfare weapon of the war, but the Army did not receive a reliable grenade until May, 1915 – too late for use at Aubers Ridge. This was the 'Mills' bomb, named after its inventor, Mr Mills of Birmingham. It had a five-second fuse, no stick or handle, and, with a range of thirty yards, it became the standard British hand grenade for many years.

It is hard to believe, but at the outbreak of the war the Army did not possess a single trench mortar. In response to need, a variety of curious and ineffective improvisations appeared. In February, 1915, a young Territorial officer described his introduction to an early type which, in design, foreshadowed the Stokes mortar:

31

It was most exciting and more like a glorified fifth of November than anything else. The trench mortar consists of a section of ordinary pipe about 2ft 6in. long blocked up at one end, with a touch hole in the manner of the old muzzle loaders. A large canister of gun-cotton with suitable detonators and so forth is dropped into the gun and then fired with a charge of black powder. The canister hurtles through the air, drops to the ground and goes off with a fearful bang, the time required being dependent on the length of fuse attached. It blows a hole in the ground about 4ft across by 1ft deep. The extreme range is about 250 yards and of course the accuracy is very low.

Like the early grenades, these home-made mortars could be a danger to both friend and foe. Only a few weeks later a new trench mortar, not dissimilar to the one described above, was being demonstrated to a battery of RHA:

The barrel looked like a bit of gas piping on a stand and fired bombs consisting of jam tins filled with high explosive and nails. The Battery intended to practise first. They formed up in a hollow square round the mortar. The first three bombs were fired successfully; the fourth exploded in the bore and killed the Major and thirteen men and wounded about thirty others.

There was also a bomb-thrower invented by a Captain A. West. This was basically a catapult, powered by twenty-four springs, which hurled a spherical bomb. It was accurate and certainly silent but it was heavy and expensive to make and its bombs were expensive and difficult to manufacture as well. By far the most effective mortar of this period was the 2-inch tube, used particularly by the BEF against snipers and machine-gun posts. It fired a spherical bomb weighing about 40lb attached to a metal stick about three feet long; the bombs were inevitably nicknamed 'toffee apples' (see illustration no.2). They were supposed to land on their nose and explode on impact but many either failed to explode or simply broke in two. This mortar, both clumsy and innaccurate, was the one used by trench-mortar sections at Aubers Ridge. All these variations on a theme were swept away when a new and efficient trench 3-inch mortar, designed by Sir Wilfrid Stokes, was introduced in April, 1915. So effective did the Stokes mortar prove that it became the standard trench mortar for the rest of the war and continued to be used throughout the Second World War.

Fortunately, the musketry skills of the soldiers of the BEF were to compensate to some extent for these deficiencies and to excite the admiration and respect of the enemy. The standard of musketry had been much improved since the Boer War. Now, armed with the short-muzzle Lee-Enfield rifle with its ten-round magazine and carrying one hundred and fifty rounds in their pouches, our well-trained regulars were capable of firing fifteen aimed shots per minute. Sadly, this level of skill was to decline with the demise of the original BEF.

Thus armed and organized, the First Army awaited orders for the forthcoming offensive. In fairness, our leaders could hardly be blamed for being ill-equipped for the special demands made by the new warfare; France and Germany were no better placed. It was some time before our senior commanders realized they were embroiled in siege warfare of a most difficult and puzzling kind, presenting problems which it took them virtually three years to solve with weapons and tactics undreamed of in their Edwardian heyday. Even Lord Kitchener, a man of massive authority and experience, was heard to remark, 'I don't know what is to be done . . . This isn't war.'

CHAPTER FOUR

'Sweat Saves Blood'

While the Allies were formulating their plans for a joint Anglo-French offensive, the Germans in front of Aubers Ridge had not been idle. Their staff officers were quick to learn the lessons of Neuve Chapelle. There they had held rather flimsy defences, consisting mainly of a breastwork of piled sandbags, with insufficient troops, and this had nearly led to their undoing. Appreciating that another attack upon the Ridge was certain to follow soon, they realized that much stronger front-line defences were needed to stop a determined attack by the First Army.

They did two things. First, they increased the density of the trench garrison in this sector from two divisions to three. Four regiments of the 6th Bavarian Reserve Division took over the right sector (8000 yards) of the front of the 13th Division running from Bois Grenier to Fauquissart. The 13th and 14th Divisions, which had been reduced to three regiments before the battle of Neuve Chapelle, were now redistributed, the 13th on a front of 7000 yards from Fauquissart to Chocolat Menier Corner, and the 14th on a similar front of 7000 yards from Chocolat Menier Corner to Cuinchy. Each regiment now held about 2000 yards of front instead of the 3000 before Neuve Chapelle. It is significant that from this time onward there were generally more Germans for each yard of front held by the British than for each metre held by the French.

Next the Germans set to work in earnest to strengthen their defences before the Ridge, using these additional troops plus extra working parties sent up from recruit depots and training centres. There is an old German Army saying, 'Sweat saves blood', and their efforts were to illustrate this. They worked day and night with great energy and by the beginning of May their position was immeasurably stronger. The Official History offers a detailed description of these German counter-measures which had such a vital bearing on the outcome of the battle:

> The width of the parapet was doubled or trebled to measure fifteen to twenty feet across and heightened to six or seven feet. It was then considered to be proof against the shell of all but the heaviest calibre armament on the British front. The wire entanglement, which, in combination with the machine guns, made the position so formidable, had been increased in breadth, and in many places remade with stouter wire. Further, wire had been erected in the excavations in front of the parapet – dug to obtain earth to build the parapet – which was not visible from the British trenches.

Incidentally, in the construction of their breastworks the Germans used sandbags of various colours and materials, such as white linen, and the resulting random patterns made an impression on our observers. A young officer wrote: 'Just in front of us is a long German breastwork, shining in the sun and, with its black and coloured sandbags, it looks like a long chessboard'. It also made it more difficult for us to spot the enemy loopholes.

In front of these breastworks the German wire varied in depth from six to fifteen yards at this stage of the war. It consisted of two or three rows of 'knife-rests', wooden frames consisting of a horizontal bar twenty-five to thirty feet long with cross-pieces three feet long at either end. Strands of barbed wire were wound round the frames and pulled tight. Between the knife-rests and the front line there was frequently another belt of low wire strung between wooden posts. Later in the war the German wire entanglements became much denser, culminating in great belts of staked wire up to fifty yards in depth in front of strongpoints in parts of the Hindenburg line.

Every few yards along the line, small wooden dug-outs covered with sandbags had been built into the thick wall of the breastworks. At regular intervals there were special emplacements for machine guns built with loopholes close to the ground so that the machine guns were able to sweep no-man's-land with grazing effect. The improved state of the enemy trenches is confirmed by those officers of the 8th Division who occupied the German front line temporarily during the battle. They reported that the front-line trenches were very well built, narrow but with boarded bottoms and good fire steps, and that the dug-outs were particularly well constructed. Machine-gun emplacements were in some cases built in the form of large box-loopholes with plenty of splay for traversing. They also noticed that there were more rifle loopholes than we had in our trenches.

Behind the front line massive sandbag mounds providing well-protected dug-outs and accommodation (*Wohngraben*) were built at distances varying from 50 to 200 yards. And there were other improvements which the Official History goes on to describe:

> The trench for the supports, 200 to 800 yards in rear of the front line, had also been reconstructed. Though not so strongly built as the front line, it offered sufficient protection to ensure that determined men could check any part of an infantry advance that might succeed in passing the front line. Special attention had also been given to the communication trenches, which at the time of the battle of Neuve Chapelle had been in a very unfinished condition. There was now in every regimental sector an 'Up' and a 'Down' communication trench between the front position and some central point, a thousand yards or so in rear. These communication trenches had fire steps on both sides so that they could be used for defence.

Another development in the enemy defences stemming from what happened at Neuve Chapelle was the siting of machine-gun posts well behind the support line to act as rallying points in the event of a breakthrough. This can be seen as the beginning of that defence in depth which was to be perfected by the Germans later in the war – and which was to cost us so dear. One or two of the regimental commanders wanted to connect up these strongpoints to form a further defensive line but the Corps Commander, General von Claer, would not hear of it. He made it clear that the battle was to be fought in and for the front line and that the improved breastworks must be held or retaken at all costs. German tactics if a breakthrough occurred were to seal off the flanks of the breach with the support companies, who would take up defensive positions along the communication trenches, assisted by their machine-gun nests. In this way the attack would be contained until the reserves arrived and a counter-attack could be launched with artillery support.

Undoubtedly the main feature of the German defences at Aubers

Ridge and throughout the war was the skilled use of the heavy machine gun – 'the concentrated essence of infantry' in Liddell Hart's memorable phrase. Something of its influence in static defences had been shown at Neuve Chapelle but its deployment in the reinforced defences in front of Aubers Ridge was to demonstrate its awesome stopping power. As defences developed in strength and complexity, heavy machine guns dominated the battlefield from their increasingly strong emplacements.

The German Army had been the first to realize the importance of the machine gun in modern warfare. Tests of experimental weapons in the 1890s convinced the Germans of its great potential, and its value was one of several lessons they learned from the Russo-Japanese War of 1905. This conflict also introduced to the many European observers such valuable novelties as barbed wire, trench lines, artillery in concealed positions, hand grenades and quick-firing guns. As a result, in 1908 the Germans introduced the Maxim heavy machine gun (it weighed 176lbs!), with a rate of fire of 400 to 500 rounds per minute and sights graduated to 2200 yards. It proved a thoroughly reliable weapon and mass production began soon afterwards. By the outbreak of war there were some 2400 machine guns already in service. German machine-gunners were specially selected and intensively trained and they could achieve a high degree of accuracy even at very long ranges. Machine-gun companies were added to existing formations so that in 1914 there was one company consisting of four officers, ninety-five men and six machine guns for each infantry regiment. Their employment during the war provides a good example of tactical effectiveness. Time and again during the great battles of 1916 and 1917, when they were on the defensive, the Germans turned to the Maxim to compensate for their numerical inferiority.

The importance attached to the machine gun by the German General Staff contrasts sharply with the attitude of the Allies towards the new weapon. Senior British commanders showed little interest and less faith in it, and in 1914 only two machine guns were allocated to each battalion. Haig himself, in a much-quoted comment from a minute to the Army Council on 14 April, 1915, considered the machine gun to be 'a much overrated weapon' and that two machine guns per battalion were 'more than sufficient'.

The German troops were organized and directed by a General Staff unrivalled in Europe. Like other major European powers, Germany possessed a very large conscript army. Every male was liable to be called upon to serve his country over a period of

37

twenty-seven years. In the conscript army a man served two or three years full-time according to his branch of the service, followed by four or five years in the reserve. He next served a further twelve years in the *Landwehr* and then, from the age of thirty-nine until he was forty-five, in the *Landsturm*. This system produced a very large reserve by which the regular army could be rapidly expanded on the outbreak of war.

At this time the standard German infantry division at full strength consisted of three brigades, two of infantry and one of field artillery, totally some 17,500 all ranks. There were two regiments to a brigade; the regiment was the basis of the army and was an operational unit roughly equivalent to a British brigade. A regiment, in addition to the regimental staff, contained three battalions, numbered I, II, and III, and a machine-gun company. The battalion closely resembled its British counterpart, being comprised of four companies, numbered in sequence through the regiment 1–4, 5–8, 9–12. It was commanded by a major, who had four captains, eighteen lieutenants and some 1054 men under him. In a company there were five officers and 259 men. It was divided into three platoons consisting of four sections, and each section was further sub-divided into two *Gruppen* of eight men each.

Across the short strip of no-man's-land, manning the trenches where the British attack would fall, were men from the 13th and 14th Divisions and the 6th Bavarian Reserve Division. It is interesting that, within an Imperial Germany Army dominated by Prussia, the Bavarian Army, at the insistence of its king, still managed to retain its identity. Bavaria had a long military tradition, possessed its own officer corps and was jealous of its independence. All in all these troops were not to be taken lightly. Certainly, experienced regimental officers of the BEF, regular officers who had commanded companies and battalions in action, considered that the German infantry of 1914 and 1915 were of very high quality. They found them to be well-trained, resolute in defence and brave and skilful in attack. This is not to say they were superior to our regulars; they simply appeared to General Jack to have 'a more soldierly manner of carrying out their duty'.

The German infantryman was armed with the *Gewehr* '98 rifle with a magazine housed in the stock holding five rounds of 7.9mm ammunition. This was the standard rifle during the Great War and it remained so during the Second World War. A trained man could theoretically get off ten aimed shots per minute but, because of the nature of German tactics, his standard of marksmanship was much inferior to that of the regulars of the BEF. He was fortunate in having a reliable and effective hand grenade, the stick bomb (or 'potato masher') activated by a time fuse of either 5.5 or 7 seconds. It consisted of a metal cylinder filled with an explosive charge, attached to a hollow wooden handle. Through this handle ran a cord to ignite the charge by friction. The infantryman simply pulled the exposed cord and threw it; its range was sixty yards, twice the range of our later Mills bomb. The Germans also had a small 'egg' grenade which could be thrown about fifty yards and a segmented type of ball grenade which our troops called 'pineapples'. The helmet worn by the Germans at this time was the traditional *Pickelhaube*; the steel helmet or *Stahlhelm*, a more effective design than the British, was not introduced until early 1916.

The Germans also possessed a most effective trench mortar. This was the 25cm *Minenwerfer* (literally 'mine-throwers'), always referred to as 'Minnies'. It fired a missile weighing just over 200lb which looked like a 5-gallon oil drum as it shot high in the sky; Blunden calls them 'small black casks'. They could easily be seen as they descended, slowly turning over and over, and the troops learned to watch their descent and take rapid avoiding action. These 'moaning Minnies' proved disastrously effective; if they landed in a trench, they exploded with a tremendous roar, bringing down sections of the trench, smashing in dug-outs and maiming and burying those troops nearby. Thus the Germans found themselves rather better equipped than the British for trench warfare. Ironically, the machine guns produced for a traditional (and brief) war of movement proved most advantageous when the opposing armies became bogged down in the trenches.

These troops were supported by an effective artillery organization, not too dissimilar from the British. The Field Artillery, which included both field and horse, manned the field guns and light howitzers of the divisional artillery while the heavy calibre pieces were the responsibility of the Foot Artillery at corps level. At this stage in the war the Field Artillery was organized into brigades, each of which was permanently attached to an infantry division whose number it took. A brigade consisted of two regiments, each composed of three battalions; there were three six-gun batteries and a light ammunition column to a battalion. There were two types of gun. The first was the 7.7cm field gun which had been introduced in 1896 and after subsequent modifications remained the principal field gun throughout the war. It fired a high velocity 15lb shell called a 'whizzbang' by our troops because its sudden arrival was followed immediately by an explosion. 'All you hear is a whizz and a bang.' The other weapon was the 10.5cm light howitzer.

In the Foot Artillery, one battalion of 15cm and 21cm howitzers was allotted to each army corps. It was the use of the 15cm how-itzer (5.9-inch) as a heavy field gun which surprised us at Ypres and had such a shattering effect upon our troops. It fired high-explosive shells called either 'coal boxes' or 'Jack Johnsons' because of the clouds of black smoke which followed their explosion. (Jack Johnson was the negro heavyweight champion of the world from 1908 to 1915 and was nicknamed 'The Big Smoke' by the Americans.)

Bruce Bairnsfather, creator of 'Old Bill', encountered them early in the war in Flanders and referred to their arrival in the vicinity as 'that slow, rotating whistle of a "Johnson" and then a reverberat-ing, hollow-sounding Crumph!' When they landed close by they exploded with a tremendous crash; if they fell in a section of trench, they would kill or mutilate all those sheltering within it. As the war developed and the demand for heavier calibre guns grew ever more clamorous the Foot Artillery expanded to almost six times its pre-war strength.

There was now a very different situation facing the First Army. At the end of April Haig found himself confronted by an immensely strengthened front line, held by a resolute and skilful enemy. Instead of the light field defences encountered at Neuve Chapelle, there were now defences which could only be demolished by sus-tained pounding by heavy guns.

Haig seems not to have grasped the extent of the problem. Instead he and his staff set to with a confidence born of their early success at Neuve Chapelle to draw up detailed plans for the attack. The atmosphere at AHQ was tinged with euphoria; as some officers put it: 'This should be Neuve Chapelle all over again, and much more successful because we have learnt its lessons and shall know what to avoid this time.' What those lesson were was underlined by a cheering memorandum from AHQ on 4 April, stating that a stretch of the enemy's front-line defences could now be captured with comparatively little loss by a combination of careful attention to detail (Haig's forte) and accurate registration by our artillery on the enemy trenches.

It was, indeed, to be Neuve Chapelle all over again, but not quite in the way the higher command anticipated. One would have expected them, in preparing their battle-plan, to examine the latest intelligence reports about the enemy's numbers and defences with care, but there appears little evidence of their doing so or, if they did, even less evidence of their plans being affected in any significant way. The work of Military Intelligence had been disrupted by the unexpected consolidation of the Western Front into a continuous line of trenches. Since there were no longer any flanks and thus no opportunity for cavalry reconnaissance, Military Intelligence was forced to rely upon patrolling and trench-raids to discover the layout of the German defences and the capture of the occasional prisoner to identify enemy units.

There was another source of information, of course, the Royal Flying Corps, which had done valuable work during the invasion of France. But the RFC found that aerial reconnaissance was now much more difficult with a static defence line. This was especially true in relation to the terrain in front of the ridge, where photographs gave little idea of the improved enemy defences, where there were few points of reference, and the variety of dykes, drainage ditches and channels made it hard to map the water hazards accurately for the infantry.

The British High Command had been reluctant to believe RFC reports in August and September, 1914, and those produced for many months afterwards were either ignored or damned with faint praise. This was still true of RFC and Military Intelligence reports furnished to First Army in the spring of 1915. We have seen earlier in this chapter how rapidly the Germans had reacted to the defensive deficiencies shown up by Neuve Chapelle. This did not go unobserved. As early as 1 April the First Army Intelligence Summary, edited by Major Charteris, carried a report from the RFC that during the previous fifteen days the whole of the German efforts opposite the First Army had been devoted to strengthening their defences in front of the ridge.

Again, throughout the latter part of April and the first few days of May there were numerous references in the daily Intelligence Summaries to increasing enemy activity. More wire and *chevaux-de-frise* appeared near Rouges Bancs, machine guns capable of enfilade and cross-fire were located, higher and stronger parapets were noticed, and Germans were seen to be increasing the wire in front of their second position. The enemy was also observed to be cutting down the large trees along his front opposite the Rue du Bois and improving his trenches and wire-entanglements there. More sinister than reports of flashes from the rifles of snipers lodged in the trees of the Bois du Biez was the identification of what appeared to be a redoubt under construction at the south-west corner of the Wood. This particular strongpoint was to cost us many lives during the battle.

Yet Haig, a cavalryman displaying a cavalier attitude, remained unimpressed. In any case he was, by temperament, most reluctant to recognize information which conflicted with his own preconceived ideas. Obdurate by nature and confident in his own judgement and experience, he seems to have made little effort to modify his plans in the light of any new information. One accepts that it could not have been easy to make major alterations or last-minute amendments to the detailed plans for which Haig was noted, but it is still hard to understand how he and his staff chose to ignore reports of the strengthening of the German defences. After all, there was simple visual evidence of this from his own front line. Moreover, Rawlinson had told him about the construction of strongpoints (*Stützpunkte*) and large dug-outs (*Wohngraben*) by the enemy. One senses that he was more concerned with the completion of a meticulously detailed plan, in a vacuum as it were, rather than with tailoring it to take account of alterations in the German defences.

If taxed with this, Haig would no doubt have countered by stressing that he was undertaking an offensive in conjunction with the French, based on a plan originated by an ally, with an inadequate number of guns and limited stocks of ammunition – a deficiency he had drawn several times to the attention of his Commander-in-Chief. He would claim that he had no alternative to a frontal assault and that he had every reason to believe that his numerically superior forces would storm the defences of Aubers Ridge as they had done those of Neuve Chapelle. In any case, his plan was now ready.

CHAPTER FIVE

Plans and Preparations

Haig proposed to launch a simultaneous pincer attack against the German defences north and south of Neuve Chapelle, the points of the two attacks being some 6000 yards apart. It would be preceded by a short, intensive, forty-minute bombardment, as at Neuve Chapelle. This would retain the element of surprise and prevent the enemy alerting and moving up his reserves before the offensive was launched. The initial pincer attack would develop into a rapid advance in order to gain a secure footing on Aubers Ridge a mile and a half away (see map on p. xx).

The main thrust, the southern prong of the pincer movement, would be made by the 1st Division and the Meerut Division of the Indian Corps. They would attack side by side on a front of 2400 yards between Chocolat Menier Corner and Port Arthur, with the Meerut Division swinging north-eastwards to capture La Cliqueterie Farm. This farm had been transformed by the Germans into a formidable *Stützpunkt*, a little over one and a half miles behind the centre of their front. Thus the southern attack planned to secure a line running from the Rue du Marais–Lorgies–Ligny le Grand to the farm.

The northern prong would be spearheaded by the 8th Division attacking south-east towards Rouges Bancs across the Sailly–Fromelles road. As soon as its leading brigades had broken through the enemy defences, they were to spread out and secure a line running from Rouges Bancs to Fromelles and along the Ridge to Aubers, with their right joining up with the left of the Meerut Division at La Cliqueterie Farm.

If Haig's plan succeeded, some six or seven German battalions and a number of guns would be cut off on a three-mile front west of the Ridge. To deal with them, i.e. keeping the net closed and beating off counter-attacks, units from the inner flank of IV Corps and the Indian Corps were instructed to seize certain key-points such as the village of Aubers and the group of farm buildings at the north-east corner of the Bois du Biez known as La Russie.

Once the army's advance on to the Ridge had been consolidated, and with the guns moved forward and reinforcements brought up, it would then be in a jumping-off position for the second phase of the offensive. Sir John French and Haig envisaged this as a further advance of some five miles to a line running from Bauvin to Don on the Haute Deule Canal.

It would be helpful at this stage if we looked briefly at the British position in front of the Ridge. As we have seen earlier, the flat ground across which the British and Indian troops were to advance was intersected in both attack sectors by drainage ditches of various sizes, some of them almost wide and deep enough to qualify as dykes. There was, for example, a prominent one, some ten to fourteen feet across with three feet of water in it, in the southern sector snaking right across no-man's-land, parallel to the front line and some fifteen to twenty yards in front of it. In May all these were filled with mud and water. The opposing trench lines were crossed at right-angles in the southern sector by the main road from Estaires to La Bassée and, in the northern, by the road from Sailly to Fromelles.

In the southern sector the main feature was the Rue du Bois, connecting Béthune to Neuve Chapelle, which crossed the Estaires/La Bassée road at a junction called Port Arthur. Port Arthur had been strongly fortified to command these vital crossroads and was a key position in our defensive line. About halfway along our attack sector on this part of the Rue du Bois was a cinder track leading to the Ferme du Bois (in German hands). Also along this stretch two narrow roads, known as Albert and Edward, ran north-west to join the Rue des Berceaux. The British trench system here is easily grasped. The front line ran three hundred yards south of, and parallel to, the Rue du Bois, while the second, or support, line of breastworks was fifty yards south of the road.

The northern sector is more straightforward. The Rivière des Laies, a sluggish stream varying from six to ten feet wide and between three and six feet deep according to season, flowed behind our front line until on the far right of our attack sector it sliced through our trenches at an angle close to a small orchard protruding into no-man's-land. Crossing no-man's-land it then ran behind the German lines for about two and a half miles before petering out at Port Arthur. The Sailly–Fromelles road (the Rue Delvas) crossed the Rue Tilleloy at the small hamlet of Petillon. Halfway between this crossroads and the Rivière des Laies ran the Rue Petillon and 1300 yards away beyond the river was our front line. The road continued through the German trenches to the straggle of buildings forming the hamlet of Rouges Bancs and then across the fields and up the slope to the village of Fromelles on the Ridge. The trench system was similar to that on the southern front.

Despite Haig's reluctance to recognize reports from Military Intelligence, his was a sound and imaginative scheme given the circumstances and resources available. It is difficult to quarrel with a plan combining a classic pincer movement with a general advance to establish the First Army on a plateau from which, now on dry ground and no longer under enemy observation, it would threaten communications between La Bassée and Lille. Admittedly it involved a frontal attack against a resolute and entrenched army, but Haig felt confident after Neuve Chapelle that he could break through the German defences before the Ridge and win a resounding victory. Haig, in fact, was faced with the problem that baffled all the allied commanders until the tank provided the solution in 1917. Once there are continuous lines of strongly defended trenches, how do you attack and outflank an enemy who has no flanks? General Castelnau felt that Napoleon would have found an answer; he would have thought of what Castelnau called 'the something else' to break the deadlock. Haig was no Napoleon and it is fair to ask what alternative he had to a frontal infantry assault. One may quarrel with the execution (ominous word) of his plan but, in my opinion, the plan itself was sound.

Two aspects of the plan, however, need comment. First, although his staff were keen to take note of the lessons of Neuve Chapelle, they paid little heed to the wish of the battalion commanders to have definite objectives specified for each day. The latter preferred the French Army's tactic of advancing by stages; once the objective had been reached and consolidated, the artillery would prepare the way for a further advance. Haig's attacking brigades were simply encouraged to press on, particularly in the second phase of the offensive, from objective to objective towards the line of the Haute Deule canal. Thus, once the initial breakthrough had been achieved, the course of the battle would be determined to a large extent by the local commanders because of the problems of communication on the modern battlefield.

45

This was a very real problem. Prior to 1914 battles had been small enough to allow direct voice command, bugles and orders sent by galloper or runner. Even during the fighting in the autumn of 1914 senior commanders, with the help of their liaison officers, could frequently keep in touch with the action by using their binoculars. But from this time onward the size of the battlefield and the sheer intensity of the fire made this virtually impossible. The further a battle developed, the less control commanders could exercise over it or give orders affecting its outcome. This led to the imposition of rigid time-tables on the attacking troops, mainly so that commanders might have some idea where their troops were and what they were doing, providing they stuck to the time-table.

Admittedly, telephone cables could be run out by the signallers behind the advancing infantry once the first objective had been taken but this was a hazardous and often ineffective undertaking. It led directly to the employment of intelligent and active soldiers as runners – an equally hazardous and short-lived occupation for most. It is true that behind the front line telephone cables could be buried or strung along the communication trenches but these were easily broken by artillery fire or human frailty. Again, at this stage in the war, although division could speak to its brigades, and brigade, with good fortune, to its battalions, battalions were not connected with one another. Thus neighbouring battalions could only communicate via HQ and this often proved impossible in action.

Second, there was the involvement of the fledgling Royal Flying Corps. It is not always realized that, even at this early stage of the war, barely nine months after the German invasion, aircraft of the RFC were already playing a part in the British offensives. Their role was a very minor one but it was to develop rapidly within a short time. At Aubers Ridge, under the direction of Lieutenant-Colonel H.M. Trenchard, three squadrons of the 1st Wing, RFC, equipped with BE2s were attached to the First Army. These satisfactory two-seater biplanes had been designed before the war by Geoffrey de Havilland and they remained in production until 1916 with over 3500 being built. The 'B' stood for 'Bleriot' and the 'E' for 'Experimental', but both terms were irrelevant. Their task was to fly defensive patrols for four days before the battle to deal with any reconnaissance attempts by enemy aircraft. During the actual battle three BE2s, fitted with experimental wireless equipment, were to cruise at 4000 feet to report on the progress of the assault.

For this purpose the infantry were provided with strips of white cloth, 7 feet by 2 feet, to drape over the parapets of the German trenches they captured. The RFC was also to mount bombing raids on enemy rest billets in villages behind the lines and on selected railway junctions in the Lille area. Sadly, the infantry were never to reach the enemy lines in strength nor did the RFC manage to score a direct hit on any of its targets.

Having examined the infantry's part in the plan, let us turn to the preparations for the artillery bombardment which was to precede the attack. Haig knew that the success of his attack depended upon his artillery destroying the enemy wire, smashing the German front-line breastworks and forcing the defenders to remain under cover, neutralizing his strongpoints, and thus opening the way for the infantry to breach the German defences. He was only too well aware of the deficiencies in his artillery and supply of ammunition.

He had seen the war of words between GHQ and the War Office suddenly flare up yet again in mid-April. Kitchener met French to discuss his latest demands and he wrote a brief letter to the Prime Minister on 14 April:

> I have had a talk with French. He told me I could let you know that with the present supply of ammunition he will have as much as his troops will be able to use on the next forward movement.

Considering that Sir John was in the middle of planning an offensive in conjunction with the French and in view of all that had taken place, this seems an astonishing statement. We shall never know the truth of what happened; was it a genuine misunderstanding on Kitchener's part or did he wilfully choose to misinterpret French's remarks? A furious French was convinced he did and said so.

Kitchener's letter led Asquith to make an unfortunate speech at Newcastle a few days later when he denied reports that our army was being handicapped by lack of shells and that the armament firms were not pulling their weight. It is not difficult to imagine Sir John's reaction when he read about it. He had much to be choleric about and he was unable to conceal his feelings from the War Office.

By the beginning of May the number of guns and howitzers available to Haig's First Army for his offensive was as follows:

TYPE	NUMBER

Field artillery : light guns and howitzers

13pdr QF (Quick-firing)	84
18pdr QF, the standard field gun	276
4.5-inch QF, howitzer, used as a field gun	60
15pdr BL (Breech-loading) – obsolete	84

Heavy artillery: Howitzers

15-inch	3
4.7-inch QF Mark 2 (obsolete)	28
5-inch (obsolete)	20
6-inch BL Mark 7 (later superseded)	40
60pdr BL	20
9.2-inch BL Mark 10	10

The paucity of heavy guns was accompanied by an acute short-age of ammunition for all types of gun. Under the circumstances Haig saw little point in making further representations to his chief, particularly as French had told him rather brusquely, after his last appeal had been rejected by Kitchener, that he must get on and do his best with what he had. Haig did ask if he could borrow a number of batteries from the Second Army but, as this request coincided with the Second Battle of Ypres, nothing was forthcoming. So, despite the strengthening of the German defences, the number of guns Haig eventually brought to bear against them was not much greater than the number he used at Neuve Chapelle. For example, in the 1st Division's sector there were forty-six howitzers on a front of 1500 yards; at Neuve Chapelle there had been sixty on an attack frontage of 2000 yards.

The First Army's artillery programme was soon settled. No gunner likes flat country. It is bad for observation at the guns and also bad for the wagon lines, which usually have to be sited rather too far behind them. However, the commanders of the various divisional artillery concerned and of the Heavy Artillery Reserve (HAR) made their preparations in great detail, with each battery being allotted a specific task. As we have seen, the preliminary bom-bardment was to last forty minutes. Haig had presented this programme as a short, intense, surprise bombardment, similar to that which had contributed much to the success at Neuve Chapelle. In fact, he was making a virtue out of necessity. He would have preferred a longer bombardment with heavy calibre howitzers capable of destroying the enemy defences but he simply did not have either the guns or the shells. He must have looked with envy at General d'Urbal, who was mounting a bombardment lasting five days at Vimy with some 1250 guns, of which nearly 300 were heavies. After their winter fighting the French had given up the idea of a short, intensive bombardment and they now opted for a prolonged bombardment by heavy guns. They abandoned the element of surprise in favour of sheer weight of shell per square metre.

The artillery arrangements for the southern and northern sectors of attack had much in common. For the first ten minutes the 18pdrs would concentrate on destroying the German wire and cutting passages for the infantry. Although 18pdrs were normally used for this work, here it was not really the ideal gun for cutting barbed wire at a range of 1500 to 2000 yards because of its low trajectory and the flatness of the ground. At the start of trench warfare the 18pdrs fired high-explosive shells against wire but it was slowly realized that these simply blew sections of German wire up into the air and that, when they came down, they formed a jumbled barrier almost as difficult to cross as the original one. The guns then switched to using shrapnel, which was a sensible move since there were vastly more shrapnel shells available at this time than high-explosive ones. Given sufficient volume and accuracy of fire, shrapnel proved much more effective in cutting wire, but it did need a sustained and accurate bombardment to do the job properly and so often this was not achieved.

After a ten-minute concentration on wire-cutting, the 18pdrs would lift and join the 4.5-inch and 6-inch howitzers in pounding the enemy breastworks and attempting to breach their parapet. Batteries of 13pdrs were to put down a barrage behind the German defences to isolate the troops in the front line and prevent them being reinforced. In fact, the only heavy guns capable of destroying the massive German breastworks were the 9.2-inch and the 60pdrs of the HAR. Yet just before the offensive there were only six of the former and twelve of the latter available and these were already reserved for demolishing strongpoints and blockhouses and the fortified farms, such as Cour d'Avoué Farm and Deleval Farm. Anticipating a Neuve Chapelle-type breakthrough, arrangements were also made for getting the guns forward behind the advancing troops. In a similar spirit of optimism certain heavy batteries were instructed to prepare to move up on to Aubers Ridge itself as occasion offered.

While the artillery commanders were planning to demolish the enemy defences with howitzers, the Royal Engineers were arranging to blow up a section of his front line by tunnelling underneath it. That mining developed so rapidly and on such a scale during the war was mainly due to the efforts of one man, Major Norton Griffiths MP. He was a contractor in civilian life whose firm specialized in the construction of underground sewers. His energy and enthusiasm for mining led in due course to the formation of the tunnelling companies of the Royal Engineers. It was the 173rd Tunnelling Company which drove the two mine galleries, 285 and 330 feet long respectively, out under no-man's-land in the northern sector. Then two mines, each containing 2000lb of explosive, were placed seventy yards apart under that section of the German front line to be assaulted by the 1/13th London Regiment.

The Germans also had tunnelling companies active in this sector, but they had abandoned their workings owing to the amount of surface water. Our tunnellers had overcome the problem by digging deep and penetrating into the stiff blue clay which lay underneath. This was arduous and perilous work, even for the experienced miners employed in the Tunnelling Companies. They had to work in narrow tunnels, hampered by lack of oxygen, and often in danger from enemy counter-mining measures. Fortunately, the miners were able to gouge out the clay; it came away in lumps and was fairly easily cleared back to the surface. Here the disposal of the soil presented another problem. It could not be left in colourful heaps near the workings because this would betray our activity to the enemy. In chalky areas it had to be carried in sandbags to the rear and dispersed, and this was equally true of the blue clay in front of Fromelles. Despite all our efforts, the area near the mine shafts became discoloured, but luckily this was not spotted by the Germans.

During April preparations for the offensive were pushed ahead. The preliminaries were on much the same lines as those for Neuve Chapelle with improvements and additions suggested by that experience. Approach roads to the forward areas were improved, new gun emplacements built, ammunition and supply dumps formed and the communication trenches renewed. The infantry battalions who were to take part in the attack underwent special training, including exercises in extended order. Their officers visited the assembly areas and the front-line breastworks and studied the ground across which they were to attack. It was not an inspiring sight and must have given them more than a *frisson* of unease. The terrain was unappealing, being flat, featureless and devoid of cover, while those elements which were to play a part in the battle, the various dykes, ditches and drains, were hard to distinguish. Beyond the German defences they could see the modest slopes dotted with trees rising to the Ridge, where the church towers of Aubers and Fromelles stood out clearly on the skyline.

One of the main problems was finding adequate cover for the infantry before the actual attack. The staff's solution to this was to reclaim and repair disused trenches beyond the front-line breast-works and to construct extra breastworks in the rear behind which troops could assemble with some degree of protection. For example, on the southern sector, a line of breastworks was built behind the Rue du Bois. Supporting troops would shelter here, until the time came for them to cross the road and move up to the front line.

It was not easy, of course, to conceal all traces of this activity from the enemy. He became a little restless and began to increase his artillery fire as the month wore on. However, despite some casualties among troops holding the front line and among engineer and infantry working parties, the work went steadily forward.

CHAPTER SIX

Into the Line

Now the pipes are playing, now the drums are beat,
  Now the strong battalions are marching up the street,
But the pipes will not be playing and the bayonets will not shine,
  When the regiments I dream of come stumbling down the line.

E.A. Mackintosh, 'Before the Summer'
(killed in action at Cambrai 1917)

Haig now proceeded to reorganize his troops to get them into the right positions to launch the offensive. During April the Indian Corps took over 1500 yards of the I Corps front south of Neuve Chapelle, their line stretching across the Estaires–La Bassée road and along the Rue du Bois as far as the Orchard Redoubt. This (there were several orchards in the area) was a fortified post between the front line and the Rue du Bois about 600 yards beyond Port Arthur. At the same time the 47th (London) Division took over 6000 yards of the southern part of I Corps front stretching from Cuinchy to Chocolat Menier Corner. This meant that the 2nd Division (Major-General H.S. Horne) could be assembled in reserve behind the 1st Division (Major-General R.C.B. Haking), which was then concentrated on its attack frontage of 1600 yards. In the Indian Corps, on the left of I Corps, the Meerut Division was assembled on a frontage of 800 yards, side by side with the 1st Division. It was commanded by Major-General C.A. Anderson, late of the Royal Artillery. A typical Irishman, he was a fearless soldier who understood his Indian troops and gained their respect and affection by constant visits to the front-line trenches. It is a pity that other senior commanders did not follow his example.

Meanwhile a similar rearrangement took place in IV Corps holding the northern section. The 49th (West Riding) Division took over most of the line, enabling the 8th Division (Major-General F.J. Davies) to concentrate in depth on its attack frontage along the Sailly–Fromelles road. The 7th Division was duly assembled in its rear. It was commanded by a friend of Haig's, the ebullient Major-General H. Gough, of whom we shall hear more later. 'Goughie' was a cavalryman from a famous military family; impetuous, energetic, resourceful and brave, he had, to the chagrin of some, gained rapid promotion during the war. Unlike his chief, he was able to talk easily to the men under his command. He constantly visited his various units, in the line and out of it, and his cheerful presence and encouragement helped morale considerably. One characteristic he shared with several of his contemporaries was a quick temper, but he was aware of this fault and usually regretted his hasty outburst.

Then, suddenly, on 22 April, the Germans struck at Ypres with a terrifying gas attack. We know now that this was not the prelude to a full-scale attempt to break through to the Channel ports, but a critical situation rapidly developed as a five-mile gap opened up in our defences north-east of Ypres. The Canadians, gallantly and at great cost, held the line together, while reinforcements were rushed up to stem the enemy advance and to counter-attack. On 24 April the Lahore Division was pulled out and sent north to help the Second Army and was soon heavily engaged in the St Julien sector. So concerned was Sir John French with the German threat to the Salient that on 28 April he ordered two brigades from Gough's 7th Division to be moved into GHQ reserve in case they might be needed at Ypres; fortunately they were not.

While the fighting at Ypres continued, Haig suddenly started to have qualms about the outcome of his offensive. He began to wonder if the bombardment and the force he had assembled would be sufficient for the task. He realized, or rather it was brought home to him, that the quantities of men, guns and ammunition he wanted were not going to be available. By 30 April he was even becoming rather doubtful of success. He wrote in his diary:

I . . . told the C. in C. that in my opinion we had not enough troops and guns to sustain our forward movement and reap decisive results . . . In my opinion, three more good divisions are required (in addition to my eight divisions) . . . Sir John said Lord K. would not send his new Army because he was afraid they might be wanted at the Dardanelles or elsewhere. He wished me to attack and do the best I could with the troops available.

Those less charitably disposed towards Haig might suggest that here he was already insuring against possible failure. Driven hard by a need to succeed, this fear of failure underlay several aspects of his enigmatic character. He would do his best, of course, with what he had been given, even though this might not be enough to guarantee success. He would not blame his Commander-in-Chief directly (he would merely continue his intrigues against Sir John using his royal connections), but a lack of resources for his offensive, rather than any reflection upon his planning or conduct of the battle, would provide a convenient excuse if things went awry.

Early in May the Lahore Division, considerably reduced in numbers, was returned to the First Army with the two brigades from the 7th Division and Haig was then able to complete the reorganization of his front.

Although Sir John French and his Second Army were critically involved in the Ypres Salient, Joffre saw no reason to alter his plans to secure Vimy Ridge. On 2 May Sir John was told by Foch that the French Tenth Army would attack on 7 May and he agreed, with reservations he did not choose to press, to launch his own offensive on the following day. Privately he made no secret of his desire for the French and British attacks to be launched on the same day. Foch's idea was for German reserves to be attracted and sucked in as they were moving south towards Vimy Ridge. This may have suited Foch, but it meant that, once the element of surprise was lost, the British divisions would be attacking an enemy already alerted to the danger of a subsidiary attack.

The Commander-in-Chief now issued (4 May) his brief, formal orders for the battle from British Advanced Headquarters at Hazebrouck:

The First Army will take the offensive on 8th May. Its mission is to break through the enemy's line on its front and gain the La Bassée–Lille road between La Bassée and Fournes. Its further advance will be directed on the line Bauvin–Don. The Cavalry Corps, Indian Cavalry Corps, Canadian Division, Highland (51st) Division (less one brigade RFA) and

Northumbrian (50th) Division will be in general reserve at the disposal of the Field Marshal, Commanding-in-Chief, and will be ready to move at 2 hours' notice.

The idea of sending the cavalry racing through the gap at some stage of the offensive was obviously very much in the minds of French and Haig. Two days later, on 6 May, Haig held the second of his two conferences at which he explained his battle plan to his corps and divisional commanders. As usual Haig was confident of success and full of determination, and his mood communicated itself to his audiences. Nothing, he assured them, had been overlooked; all had been prepared. When the meeting broke up the senior officers returned to their headquarters with the conviction that a breakthrough and a successful advance onto the Ridge were within their grasp. The die was cast.

Haig's orders for his attack were issued later that night from his advanced headquarters at Merville, a small village on the River Lys, five miles west of Estaires:

1st ARMY OPERATION ORDER NO.22

6th May 1915

1. (a) The 1st Army will advance on 8th May and operate so as to break through the enemy's line and gain the La Bassée-Lille road between La Bassée and Fournes.

   Its further advance will be directed on the line Bauvin-Don.

   (b) Two Cavalry Corps and three infantry divisions are being held in readiness, as a General Reserve under the orders of the Field Marshal Commanding-in-Chief, to exploit any success.

2. (a) The artillery, disposed in accordance with special instructions which have been issued, will complete such registration as may be necessary by 5 am, at which hour the preliminary bombardment will commence.

   At 5.40 am the infantry assaults will be carried out simultaneously at all points. All troops holding the line will at the same time co-operate by a vigorous fire attack along their entire front.

(b) The 1st Corps, maintaining its right at Givenchy, will attack from its breastworks in the vicinity of Richebourg L'Avoué in accordance with instructions already issued, and advance on Rue du Marais-Illies.

(c) The Indian Corps (less 1st Highland Division) will attack from its breastworks in the vicinity of Rue du Bois in accordance with instructions already issued. It will operate so as to cover the left of the 1st Corps, and will capture the Distillery and the Ferme du Biez.

Its subsequent advance will be directed on Ligny le Grand-La Cliqueterie Farm.

La Ferme du Biez-Ligny le Petit-Ligny le Grand road inclusive is assigned to the Indian Corps.

(d) The 4th Corps will operate so as to break through the enemy's line in the vicinity of Rouges Bancs, in accordance with instructions already issued, with the object of:

i Organizing a defensive flank from the vicinity of La Cordonnerie Farm to Fromelles and

ii Turning the Aubers defences by an attack from the North-East and effecting a junction with the Indian Corps in the direction of La Cliqueterie Farm.

3. The 1st Highland Divison (less 1 Bde RFA) will be in General Reserve at disposal of the Field Marshal Commanding-in-Chief.

4. The 1st and 4th Corps will each detail one infantry brigade as Army Reserve under the orders of GOC 1st Army.

5. Advanced 1st AHQ will be established at Merville at 3 pm on 7th May.

R. BUTLER
Brigadier-General

Issued at 10 pm   General Staff, 1st Army

There was now much feverish activity among the staff of the two Corps. A little before noon on the following day (7 May) Corps Operational Orders were sent out to the various divisional generals concerned. (An example of the orders from I Corps is given in Appendix 3.) These in their turn were translated by the divisional staffs into more detailed instructions for their brigades and battalions in the attack, including the arrangements made for the artillery bombardment. These were sent off at 4.45 pm.

There are two points of particular interest in the divisional orders. It was stressed that at 5.30 am under cover of the opening bombardment the assaulting troops should emerge from their trenches, deploy, cross no-man's-land and lie down eighty yards from the enemy breastworks. Secondly, there were precautions against gas. This, as we saw earlier, had only been used by the Germans for the first time on 22 April. Yet already the men of the First Army had been issued with a rudimentary 'muffler' or respirator. This primitive device was to be dampened shortly before the attack with a solution available from containers placed at intervals along the breastworks. At least it was better than having to urinate on a handkerchief or piece of gauze.

The tempo of the First Army's preparations had been considerably stepped up during the past week, though most of the work had to be done at night. In front of our breastworks in some parts of no-man's-land were some old trenches. Now that the offensive was imminent, working parties filed out to them under cover of darkness and cleared and improved them so they could be used as 'jumping-off' trenches by the leading companies.

The Germans had certainly become uneasy and may have expected an attack, yet even towards the end of April they still had no hard information about when it might be launched. Then, on 30 April, for some reason they became nervous. Concerned about a possible attack at dawn on 1 May, they opened a heavy bombardment lasting for an hour and a quarter on our support trenches near Richebourg l'Avoué. They also briefly bombarded the village of La Couture north-west of Richebourg where the Cameron Highlanders were billeted and caused them some casualties. The Garhwal Brigade, which was close to the heavily defended position of Port Arthur, was also singled out by the enemy artillery and had forty-four men killed or wounded. Our own artillery replied and, when it became apparent that no attack was forthcoming, the enemy shelling gradually died away. It seems likely that, suspecting an attack, the enemy was searching the support and reserve areas and seeking to damage our communication trenches. Again there was some desultory shelling during the early days of May but nothing to suggest the Germans anticipated an early offensive. On Friday, 7 May their artillery concentrated on searching the Rue du Bois and the Orchard Redoubt but it did not develop into a serious bombardment and caused few casualties.

Since zero hour was to be 5.40 am on Saturday, 8 May, this meant that our attacking battalions would have to start moving up to the front line early on Friday evening to ensure they were in position by the early hours of Saturday. Instructions were given for the troops to leave their billets and parade, ready to move off at 6 pm.

It rained heavily all day on Thursday, while on Friday morning, 7 May, the men woke to find a thick mist covering the area with visibility down to fifty yards. This unkind weather played havoc with the French Army's artillery programme. As a result, General d'Urbal decided to postpone his main infantry attack planned for Friday morning until Saturday, 8 May. Later in the day he was forced to defer his attack once again until the morning of Sunday, 9 May. He also decided that the four attacks forming his offensive, that is the main French attack, their two subsidiary attacks on the flanks and Haig's First Army attack, should all take place on Sunday morning. This new arrangement suited Sir John French very well; all along he had wanted a simultaneous operation, though he had been forced to give way to his ally.

The decision to postpone the offensive until Sunday reached Haig at his advanced headquarters at Merville at 5 pm on Friday. He immediately sent orders halting the movement of his troops towards the front, but, by the time these orders were received, several battalions (the 2/Royal Sussex was one) were already paraded and about to move off. The men, therefore, had to settle down uneasily where they were for the night. As was usual just before an attack, blankets and packs had been dumped in the rear, so it was just as well that the mist had cleared and the weather was fine.

Visibility was good enough on Saturday morning for the French bombardment to continue, increasing in intensity as the day wore on. The British guns remained silent. The only major explosion heard on the First Army front that morning was caused by the destruction of a factory chimney in the Rue du Bois because it obstructed the fire of our 18pdrs. This again aroused the suspicions of the Germans. Early on in the battle the following morning German soldiers shouted at troops of the 2nd Brigade pinned down in front of the enemy wire that they had been expecting an attack for twenty-four hours. The only other excitement during the day was a sudden raid on a post on the Sailly-Fromelles road by men of the 1st Company of the 16th Bavarian Reserve Regiment, armed with knives and bayonets. They were driven off after a brief skirmish, having learned nothing of our intentions and leaving four dead behind. The First Army spent the day making sure everything was in place for the offensive and then in the evening, after all these irritating delays and postponements, the troops finally began to move off to the front-line trenches and the assembly areas. As they did so, several battalions struck up a new ditty:

> We beat the Germans every time.
> We beat the Germans at Mons,
> We beat the Germans at Neuve Chapelle
> And now we're going to give them hell.

Sir John French decided to watch the battle from a lofty but secure vantage point, the ruined church tower in the village of Laventie, not far from IV Corps HQ. In addition to his staff, he was accompanied by Colonel Repington, the egregious military correspondent of *The Times*, who was an old friend of his and thus afforded facilities not extended to other journalists. At the time Repington happened to be staying at French's Headquarters; he was 'touring' the front. There was also a much more important guest at the battle, none other than Winston Churchill, First Lord of the Admiralty. On 7 May Churchill was on his way back from Paris where he had been negotiating a Naval Convention with France and Italy. He thought he would break his journey and spend a day with Sir John French with whom he was on intimate terms. When he arrived at St Omer he learned to his satisfaction that Sir John was about to launch an offensive against Aubers Ridge at dawn on the 9th. Churchill decided to stay on to watch it; at least it would serve to keep his mind off the Dardanelles.

Dr Jocelyn Nangle, Medical Officer of the 1/Loyal North Lancashire in the 2nd Brigade, found himself in the southern sector with the 1st Division. Before a battle, a battalion established its Regimental Aid Post under cover or out of the line of fire in a support or reserve trench. Here the wounded reported or were brought by stretcher-bearers for attention. The non-walking wounded were then taken on stretchers to an Advanced Dressing Station from there they were carried either by field ambulance or by stretcher-bearers to the Casualty Clearing Station serving their particular division. Dr Nangle set up his post in a house in the Rue du Bois. In a letter to his parents he wrote:

> On the night of Saturday the 8th, with the rest of the brigade, we moved into position behind the breastworks in front of the German line. A fine night, but rather cold. The men, however, were wonderfully cheery, and talked and joked as if they were setting out for a spree.

Their high spirits were echoed by men of the 1/Northamptonshires of whom it was reported, 'All ranks are keen and eager for the coming fight'.

Other men took a more pragmatic view of what was to come. In the 3rd Brigade were the 2/Welch whom Robert Graves joined a few days after the battle. Graves had left Charterhouse in 1914 where he had been in the Officers' Training Corps. In early August he applied to the Royal Welsh Fusiliers and was commissioned into their Special Reserve Battalion. Crossing to France in early May, 1915, he was then posted to the 2/Welch. In his platoon he found a certain Sergeant Beaumont, distinguished for being the last unwounded survivor of the original battalion, apart from the transport men. Beaumont had again been one of the survivors at Aubers Ridge but sadly he was to be killed in June. In *Goodbye To All That* Graves writes that a few days before his death:

> Beaumont had been telling me how he had won about five pounds' worth of francs in the sweepstake after the Rue du Bois show: a sweepstake of the sort that leaves no bitterness behind it. Before the show, the platoon pools all its available cash and the survivors divide it up afterwards. Those who are killed can't complain, the wounded would have given far more than that to escape as they have, and the unwounded regard the money as a consolation prize for still being there.

For some soldiers the night before an attack entailed something rather more than the usual fear for their safety on the morrow and concern about their dependants. Many men of the 1/Royal Irish Rifles took the opportunity of attending a field Communion Service before parading and moving off to the front line. In the Rue du Bois

60

men of the 2/Munsters received their last absolution from their chaplain, Father Gleason. This scene was later painted for the Christmas number of *The Sphere* by that popular illustrator and titillator, Fortunino Matania, under the title of 'The Last Absolution of the Munsters' and caused a minor emotional storm.

It was now getting on for midnight as the four battalions from the 2nd and 3rd Brigades, who were to lead the attack on the 1st Division front, crossed the Rue du Bois and took up their positions in the front trenches. On their left the three assault battalions of the Dehra Dun Brigade similarly moved up into the front breastworks.

In the northern sector the two attacking brigades of the 8th Division, the 24th and 25th, moved forward to their battle positions in roughly dug assembly trenches facing the German line before Rouges Bancs. To ensure a continuous flow of reserves both brigades were disposed in depth, battalion behind battalion. In their rear, in front of the Rue Tilleloy, waited the 23rd Brigade, the divisional reserve. Further back, grouped west of the hamlet of Petillon, was the 7th Division. By 2.30 am all the troops of the 7th and 8th Divisions were in position for the attack – no mean feat on the part of the much-maligned staff officers.

The men were in battle-order: haversack moved to the back below the shoulder blade, rolled groundsheet in the small of the back, extra ammunition in a bandolier over the right shoulder, water bottle and white linen bag with the iron ration on the right side. In both sectors the infantry found themselves crowded into front-line breastworks already occupied by the troops whose job it was to hold the line during the offensive. There were scaling ladders propped up against the side of the trench to enable them to climb out quickly and steps cut at intervals in the breastworks for the same purpose. Wooden ladders and light footbridges further cluttered up the trenches. These had been drawn earlier from stores by the troops to help them cross any dykes, ditches or streams which might hold up their advance. One or two battalions, notably in the Indian Corps, had already climbed out under cover of darkness and placed their ladders over the wide dyke that ran in front of their trenches some fifteen yards away. At points just behind the breastworks were small dumps of ammunition, bombs and those stores needed to strengthen and defend captured sections of the enemy trenches.

Jammed together with little room to move, the troops made themselves as comfortable as they could while they waited for the dawn. It was a fine, clear night and the 2/Royal Sussex, like other battalions, enjoyed an issue of tea and rum at 3.30 am. There was still no sign of any unusual activity in the German lines opposite; indeed there was no sign of any activity at all. The troops of the First Army were now in position. In front of them the Ridge stretched like a black band across the night sky. A silence fell upon the crowded trenches.

> . . . The poor, condemned English,
> Like sacrifices, by their watchful fires
> Sit patiently, and inly ruminate
> The morning's danger.
>
>> William Shakespeare,
>> *King Henry the Fifth*, Prologue to Act IV

Sunday, 9 May: Sunrise 4.4 am. Sunset 7.16 pm

CHAPTER SEVEN

Battle: The Opening Assault – South

> The night is still and the air is keen,
>> Tense with menace the time crawls by . . .
>> The darkness moves like a curtain drawn,
> A veil which the morning star will tear
>> From the face of death. – We charge at dawn.
>>> Patrick MacGill, 'Before the Charge'

Night. A fine night with a clear sky. A multitude of stars glittering above a dark swathe of battlefield. A quiet night. No shell-burst or rifle shot, no ugly rattle of a traversing machine gun. Only the muffled sound of the assaulting battalions moving up from the rear to the assembly area, filing along communication trenches in thin streams of khaki, filling the support line and steadily pressing forward towards the front-line breastworks. Night. Under cover of the soft darkness thousands of men take up their positions for the attack. A few noises disturb the stillness: nervous coughs, smothered curses, the chink of equipment, quiet orders and brief, whispered conversations. Well before dawn the troops stand ready, waiting. In a little while the stars will fade and the dawn break, heralding the last Sunday that thousands of those now crowded into the front-line will ever see.

Now our bombardment bursts upon the enemy trenches. An appalling, continuous thunder. The ground shudders; the air vibrates. Ten minutes to zero hour. Fix bayonets! Soon it will be time to leave the protection of the breastworks, climb out over the parapet into no-man's-land, form up and, on command, walk through the enemy fire towards the German line.

As the sky lightened and the stars faded, all were agreed that it had the makings of a splendid day. One eye-witness recalled:

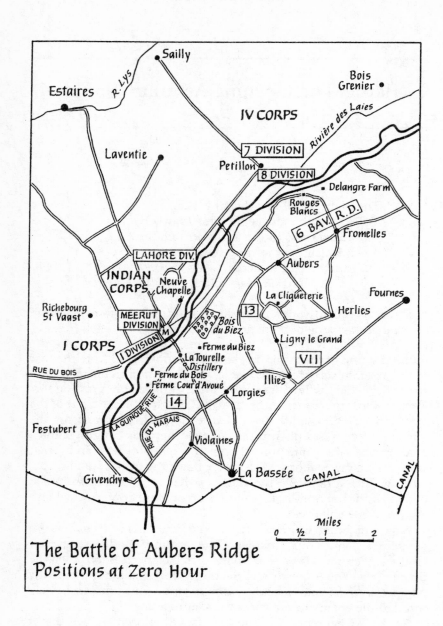

The Battle of Aubers Ridge
Positions at Zero Hour

The scene in front of our line was the most peaceful imaginable. Away to our right were Cuinchy, with its brickfields, and the ruins of Givenchy; to the north of them lay the low ground where, hidden by the trees and hedgerows, ran the opposing lines which were about to become the scene of conflict; and beyond, in the distance, rose the long ridge of Aubers, the villages crowning it standing out clear against the sky.

Another witness, much closer to the action, was 2nd Lieutenant K.H.E. Moore of the 1/7th Middlesex, 23rd Brigade, which was in the trenches opposite Fromelles with the task of manning the front line during the attack. He wrote:

Sunday broke a glorious day with the corn and fields looking perfect. It was light about three but it was not until five that the show was to start. The first-line trenches in which we were and the assembly trenches were by this time simply packed with troops and of course it seemed an eternity waiting for our watches to point to five o'clock. However, it came at last and to the very tick hundreds and hundreds of guns started pounding away.

Suddenly 600 guns shattered the quiet of the dawn and the roar and thunder of the bombardment contrasted with the silence that had preceded it. For those in the trenches the noise was deafening; the earth shook under their feet, while further back in the various headquarters along the Rue du Bois the ground trembled and quaked. For the first ten minutes the 18pdrs concentrated on cutting the enemy wire with shrapnel. Then, at 5.10 am, the bombardment lifted and the 18pdrs, now joined by the howitzers, began to pound the front-line breastworks. Observers in our front-line could see little through the clouds of smoke, dust and débris rising from the German breastworks as a multitude of small explosions erupted along their line. To our waiting infantry, the flame and the smoke from the shells bursting along the enemy trenches was an awe-inspiring and cheering sight.

About 5.20 am a strong breeze suddenly got up and blew across the southern sector of the attack and for a brief moment the clouds of smoke and dust were dispersed. The troops in the front line could now see their objective clearly. They could also see the helmets and bayonets of the enemy behind his breastworks. The Germans had been ordered out of their dug-outs by their officers to stand to and were now manning their trenches, undeterred by the fire of our guns. Then the fickle breeze died away as quickly as it had arisen and once more the enemy's position was shrouded in smoke and hidden from view.

The bombardment now entered its final intensive phase and the shells roared and whined over the heads of our waiting troops in an ear-splitting crescendo. As zero hour drew near, the order was given to fix bayonets. Officers glanced at their watches, made last-minute checks on their platoons and companies and exchanged a few, final words with their NCOs. The men, keyed up by nervous tension, shook hands with their comrades and muttered wishes of good luck and brief words of encouragement. Although quiet, they were confident and in good spirits.

A little before 5.40 am along the front of both sectors, thousands of men, British and Indian, could be seen climbing out over the parapet and attempting to form up for the attack. Zero hour! The guns lifted 600 yards from the German breastworks. Whistles shrilled, officers waved their men forward and long lines of khaki figures started to advance across no-man's-land.

At this point, what I planned as a detailed and orderly narrative begins to bear little resemblance to the progress of the battle. From the time that the infantry start out to cross no-man's-land confusion and ignorance reign. The Official Historian puts it succinctly:

> The historian is forced to depict a battle with an orderliness which was not apparent during the actual events; it is quite impossible to give an adequate representation of the organized confusion of modern warfare.

Aubers Ridge, even though it was only a one-day battle and on a relatively small scale, poses the same problem. One remembers the Duke of Wellington's reply to a writer who sought his help in writing an account of Waterloo: 'Write the history of a battle, Sir! You might as well write the history of a ball.'

Like a theatre gauze, the fog of war descends upon the vivid scene. Quite suddenly many things start to happen at the same time in different places. Like breakers on a beach, lines advance, waver, fall and then recede, leaving bodies strewn like pebbles upon the shore; small groups emerge, penetrate, are lost to sight, only to reappear at intervals, fitfully glimpsed. Fresh lines emerge to join and merge with those in front; another wave dissolves and men disperse to seek the safety of the parapet. All this seemingly haphazard activity takes place amid a numbing tumult of noise, the rattle of machine-gun fire, the crash of bursting shells, where the shouts and screams of the participants are barely audible. Unwholesome clouds of dirty smoke swirl across the enemy defences, masking the death waiting within.

This fog of war, which accounts for so many misjudgements, errors, minor and major tragedies, so much apparent blindness and stupidity, is compounded of many ingredients. Among these are: inadequate knowledge of the enemy's forces, their deployment and the nature of their defences; the inability to see 'behind the hill' or to observe troops hidden from view in trenches; and the inability of commanders, once an attack has gone in, to see what is happening to their men or, indeed, to see more than a small area of the immediate battlefield. Above all, at this particular period, as we saw earlier, was the sudden loss of communication in the forward areas. Once troops were out of sight, it became difficult, owing to telephone wires being constantly cut by shellfire, officers killed and runners shot down, to send back the simplest message. These factors, in various combinations, contribute to the ignorance of senior commanders about what is happening to their plan of attack. Ignorance accounts for their failure to respond rapidly to the ebb and flow of conflict and, when allied to a natural intransigence or arrogance, often leads to disaster.

In describing the battle, I shall move from right to left in the customary way, dealing first with the southern attack, which was the main thrust or right pincer, and then with the northern attack or left pincer.

The Southern Attack

The southern assault was made by the 1st Division of I Corps on the right with the Meerut Division of the Indian Corps on its left, attacking side by side. Our troops were faced on their right by three companies from the 1st and 3rd Battalions of the 57th Royal Prussian Regiment (Herzog Ferdinand von Braunschweig) and on their centre and left by nine companies from the 1st and 3rd Battalions of the 55th Regiment (Graf Bülow von Dennewitz). More importantly, as we shall see, there were numerous machine-gun posts, cleverly sited and well-protected, along the enemy line.

The attack of the 1st Division was to be delivered by the 2nd and 3rd Brigades on a four-battalion front of some 1600 yards, stretching eastwards from Chocolat Menier Corner to the Orchard Redoubt. The dividing line between the two brigades was the cinder-track leading to the Ferme du Bois. Their immediate objective was to take the three lines of German trenches opposite them and storm the two fortified farms, the Ferme Cour d'Avoué, plus the buildings nearby, and the Ferme du Bois. They would then reform along the line of the Rue des Cailloux and la Quinque Rue which leads to the hamlet of La Tourelle on the main Estaires–La Bassée road. In the 2nd Brigade the two assaulting battalions were the 1/Northamptonshire (Lieut-Colonel L.G.W. Dobbin) and the 2/Royal Sussex (Lieut-Colonel E.B.W. Green), supported by the 2/King's Royal Rifles (Major L.F. Philips) and the 1/5th Royal Sussex (Lieut-Colonel F.G. Langham). In the third line, in reserve behind the Rue du Bois, were the 1/9th King's (Major T.J. Bolland, who was to be killed later in the day) and the 1/Loyal North Lancashire (Lieut-Colonel W.D. Sanderson). On the other side of the track were the two leading battalions of the 3rd Brigade, the 2/Royal Munster Fusiliers (Lieut-Colonel V.G.H. Rickard) and the 2/Welsh (Lieut-Colonel A.G. Prothero), supported by the 1/4th Royal Welch Fusiliers (Lieut-Colonel T.C. France-Hayhurst). In reserve, waiting behind the Rue du Bois, were the 1/Gloucestershire (Lieut-Colonel A.W. Pagan) and the 1/South Wales Borderers (Lieut-Colonel A.J. Reddie).

General Haking, commanding the 1st Division, had established his headquarters in a house in the Rue du Bois and further along the road were the headquarters of Brigadier G.H. Thesiger's 2nd Brigade and Brigadier H.R. Davies's 3rd Brigade. For most of the battle Brigadier E.A. Fanshawe, who controlled the artillery on the front of I Corps, was in Divisional Headquarters, which made it easier for him to alter the artillery programme or arrange a special bombardment.

On the front of the 1st Division the bombardment was carried out by ninety-six field guns, mainly 18pdrs, placed along the line of the Rue des Berceaux some 1600 yards from the German wire. Another thousand yards to the rear forty-six howitzers were ranged around Richebourg St Vaast. Strongpoints and targets beyond the range of the divisional artillery were shelled by the heavy howitzers of No.1 Group, HAR, situated between Vieille Chapelle, four miles west of Neuve Chapelle, and the Rue du Bois. Other heavy guns of No.1 Group and the three French heavy batteries at Annequin, south of the La Bassée Canal, engaged German batteries in the rear. The British guns concentrated on targets between Violaines and Ligny-le-Grand, while the French shelled batteries in the area between the canal and Violaines.

Against the Allied artillery in the southern sector the Germans could muster the eight heavy batteries of their VII Corps artillery on the line of Violaines–Lorgies–Ligny-le-Grand. There were also six batteries of the 14th Divisional Artillery near Canteleux (a mile west of La Bassée), the Rue du Marais and Lorgies, while nine batteries of the 13th Divisional artillery were concentrated in the area bounded by Lorgies, La Tourelle, Ligny-le-Petit, and Illies. The enemy artillery, of course, had the exact ranges of our trench system and assembly trenches and was to perform with typical effectiveness during the battle. Their military observers along the Aubers-Fromelles Ridge had superb observation over our positions and no-man's-land and could rapidly adjust the fire from their batteries as the battle developed.

As our bombardment proceeded, problems began to arise. Officers in the front line reported that many of our shells, especially the 4.7s used for counter-battery work, were falling short. This was partly due to wear and tear in the gun barrels and partly to faulty ammunition. In the case of the 4.7 shells, the copper driving bands stripped off as they left the muzzle and the shells turned over and over and were likely to fall anywhere, in some cases hundreds of yards behind the British front line. Thus it was proving difficult to assess the effects of our counter-battery fire and our attempts to smash enemy strongpoints. The approximate position of the German batteries had been fixed by aerial reconnaissance in the weeks before the offensive. But because the ground was so flat it was difficult for the Forward Observation Officers to locate the guns in action, and the trees along the water-courses, being in leaf, hindered observation of the fall of shot. In the event, artillery commanders had to rely for counter-battery work upon messages from two sources: divisional headquarters, giving details of the direction from which fire was being received and, equally unreliable, radio messages from the three BE2s attached to No.1 Group, HAR and the four attached to No.2 Group. Unfortunately, although over forty messages and calls were sent down during the battle, they proved of little value as our observers had great trouble distinguishing friend from foe.

Our troops in the trenches, waiting to go over the top, were naturally unaware of these difficulties. They were more concerned with how well the German wire had been cut; they were soon to find out.

★ ★ ★

At last the barrage roars its opening range
The air's a cloud of shell-fumes and the stench
Of new-churned graves. We surge up from the trench.
Leonard Barnes; 'Youth at Arms' (XVII)

It is not often at this early stage in the war that we have eye-witness accounts from the German side of how our attacking battalions appeared to them. But in the case of Aubers Ridge we have such descriptions from both the regiments opposing the 1st and Meerut Divisions. Although perceptions naturally vary from company to company and according to their position in the front line, there is sufficient evidence from our own records to suggest that the German Regimental Histories, published after the war and relying heavily on their battalion war diaries, give an accurate picture of the opening stages of the battle. Their accounts stress the great courage (*ungeheure Bravour*) with which our attacks were carried out and how the discipline and determination of our troops won the admiration of the defenders.

At 5.30 am, as the bombardment increased in violence, the leading companies of the four attacking battalions clambered up their assault ladders and over the top of the breastworks with the intention of forming a line about eighty yards from the German breastworks. They had hoped to carry this out without interference but they were seen by enemy look-outs, alerted by the shelling to an imminent attack. These Germans were watching from their front line, seemingly unaffected by our bombardment and with no covering rifle fire to make them keep their heads down. So immediately our men appeared on the parapet they were met by a storm of accurate machine-gun and rifle fire. On the right, in the 2nd Brigade, as enemy machine guns swept the parapet, men of the 1/Northamptonshires and the 2/Royal Sussex crumpled on their ladders and fell back into the trench; others fell dead or wounded on the parapet or a few yards in front of it. The rest doubled forward and managed to form a line, lying down about half-way across no-man's-land, which was some 300 yards wide here. At 5.40 am our bombardment lifted from the German front line and in this area concentrated on the communication trenches on the enemy left (1 Battalion) to form a defensive barrier to protect the right flank of the 1/Northamptonshires. As it did so, the men of the two battalions rose to their feet and, cheering and shouting, made for the enemy wire.

At the same moment, as the smoke of the explosions thinned and drifted away, men of the German 57th Regiment could see the battalions of the 1st Division advancing in three long waves across the bare fields. Despite their initial losses, the first wave, advancing in extended order, was already within fifty yards of their wire; the second wave was half-way across no-man's-land, while the third was making its way through the gaps in the British wire, preparatory to forming up. Behind them, elements of the fourth wave were climbing out over the breastworks.

The German machine guns now got to work with a vengeance. Firing from well-protected positions sited low down in the breastworks, they began to traverse along the lines of khaki figures sharply etched in the morning sunlight. Our first wave was simply mown down before they could even reach the enemy wire; while the second was savaged by machine-gun fire from the right flank of the I Battalion. The third wave, more closely packed, was virtually annihilated by the same machine-gun on their right and by furious rifle fire from the III Battalion. The fourth wave suffered heavy casualties as they were caught by accurate artillery fire attempting to climb out of their front line.

It immediately became apparent that our artillery had failed to destroy the enemy wire and had been unable to locate and knock out his machine guns, which required virtually a direct hit to put them out of action. One battery commander, who spent the day in the front breastworks, admitted later that he had never spotted the position of a single German machine gun.

The wire-cutting guns, the 18pdrs, had failed to do their job. For many of our batteries it was their first experience of wire-cutting and their fire was neither sustained nor violent enough to be effective. Only a few gaps had been cut in the German wire, which still presented a formidable barrier. Our howitzers, too, seemed to have caused relatively little damage to the much-strengthened enemy breastworks, while the 18pdrs had had no visible effect on them whatsoever. So, despite the noise and the flames and the smoke of the bombardment, the damage to the enemy defences was more apparent than real. The bombardment, in effect – or in its lack of effect – merely served to confirm to the Germans that an attack was about to start.

The previous paragraph is based on the fairly scathing comments made about the shortcomings of our artillery performance in the Official History. Although justified in general, this is not how our bombardment seemed at the time to the Germans holding certain stretches of their line. As the roar and explosion of shells along their breastworks blended into a continuous and deafening cacophony, the effect of this drum-fire soon became apparent. The signallers only just had time to report the concentration of fire on the front trenches before the telephone lines were cut and contact with battalion HQ was lost. From then on runners had to brave the shellfire with messages and orders. Soon even the immensely strengthened breastworks were suffering damage with some stretches in the northern sector virtually levelled. Casualties mounted and the survivors were forced to take cover in dug-outs and *Wohngraben*.

Despite the enemy fire, some men of the 2nd Brigade did reach the enemy line. A party of twenty-one men of the 1/Northamptonshires found a gap in the wire and passed through it, only to find that a deep ditch, dug in front of the German parapet for earth to fill sandbags for the breastworks, had been filled with coils of barbed wire. They managed with difficulty to cross this and enter the German trench through a small breach. None of this party ever returned; according to German accounts they were dispatched either by bomb or bayonet in hand-to-hand fighting.

At this time the 2/Royal Sussex rejoiced temporarily in the unofficial title of 'The Iron Regiment'. It was not the kind of nickname an English county regiment would normally seek. They received it during the First Battle of Ypres as an unsolicited testimonial from German prisoners who had been intimidated by the battalion's determination not to be ousted from their positions despite the overwhelming numbers flung against them. However, their bravery on 9 May availed them nothing. As they advanced, they came under enfilade machine-gun fire from their right and especially severe fire from their left, where a machine gun, sited at an angle in the German trench opposite the Royal Munster Fusiliers, fired almost at right-angles to their line of advance. Most of the Royal Sussex officers were quickly killed or wounded; German marksmen were instructed to pick off officers, easily identified at this stage in the war by their uniforms and revolvers. Seeing his officers shot down, Company Sergeant-Major Butcher took command of the first line and ordered the men to dig in and take cover.

At this point the supporting battalions arrived. The task of the 2/King's Royal Rifle Corps was to follow up the advance of the 1/Northamptonshires and then secure the right flank of the brigade

72

by capturing the stretch of German trenches running south, almost at right angles to their front, towards la Quinque Rue. This plan proved illusory. Their leading companies were cut down by machine-gun fire as they crossed the parapet and debouched into no-man's-land and they soon found themselves pinned down.

On their left the 1/5th Royal Sussex, a Territorial battalion, had made a prompt start at 5.40 am. The men left the shelter of the breastworks in the second line in front of the Rue du Bois and moved rapidly across the 250 yards of open ground to the front line. They advanced so quickly that they actually arrived before the supporting companies of the 2/Royal Sussex were clear of the front-line breastworks. Their orders were: 'to follow immediately in the rear of the assaulting battalions – feed them up as necessary – clear all hostile trenches still occupied in rear of both assaulting battalions – secure all prisoners and send them to the rear and then follow in support'. Although they had already suffered casualties crossing the space between the first and second lines of breastworks, the Territorials, nothing daunted, went straight over the parapet to support the advance of their 2nd Battalion, mingling with the two rear companies as they went. They ran into the same enfilade machine-gun fire from their left and suffered heavily, and their situation worsened as the enemy started to shell the area before and behind the breastworks. The Territorials, like their regular comrades, were forced to go to ground – but only for a brief period. Captain F.N. Grant of B Company got to his feet and, waving a large red company marking flag, led a gallant charge of survivors of both Sussex battalions. Formerly an officer in the Royal Navy, he had served as a private in the battalion for several years before he could be persuaded to take a commission and he had already been awarded the MC. He attempted to guide his men towards the 1/Northamptonshires on the right but was shot and killed. Under such devastating fire no attack had much chance of success and only a handful of men were able to get within a hundred yards of the German line.

The men of the four battalions of the 2nd Brigade were now lying out in no-man's-land, unable to advance or retire without being fired on. Those who were unable to crawl back to their own line had to lie out throughout the day (some fourteen hours) exposed to rifle, machine-gun and shell fire from the German line until darkness fell and stretcher-bearers could bring them in.

We must now consider the fortunes of the two battalions of the 3rd Brigade, the 2/Royal Munster Fusiliers and the 2/Welsh, attacking to the left of the cinder track. As the Munsters swarmed over their parapet and into no-man's-land, they were cheered on by Captain Campbell-Dick who stood on top of the breastworks waving his cap until he fell, shot through the heart. The Munsters ran into machine-gun and rifle fire as heavy as that experienced by the 2nd Brigade but, led by Lieut-Colonel Rickard, they pressed on with great determination. Some hundred men reached the enemy wire which had been reduced by our guns to a tangle of posts and wire. As they attempted to force their way through it, Lieut-Colonel Rickard was mortally wounded and half his men were shot down. He thus became the third Colonel of the Munsters to be killed or disabled since August, 1914. Yet a party of fifty Munsters managed to pass this barrier, cross a wire-filled ditch, clamber over the parapet and jump down into the German trench. One man was clearly seen for a moment, standing up on their parapet and waving a green flag, before he, too, disappeared from sight. They found that the defenders of this section of trench (the third platoon of 11/55) had been wiped out by our bombardment so they decided to press home their temporary advantage and drive deeper into the enemy defences. The sheer audacity of this move surprised the Germans and the remainder of 11 Company was soon surrounded.

But the Germans fought back vigorously, led by their commanding officer, *Oberleutnant* Herbert Reuter. He led several determined bombing attacks which gradually reduced the numbers of the Munsters until they were finally overrun and killed except for eight men who were taken prisoner. There were as many acts of bravery and daring on the German side as on ours. A bugler called Ziegenbein distinguished himself. He stayed close to his commanding officer and accounted for several Irishmen with his rifle. When he himself was shot, his dying words to Reuter were, 'Sir, the English, in our rear!' This brief episode caught the imagination of the public and later on the scene was painted by Weinberg, a German war artist, under the title: *The 11/55 in the Battle of May 1915 near La Bassée.*

Ziegenbein's words referred to a small group of Munsters who, still bearing their green flag, had carried the enemy's support position and broken out into the country beyond. However, the attackers were far too few for any possibility of success. The moment they passed through the German support line, the defenders ran back down the trench and, using the parados as a fire-step, poured a stream of fire into their backs. A little further on the Munsters were halted by a deep dyke. Some of the men tried to swim across but barbed wire had been staked across the bottom and they were drowned. The survivors took up a position along the bank, but their position was now worse than ever and all except three (who were taken prisoner) were killed by the British bombardment that preceded the afternoon attack.

On the left of the Munsters the 2/Welsh faced the same intense fire. Among the subalterns in the first wave was 2nd Lieutenant B.U.S. Cripps, who had joined the regiment straight from school. Now he was just nineteen. In a letter written on 17 May he commented:

> We were told that after the bombardment there would not be many people left in the German first and second lines. We were all quite confident of the result and were very cheery. I got about 2 hours' sleep and then I had breakfast and plenty of rum and felt quite ready for any German.

No-man's-land in front of the 2/Welsh was about a hundred yards wide and there were three deep water-filled ditches that had to be crossed to reach the German defences. Cripps gives a vivid account in his letter of what happened. His experience was a representative one and explains why his battalion, like most of the others, failed to reach the enemy line.

> My platoon was not to leave the trench for two minutes after the first two platoons had gone. At 5.37 am the first two platoons jumped up over the parapet ready to charge but they were met by a perfect hail of bullets and many men just fell back into the trench riddled with bullets. A few survivors managed to get into one of the ditches. My company commander then turned to me before my two minutes were up and said I had better try. So I took my platoon and the other platoon in the company also came and we jumped up over the parapet to charge but we met with the same fate and I with a few men managed to get into the ditch. I was the only officer left in my company, two being killed outright and my company commander and another subaltern severely wounded. So I had to take command of my company. I only had fifteen unwounded men with me and heaps of wounded and dead. There was no means of getting back to the trench except by walking along the ditch for about 50 yards in water and mud up to your middle. This method was of course impossible as we had so

many wounded. So after we had bound up the wounded as best we could we started to dig our way back. The Germans were firing as hard as they could at first with their heads and shoulders looking over their parapet and there were any amount of them. It took us about 3 hours to get the trench dug and another hour to move the wounded. All the time we were out there the Germans dropped shells all around us and our own guns dropped a lot among us. I was covered with earth once but was not hurt, I had a bullet through my hat and through my hair but it did not draw blood. I was soaked up to my middle and I had to sit with dead and dying all around me. It was absolutely past words, my best friends killed and we could not do anything about it.

Behind the German front the commander of the 57th Regiment, Major Castendyk, had been told that the violent artillery fire that had woken him up was directed at his 3rd Battalion's front. He approved the request of his battalion commander, Major Wülfing, for the reserve company (9) to march up from La Bassée to battalion HQ on the road to Estaires. A little later Major Castendyk himself arrived at his advanced headquarters at Violaine by 'car'. This was a curious vehicle consisting of a motor-cycle coupled with a kind of comfortable wicker chair on wheels. Here he learned that the initial attack of the 1st Division had been repulsed with crushing losses by his 3rd Battalion. As a precaution, however, he ordered 4 and 7 Companies, who were also in reserve at La Bassée, to move up to the Rue du Marais.

On the left of the main thrust the Dehra Dun brigade of General Anderson's Meerut Division had a difficult task. Its objectives were successively:

1. The enemy's front and support trenches
2. The hamlet of La Tourelle and houses nearby
3. The Distillery, the Ferme du Biez (a strongpoint) and the south-west edge of the Bois du Biez
4. Ligny-le-Petit
5. Ligny-le-Grand and La Cliqueterie Farm

In addition, the Bois du Biez was to be engaged simultaneously with the advance on Ligny-le-Petit by a special force under the command of Lieut-Colonel D.H. Drake-Brockman. This consisted of two battalions from the Garhwal Brigade, the 39th Garhwalis and

1. British front-line breastworks at Laventie, Winter 1914/15. (*Imperial War Museum*)

2. Mortar bombs ('toffee apples') in a reserve trench dump. (*Imperial War Museum*)

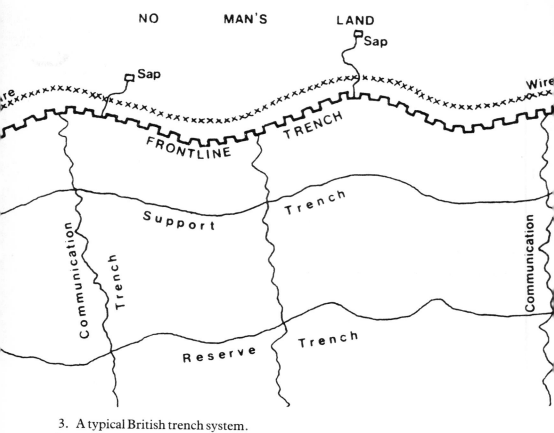

3. A typical British trench system.

4. A German strongpoint today at the foot of Aubers Ridge, west of the Rue d'Enfers.

5. A German wiring party. (*Imperial War Museum*)

6. Captured German wire, showing knife-rests. (*Imperial War Museum*)

7. Captain Hay and Jack Scott. At six foot, eleven and a half inches, Captain L.F. Hay was reputedly the tallest man in the British Army. Here, at Le Touret in France, he is pictured with fellow Black Watch officer, Jack Scott. Not long after this photograph was taken, Scott was killed leading his men in the attack on Aubers Ridge. Captain Hay was later wounded at the Battle of Loos but survived the war. (*Liddle Collection*)

the 2/8th Gurkhas, with their own staff, signals and ammunition supply. They were stationed behind the Rue du Bois with instructions to move up into the front trenches as soon as the Dehra Dun Brigade had left them and then advance through the Bois du Biez, secure its eastern edge and also capture the important buildings of La Russie at its north-east corner.

The assault was to be delivered on a three-battalion front of 800 yards. On the right was a company of the 6th Jats, temporarily attached to the 2/2nd Gurkhas (Colonel E.R.P. Boileau); in the middle were the 1/4th Seaforth Highlanders (Lieut-Colonel T.W. Cuthbert), while on the left, across the Estaires–La Bassée road and south of Port Arthur, were the 1/Seaforth Highlanders (Lieut-Colonel A.B. Richie). The Lahore Division held the line beyond them; the Bareilly Brigade was in support with the Garhwal Brigade, less two battalions, in reserve. As we have seen, in front of the Brigade's breastworks was a wide ditch or dyke some ten to fourteen feet across with three feet of water in it. During the night light bridges had been placed over the dyke, assault ladders set up at intervals along the front breastworks and our own rather flimsy wire cut.

The troops waited patiently in their positions during the preliminary bombardment by the artillery of both the Meerut and Lahore Divisions. By 5.20 am observers were becoming concerned that, although the enemy's wire seemed to have been satisfactorily cut, the German parapet seemed little damaged. Also, despite the noise and smoke, the volume of our artillery fire seemed less violent than expected and there was the usual problem of shells falling short, some of them exploding in the trenches of the 1/Seaforths and 2/2nd Gurkhas and causing casualties. At 5.40 am the guns lifted some 600 yards and began to shell La Tourelle. After bombarding the strongpoint there for thirty-five minutes, the plan was for them to concentrate for thirty minutes on the Distillery further down the La Bassée road.

Just before 5.40 am Nos. 2 and 4 Companies of the 2/2nd Gurkhas and two platoons of the 6th Jats climbed out over the parapet and attempted to form up. The moment they appeared in the open they were subjected to accurate machine-gun fire. On their left, astride the Estaires–La Bassée road, the 1/4 Seaforths and the 1/Seaforths were already out of their trenches. Brigadier Jacob had explained the plan of attack to his officers and sergeants two days before and he had impressed them as being very optimistic. His optimism was short-lived. At 5.25 am the leading companies

77

climbed over the parapet and formed up with the intention of creeping up as close as possible to the enemy wire under cover of our bombardment. So many of our shells were dropping short, however, that this idea had to be abandoned and the Seaforths were forced to lie down close to the parapet. At 5.40 am when they rose and moved to the attack they came under even heavier fire than the Indians.

The history of the 55th Regiment vividly describes the experience of their troops in the front line as they peered out anxiously through the clouds of dust and smoke. When our barrage finally lifted and the smoke thinned, they saw masses of khaki figures emerge from our breastworks, some in caps, others in turbans, and start to advance in dense waves. Those Germans who had been sheltering from our drum-fire now hurried back and took up their positions behind the breastworks. It was an amazing spectacle. No-man's-land here was only 100 to 150 yards in width and there could hardly have been a more perfect target than this solid mass of khaki, British and Indian, side by side. The crash of rifle fire mingled with the rattle of machine guns as the Germans poured a hail of bullets into the ranks of the Dehra Dun Brigade. The barrels of the machine guns became red-hot as the cooling water evaporated but the machine gunners ignored it on this occasion. The vital thing was to keep firing, to keep traversing to and fro along the lines of khaki.

As the first waves staggered under the impact of this storm of fire so shells from the German field batteries began crashing down upon the attackers. Artillery observers watched fascinated as their shells ploughed into the mass of men moving across the short stretch of no-man's-land. As the German account puts it: 'There are not many orders to be given at this crisis in the battle. Should one attempt to correct the range? Ridiculous! There is only one command: Fire until the barrels burst!'

The 6th Jats were mown down almost immediately; the Gurkhas fell in heaps as they made for the dyke in front and all their British officers who had led them across the parapet were either killed or wounded. While No. 4 Company still pressed forward on the left, the attack was halted by Lieut-Colonel T.W. Cuthbert, the Commanding Officer of the 1/4th Seaforths. He decided that it was impossible for his men to advance any further in the face of such fire, and he ordered the captain in charge of No. 2 Company of the 2/2nd Gurkhas to take cover. Lieut-Colonel Cuthbert then made his way across to the battalion headquarters of the 2/2nd Gurkhas, informed Major Boileau of what he had done and went off in person to the brigade report centre. While this was going on, No. 3 Company had climbed over the parapet and dashed forward to support No. 4 Company, but they got no further than the ditch, where their company commander fell mortally wounded. The survivors of the 2/2nd Gurkhas were now seeking cover on both sides of the ditch or sheltering in the ditch itself and the slightest movement brought a hail of bullets upon them.

On the left of the assault, the Seaforths came under murderous machine-gun fire as they started to advance, especially from the strongpoint in the corner of the Bois du Biez. Whole lines of the Seaforths were scythed down as the machine guns traversed along the extended ranks. Men threw up their arms, spun round and collapsed, others lurched forward and fell to the ground, some simply crumpled up and slid to the ground under the torrent of fire. Survivors pushed bravely forward and managed to reach the safety of the ditch, while the wounded tried to escape the merciless fire by crawling into shell holes or dragging themselves towards the ditch.

Men of both battalions turned and sought the cover of their own breastworks, only to run into the second and third waves who were trying to clamber out. Confusion reigned; the trenches were full of dead and wounded; companies and platoons lost their cohesion. The troops had lost many of their officers, a number of whom had been shot while standing on the parapet urging their men to come out and press the attack. One observer wrote later that from a distance the sound of the machine-gun fire in this particular sector resembled nothing more than 'the purring of a multitude of giant cats'.

But the German defenders in the front breastworks had suffered casualties from our bombardment. The commander of III Battalion, learning of the scale of his losses, ordered his support companies to move up and reinforce those parts of his line which appeared most under threat. The Regimental History records an act of self-sacrifice illustrating the courage and attitude of ordinary soldiers, of which there were to be many examples during the battle on both sides. As men of No. 3 Company threaded their way through the badly damaged communication trench, they came under devastating fire as they approached the front line. Almost immediately Drummer Bussmann was hit by no less than twenty-two bullets in his neck, chest and stomach. When the medical orderly found him, Bussmann, still fully conscious, refused his help, gasped that he was done for and urged him to see to his other wounded comrades.

Only twenty minutes had passed since the three brigades had attacked but it was already clear that the southern assault had failed to reach its first objectives. And a heavy price had been paid. In this short time the six battalions of the 2nd and 3rd Brigades had lost eight-three officers and 2135 men killed or wounded. In the Dehra Dun Brigade thirty-seven officers and 856 men had fallen.

CHAPTER EIGHT

Battle : The Opening Assault – North

Pulver, Rauch, Verluste!
Gefreiter 9/57 Pockrandt
(Gunpowder, Smoke, Casualties!
Corporal Pockrandt)

Some 6000 yards to the north of the southern pincer troops of
Major-General Davies's 8th Division waited for the opening of
the bombardment. Rawlinson's plan was to attack towards the

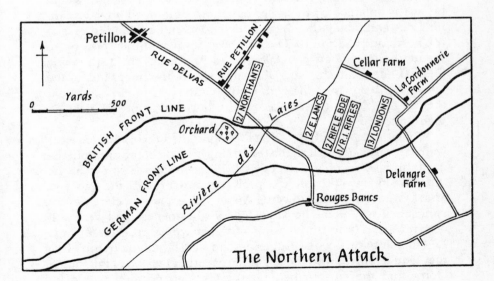

scattered buildings of Rouges Bancs and the village of Fromelles with two brigades. The 24th and 25th Brigades (Brigadiers R.S. Oxley and A.W.S. Lowry Cole respectively) were to launch three separate but co-ordinated attacks. The main thrust would be delivered by three battalions across the Rue Delvas on a 1200-yard front. The 2/East Lancashires (Major H. MacLean) of the 24th Brigade would advance on the right across the road, while the 2/Rifle Brigade (Lieut-Colonel R.B. Stephens) and the 1/Royal Irish Rifles (Major O.C. Baker) of the 25th Brigade on their left would attack Rouges Bancs.

Of the two subsidiary attacks, the one on the right, about a quarter of a mile west of the main thrust, would be made by the 2/Northamptonshires (Major C.R.J. Mowat) against an exposed salient in the German front line. It was timed to start ten minutes after the main attack. The other attack on the extreme left of the front, some 400 yards east of the central attack, would be delivered by a Territorial battalion, the 1/13 London Regiment, known as the Kensingtons, under Lieut-Colonel F.G. Lewis, immediately after the explosion of the two mines beneath the German trenches opposite them.

With these five battalions Rawlinson hoped to break through the German front line in the first assault. The gaps in the line would be swiftly enlarged by the other battalions of the two brigades fanning out and taking the German defenders in flank and in rear to the north and the south. The two brigades would then pass on to secure the Ridge between Aubers and Fromelles, the 24th taking Deleval Farm and the Rue Deleval to secure the right flank of the advance. Meanwhile, the 25th would capture Fromelles and hold the left flank from the village back to our own front line near La Cordonnerie Farm.

While the 24th and 25th Brigades continued their advance eastwards towards Fromelles, the remaining brigade of the division, the 23rd, under Brigadier-General R.J. Pinney, plus a brigade of the 7th Division, would follow closely behind through the gap and attack south-eastwards towards Aubers village and Leclercq Farm almost half-way along the Ridge towards Fromelles. If all went well with the attack, the 7th Division's Brigade would press on towards Le Plouich Farm beyond Aubers and to La Cliqueterie Farm. Here they would join up with the left of the Meerut Division of the Indian Corps and the encirclement of the German position would be complete.

Rawlinson was confident that his superiority in numbers would enable him to smash through the German front line. The sector he proposed to attack was held by three battalions of the 16th Bavarian Reserve Infantry Regiment (16 RIR). Like the 21st and 17th Regiments to the east and west of it respectively, the 16 RIR kept two battalions in the trenches holding some 2500 yards of the front line while its third battalion remained in billets in reserve. The two battalions in the line, had three of their four companies, each about 160 men strong, in the front breastworks with the remaining company several hundred yards behind in support. Early in April fresh drafts had replaced the casualties suffered at Neuve Chapelle and the rifle strength of the battalions was now about twenty-five officers and 750 men. They were supported by twelve batteries of the 6th Bavarian Reserve Division drawn up on the ridge on the line Aubers-Fromelles-Le Maisnil and by four heavy batteries in the rear between Herlies and Fournes. The British assumed that under normal circumstances there would be some eight companies (roughly 1280 men) in the front and support trenches opposite them. Since their two assaulting brigades numbered about 7000 men they had high hopes of the local superiority they had enjoyed earlier in the year at Neuve Chapelle.

While the battalions of the 8th Division were crowded into their trenches waiting for dawn, the 16 RIR across no-man's-land carried out their routine trench relief as usual. The 1st Battalion, which had been in the front line since 2 May, moved out at 3 am and marched back to their billets in Fournes to form part of the divisional reserve. Their place was taken by the 3rd Battalion under Major von Lüneschloss who noted that this relief was carried out without any interference from the enemy, which was hardly surprising under the circumstances. There was apparently no reason for him to suspect an offensive was shortly to be launched against their line. As the darkness perceptibly lightened, our men could see little sign of activity along the enemy front.

At five o'clock precisely our artillery thundered into action and some 190 guns and howitzers rained down shells upon the German positions. The bombardment was carried out by the divisional artillery of the 7th and 8th Divisions, assisted by the heavy guns of No. 2 Group, HAR, and the VII Siege Brigade. The fire of the 4.5-inch and 6-inch howitzers was particularly directed against the centre of the German defences in front of Rouges Bancs and the salient to be attacked by the 2/Northamptonshires. The heavies concentrated their shelling on the batteries along the crest of the Ridge, upon Deleval and Delangre Farms, and on the villages of

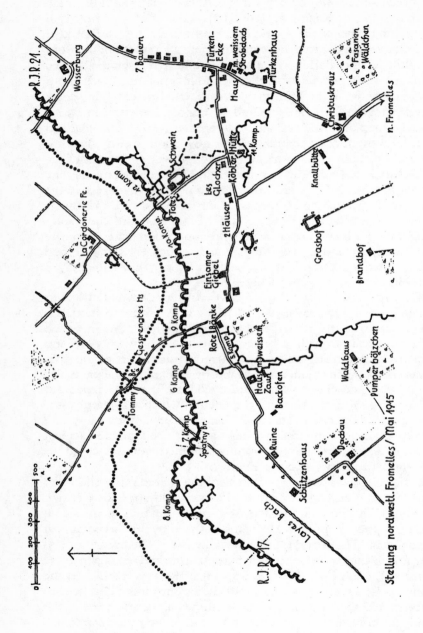

A German sketch-map showing the trench system and the disposition of the companies of the 16 R.I.R. opposite the 8th Division.

Aubers and Fromelles. At the same time, the artillery of the 49th (West Riding) Division protected the southern flank of the 24th Brigade by shelling the enemy front line in an attempt to hold his infantry in their trenches and prevent them being sent to help the regiments being attacked to their right.

2nd Lieutenant K.H.E. Moore was to remain a close and horrified spectator of the assault by the 25th Brigade. Of this early May morning he wrote:

> The first 10 minutes were allotted for cutting the German wire by shrapnel and of course as we were only 50 yards from the German trenches we were in considerable danger from our own guns which like most other things are only human. The noise was terrific and the ground simply shook like a jelly. After 10 minutes on the wire the guns were turned on the parapets of the first and second-line trenches and our heavy Lyddite and high-explosive shells simply blew them to hell. The German lines were a long sheet of flame and bursting shells.

Our troops watched with fascination as our shells roared overhead and a continuous series of explosions erupted along the German trenches. It seemed difficult to believe that the defenders could survive such an onslaught and still be able to resist a determined attack. Yet the failure of our bombardment to do its job effectively, despite the noise and the smoke, was to cause exactly the same problems for the northern pincer as it had for the southern.

At 5.30 am the shelling intensified and the noise rose to a crescendo. At a signal from their officers and under the cover of this fire, the front companies of the attacking battalions began to climb out over the parapet and form up in no-man's-land for the assault. The average width of no-man's-land in front of the 24th and 25th Brigades was about 100 yards, rather less on the left where the Kensingtons waited. On the right, however, where the 2/Northamptonshires were to attack, it widened to some 330 yards. It is fair to say that the Rivière des Laies played no significant part in the battle in this sector except on the right, where it cut across no-man's-land at an angle almost parallel to the left-hand edge of the line of advance of the 2/Northamptonshires. Occasionally the smoke and dust over the German trenches cleared and the troops could see their objective clearly in the early morning sun. But the promise of a fine summer's day was vitiated by the sight of bayonets showing above the enemy parapet.

In describing in detail what happened next, let us deal first with the two battalions of Brigadier Oxley's 24th Brigade, the 2/Northamptonshires and the 2/East Lancashires, who were attacking from west of the Sailly–Fromelles road to seize a small salient in the German line. Their assaults were complementary. The 2/East Lancashires were to capture a stretch of enemy trenches opposite them and thus secure the left flank of the 2/Northamptonshires. The latter would then advance ten minutes later against the flank of the salient. This was the salient which was later nicknamed the 'Sugar-loaf' by the Australians who attacked it in 1916.

Behind the 2/East Lancashires were the 1/Sherwood Foresters. To the right rear of the Foresters lay the 1/Worcestershires, half the battalion close up by the Rivière des Laies and the other half some 400 yards to the rear. It was arranged that as soon as the 2/East Lancashires moved out to attack, the Foresters would occupy the front-line breastworks, their position being taken in turn by the 1/Worcestershires. Then the Foresters would advance, followed in due course by the 1/Worcestershires.

Originally it was the intention for the 2/East Lancashires (always known as 'the 2E-Lan R') to attack from a trench to be dug west of the Sailly–Fromelles road. The new one had even been begun under the supervision of the Royal Engineers but the waterlogged condition of the ground and sporadic fire from the German front line had made it impossible to dig a satisfactory trench. As a result, 200 men had been assembled for the attack in two short lengths of reclaimed trench just in front of our line, while the rest of the battalion was kept under cover behind the breastworks for as long as possible. At 5.20 am the 2/East Lancashires moved out from cover with the intention of taking up a position within attacking distance of the German line under the protection of our bombardment. Their hopes were quickly dissipated for as soon as they appeared in the open they were met with heavy machine-gun and rifle fire which caused many casualties.

They also suffered from our shells falling well short, a failing that was to haunt and, in some cases, destroy our attacking infantry for much of the war. The danger is vividly illustrated by an entry in the diary of a young subaltern:

Sunday May 9th 5.30 am over the top in major attack of Battle of Festubert [sic]. My batman and I almost immediately blown up by our own barrage, 18lb shell from behind, and

86

crouched wounded in shallow field ditch, soaked by blood and brains of a soldier who was apparently beheaded and lay over us – and probably protected us from further damage. When worst storm and carnage abated, I was found and carried back by stretcher-bearers to 1st Field Dressing Station about 7 am. [He had received two shrapnel wounds.] I heard no more of my batman.

Undeterred by these setbacks, the 2/East Lancashires reformed and when the bombardment lifted moved to the attack. They had to cross 150 yards of no-man's-land and, since their objective was a stretch of German trenches lying at an angle to their line of advance, this meant they had to change direction to their left as they approached. The leading companies, already depleted by their early casualties, were swept away by enfilade machine-gun fire. Germans were even observed standing up on the parapet and firing at the stricken troops. The attackers crumpled to the ground and the attack halted half-way across no-man's-land. Seeking what little cover they could find, the survivors crawled back with difficulty to the shelter of the breastworks.

Realizing the attack of the 2/East Lancashires had faltered, Brigadier Oxley ordered two companies of the 1/Sherwood Foresters to advance in support. One cannot quibble with this decision because Haig had impressed upon all his senior commanders the need to maintain the momentum of the attack with fresh troops – not that there was much momentum to maintain at this stage. The Sherwood Foresters found themselves in trenches choked with dead and wounded and some survivors from the initial assault. Despite the confusion and the difficulties in forming up, the leading platoons of the Sherwood Foresters managed to move out from the breastworks about 6.10 am. They found other survivors of the 2/East Lancashires sheltering in the shallow trenches in front of them, while further ahead the ground on their left front was strewn with bodies. They therefore changed direction to the right and under intense fire advanced against the shoulder of the enemy salient. When they were forty yards from the German line they were suddenly brought to a standstill by uncut wire. There seemed to be only one possible gap in it; but, more sinister, immediately in front of the German breastworks they saw a ditch full of wire quite untouched by the bombardment. Pressing forward, the men of the Sherwood Foresters were shot down at close range as they sought to force a way through the wire.

Back in the front-line breastworks survivors of the two battalions, now hopelessly mixed up and disorganized, blocked the path of the 1/Worcestershires attempting to push forward. Continuous machine-gun and rifle fire swept a no-man's-land littered with corpses while German shells began crashing among the confused mass of men sheltering in the breastworks and forward assembly trenches.

It was following this repulse that Corporal J. Upton of the 1/Sherwood Foresters won the first of the four Victoria Crosses that were to be awarded on 9 May. He displayed great courage in rescuing the wounded while exposed to very heavy rifle and artillery fire, going close to the enemy's parapet regardless of his own safety. One wounded man was killed by a shell while the corporal was carrying him to safety. When not actually carrying in the wounded, he stayed out in front of our breastworks dressing and bandaging the serious cases. Corporal Upton survived the war.

Meanwhile, on the right, the men of the 2/Northamptonshires could see little of what was happening to the 2/East Lancashires, but what little they could see filled them with misgiving. They had assembled during the night in an orchard just outside their front line. D Company under Lieutenant O.K. Parker had preceded them, cleared the wire, and had dug jumping-off trenches immediately beyond it. They now had to cross about 200 yards of fields sown with rape to reach the German salient held here by 8 Company of the 16 RIR, but their attack was virtually dependent upon the success of the 2/East Lancashires.

During the night two field guns from the 104th Battery, XXII Brigade, RFA had been brought up into emplacements in our front line. This was an interesting innovation, since it was highly unusual for field guns to be placed among the infantry in the front line. This particular battery had been moved into fields a couple of miles behind Merville at the end of April. Here the left section of two guns experimented for several days firing shrapnel shells at short range at a mock-up of the German barbed-wire entanglements opposite. The results were scrutinized by senior officers and approved. On the night of 8 May the two guns, with their wheels fitted with rubber tyres to reduce noise, were brought forward and manhandled into position in the breastworks and carefully covered. They went into action with the rest of the artillery and one gun was able to make several gaps five to six yards wide in the German wire and breastworks on the right of 8 Company's position.

At 5.40 am A and D Companies climbed out of their shallow

trench and with rifles at the high port advanced across the rape fields. At once the failure of the 2/East Lancashires to secure their left flank became apparent. The two companies were exposed to a merciless enfilade fire ripping across the Rivière des Laies into their left flank. On the left, A Company reached the enemy wire but could not find a way through it and was virtually wiped out by machine-gun and rifle fire at short range. D Company managed to reach the breach in the German breastworks and a party of thirty men under Lieutenant Parker established itself in a ruined trench. He found it impossible to advance to his left because the breast-works had been smashed in and the way to the right was barred by determined resistance by men of 8 Company equipped with a seemingly inexhaustible supply of grenades. However, the battal-ion made an attempt to exploit this small success. At 6 am Major Mowat sent B Company forward to reinforce Lieutenant Parker but as soon as it left the shelter of the orchard it, likewise, came under heavy machine-gun fire from its left flank. By this time the German artillery was fully aroused and, when C Company advanced thirty minutes later, no-man's-land was being swept by machine-gun fire and was also under constant artillery fire. It was virtually impassable and the survivors of both companies were forced to take whatever cover they could find among the ditches. Because of the smoke, it was not possible to see what was hap-pening to Lieutenant Parker, but one man, Private Lapham, volunteered to brave the storm of fire to reach him. He returned to confirm the desperate situation of the remains of D Company, now cut off within the German lines. The attack of Oxley's 24th Brigade had broken down irretrievably.

The attack on the east side of the Sailly–Fromelles road by the two battalions of Brigadier Lowry Cole's 25th Brigade, the 2/Rifle Brigade and the 1/Royal Irish Rifles, was initially encouraging. Here no-man's-land was only 100 yards wide. When the two battalions went over the top they came under heavy machine–gun and rifle fire from men of 9 Company but they covered the ground rapidly in lines of platoons at thirty paces' distance. They found, for a change, that most of the wire had been cut and, although the lead-ing companies suffered heavily, they stormed over the enemy breastworks on a wide front and poured through a twenty-yard breach made by our artillery on the left of the German line. They met little resistance here because nearly all the troops in this stretch of trench had been killed by our bombardment including the com-pany commander who had only joined his regiment eight days before. Our troops took a number of prisoners, regrouped and then advanced on their first objective, the road from Rouges Bancs to Fromelles, 200 yards further on. Despite increasing enemy resistance, they seized Rouges Bancs, formed a defensive line and waited for reinforcements.

By this time the Germans had recovered their poise and the supporting companies had to make their way across a bullet-swept no-man's-land. The other two companies of the 2/Rifle Brigade with their CO, Lieut-Colonel Stephens, and his headquarters, managed to secure the captured enemy trench, some 250 yards in length, despite heavy casualties. These losses disorganized the bombing and blocking parties and Lieut-Colonel Stephens had to improvise groups to protect his exposed flanks. When reinforcements, two companies from the supporting battalion of the 2/Lincolnshire (Major F.S.G. Cox) next tried to push across no-man's-land they met fire of such intensity from the unattacked length of trenches between the 1/Royal Irish Rifles and the Kensingtons on the left that they were unable to advance beyond the trenches in front of our own parapet and were forced to seek cover short of the German line.

Much more encouraging, however, in terms of penetration, was the subsidiary attack by the Kensingtons 400 yards away on the left of the central thrust. They had waited impatiently in the trenches for the explosions that would be the signal for the charge.

Like the other Territorial battalions serving with the First Army, they were inexperienced and only partly trained, but they were enthusiastic and desperately keen to get into action. They were anxious to do well in the eyes of the regular battalions in the brigade and not to let their own regiment down in any way. The Kensingtons had an important task; they were to seize the mine-craters and then advance towards Delangre Farm (called by the Germans the 'farm of the dead pig') and there form a defensive flank.

2nd Lieutenant Moore looked at his watch and later recorded:

We all waited anxiously for 5.40 at which time an enormous mine which ran under the first and second German lines opposite us and only 50 yards away was to be exploded. It was the largest mine ever made in the world and the charge of gun-cotton in it was prodigious. The engineers themselves didn't quite know what would happen to us either. On the very stroke of 5.40 and in the middle of a frightful bombardment the button was pressed.

Suddenly there was a great roar which momentarily drowned the thunder of the guns. The ground under the enemy front line quaked and heaved upwards while our own trenches opposite shuddered under the impact of the shock waves from the explosion. Two huge columns of earth rose high into the air. They seemed to hang there for a while, as if suspended, and then slowly collapsed, falling back round the craters with a crash. Eighty yards of the enemy front line and its garrison of forty-eight men of 10 Company had simply disappeared. All that remained was a tormented desolation in which débris and equipment, torn bodies and limbs, lay scattered in two large craters. A pall of thick blackish-yellow smoke slowly settled over no-man's-land. As soon as the earth had finished falling, forming a rim round the edges of the craters, whistles shrilled along our front line and the Kensingtons clambered over the parapet and charged. Moore continued:

> Immediately after the explosion one whole regiment (the Kensingtons London Regiment) which was in the trenches with us got over the parapet and charged in lines of platoons and occupied the craters without any losses. It was a magnificent charge and a Territorial Regiment too.

Moore, who was a Territorial himself, may have been slightly prejudiced, but regulars who watched the desperate charge were very impressed by it. The Bavarian official account confirms that the explosion of the mines came as an unpleasant surprise to their troops. Observers had noticed no special preparations being made and so no one had any idea that mine shafts had been driven under the front trenches of the 16 RIR.

Breathless and excited, the Kensingtons regrouped among the ruins of the German position. The enemy, on the flanks of the breach, rapidly recovered from the shock of the explosions and now poured a heavy fire into the ranks of the supporting companies as they attempted to cross the seventy yards of no-man's-land. Undaunted, the Kensingtons climbed out of the craters and charged onwards. They burst through the enemy's main position and, despite further casualties, overran the German second line and pressed on. They captured the major *Stützpunkt* at Delangre Farm, which had hardly been touched by our guns, and pushed on beyond the German third trench. Here, as ordered, they re-formed, faced left and occupied an enemy communication trench to form a defensive flank.

Falling back under the weight of the assault and harassed by heavy British shellfire, the Germans still managed to control the wide breach in their line. They established a blocking party on their left, while on the other flank Lieutenant Schmitt, the commander of 12 Company, did two things: first, he built a strong barricade to prevent the Kensingtons moving to their left and, secondly, with the help of platoons from the 21st Regiment, he organized a defensive line to the east of Delangre Farm facing the German communication trench occupied by the Kensingtons. Schmitt now prepared plans for a counter-attack at midday.

Soon after the Kensingtons' charge, their fellow Territorial battalion, the 1/1st London Regiment, who were stationed some way back south of the Rue Petillon were ordered to move forward to support the attack. They deployed and advanced with exemplary steadiness across 400 yards of open ground under heavy shellfire, losing many men in the process. Brigadier Lowry Cole was swift to check their leading companies before they suffered even heavier losses.

Then, about 6 am, the welcome news that both the attacks on his sector had met with initial success reached the Brigadier at his advanced headquarters. He at once sent a message of congratulation to the Commanding Officer of the Kensingtons, Lieut-Colonel Lewis, who had led the attack despite having been on the sick list for ten days before the offensive. 'You have done splendidly,' he wrote, and promised to send reinforcements. At 6.10 am the remainder of the 1/1st London Regiment was ordered to advance but it lost three officers and 120 men even before it reached the Rivière des Laies. The advance was not continued. Lowry Cole then determined to direct the follow-up operations from the front breastworks and reached there about 6.20 am. On his arrival, he found to his dismay that the promising attacks had ground to a halt and that no-man's-land was being swept by heavy fire, particularly, as we have seen, from that untouched section of the enemy defences between the two points of his attack.

The Germans on both flanks of the 25th Brigade's advance had quickly realized that their own positions were not seriously threatened. They were therefore able to turn their attention to containing those of our troops who had broken into their lines and also to preventing the supporting companies from crossing no-man's-land to reinforce them. In the Rouges Bancs area two platoons from the supporting company (5) holding a trench running from Rouges Bancs to the *Haus mit weissem Zaun* (house with the white fence) were sent forward to strengthen the front line, while a third, taking up a position on the right flank, checked the 2/Rifle Brigade's advance. In due course Lowry Cole learned that advanced elements of his troops were being subjected to heavy machine-gun fire from the flank and even from the rear. They had been expecting the 2/Lincolns to pass through them and continue the advance, but, as we have seen, the 2/Lincolns failed to reach the German line. After waiting half an hour beyond the appointed time for their arrival and in danger of being overwhelmed by a heavy German counter-attack, the men were ordered to withdraw. The advanced troops, having lost almost all their officers and suffered heavy losses, now returned to the German front-line trench they had so recently captured. Here, under the energetic leadership of Lieut-Colonel Stephens, the remains of the two battalions strengthened and secured their hold on a 400 yard section of the German line.

Lowry Cole, a fine commander and a gallant officer, quickly grasped the situation and directed the two remaining companies of the 2/Lincolnshires to move down a new sap which had been hurriedly pushed out to the mine crater and then work to the right towards the Royal Irish Rifles, clearing the Germans out of the trenches as they went. No sooner had the Lincolns under Captain B.J. Thruston moved off, preceded by a bombing and blocking party, than a fresh and most damaging crisis developed. Lowry Cole saw a number of men from the Rifle Brigade and the Royal Irish Rifles streaming back over the German breastworks, bringing in their train the two companies of the 2/Lincolnshires who had gone to ground earlier and were sheltering in shell-holes behind the breastworks. Apparently someone had shouted: 'Retire at the double!' and this order, welcome news to many of the hard-pressed regulars but hardly in accord with regimental traditions, was passed rapidly along the length of the captured trench and obeyed with alacrity. To add to the confusion, German prisoners taken in the original attack and now running for cover behind the British front line were mistaken for a counter-attack. Confusion was further compounded by the inopportune arrival of companies from the supporting battalions from the rear. Brigade staff, directed by Major Dill, the Brigade-Major, tried desperately to restore order but their immediate task was to stop the retirement. Then Lowry Cole, regardless of the heavy fire, leapt up on to the parapet and by his personal example and decisive orders succeeded in stopping the rout. Yet all his efforts and those of his officers to re-form his troops

93

and renew the attack were thwarted by the increasing intensity of the enemy's fire. While standing on the parapet encouraging and urging on his men, Brigadier Lowry Cole was suddenly seen to stagger and collapse. Mortally wounded, he was carried to shelter behind the breastworks where he died shortly afterwards. Moments later Major Dill fell, badly wounded. After the battle an exhaustive enquiry among the survivors failed to discover any reason for this second retirement beyond the fact that someone had shouted out: 'Retire at the double!'. The two battalion war diaries throw no light upon this episode.

While this was happening Captain Thruston and his men had broken into what proved to be a network of German trenches and had lost direction. They became embroiled in fierce hand-to-hand fighting for some twenty minutes, suffered numerous casualties and their chances of joining forces with Lieut-Colonel Stephens began to look very slim. The situation was saved largely by one man, Acting-Corporal C. Sharpe. He had been among the first to reach the enemy position and, using bombs with great determination and effect, he cleared out a trench fifty yards long. By this time all his party had been killed or wounded but he was then joined by four other men. They again attacked the Germans with bombs and captured a further stretch of trench 250 yards long. For this action Corporal Sharpe was awarded the Victoria Cross; he survived the battle and ended the war as Company Sergeant-Major. Meanwhile, Captain Thruston managed to locate two enemy machine guns which were firing from beyond the craters and causing casualties among his men. He collected several machine guns, brought their concentrated fire to bear upon the German positions and quickly silenced them. Yet, although the Lincolns were able to consolidate their hold on the length of trenches they had captured, they were unable to make further headway towards Lieut-Colonel Stephens and communication with their own front line remained hazardous.

With the death of Brigadier Lowry Cole, command of the 25th Brigade had devolved upon Lieut-Colonel Stephens as the senior battalion commander, who was still isolated with the combined remains of the two battalions in the German front line. So Major Cox of the 2/Lincolnshires assumed temporary command and at once began to reorganize the two leading companies of his battalion which had attacked unsuccessfully before and had taken part in the 'retirement'. He also arranged for the artillery to shell that section of the enemy trenches between Captain Thruston and Lieut-Colonel Stephens. After a short bombardment the two companies of the Lincolns again moved out from behind the breast-works in an attempt to capture the trench and close the gap. Inevitably, they met with machine-gun and rifle fire so intense that they were unable to advance very far across no-man's-land and the attack simply withered away.

General Davies, commanding the 8th Division, had been wait-ing anxiously at his headquarters in the Rue du Bacquerot, south-west of Fleurbaix, for news of the progress of his two brigades. He was aware of the débâcle on the front of the 24th Brigade but he was shocked and saddened shortly before 8 am to hear of the death of Brigadier Lowry Cole. He sent his GSOI, Colonel W.H. Anderson, to the headquarters of his reserve brigade, the 23rd, to tell Brigadier Pinney that he was to assume command of all troops east of the Sailly–Fromelles road. Anderson warned Pinney he would first need to take control of a confused and worsening situation and then attempt the relief of those of our troops who had made lodgements in the enemy line. Pinney made his way to the front line along shallow communication trenches choked with wounded and stretcher-bearers making their way to the rear. He was appalled at what he found. The British front breastworks were a shambles; the trenches were full of dead and dying, littered with broken scaling ladders and the débris of the initial attack, while small groups of leaderless men tried to find what cover they could from the German shelling.

Pinney reported to General Davies about 8.30 am that there appeared to be three separate lodgements in the German line on the front of the 25th Brigade, where his troops were fighting for their lives. These were:

1. Lieut-Colonel Stephens with men of the 2/Rifle Brigade and 1/Royal Irish Rifles across and to the east of the Sailly–Fromelles road.
2. the remains of two companies of the 2/Lincolnshire on their left.
3. the Kensingtons on the far left.

General Davies knew that on the front of the 24th Brigade the small party from the 2/Northamptonshires were still holding out, but he realized that after nearly three hours of fierce fighting the offensive along the whole of his front had come to a standstill. His shattered brigades could do no more. The northern pincer was not after all going to bite deep into the German salient, seize the ridge at Aubers and meet the southern pincer at La Cliqueterie Farm. It made a gloomy report for General Rawlinson, his Corps Commander.

2nd Lieutenant Moore had watched the opening attacks going in from the front breastworks and he had seen successive waves of our regular infantry mown down by enfilading machine-gun fire as they advanced across the short, featureless strip of no-man's-land. His comment on the morning's work reads:

It was a terrible thing to watch line after line crumple up. Meanwhile the trenches were absolutely blocked with the dead, dying and wounded. If people at home really knew what a show like Sunday's was like . . .

So ended General Haig's opening attack on Aubers Ridge. Above the battle the sun climbed steadily into the sky and the bright promise of the early morning was ironically fulfilled.

CHAPTER NINE

Battle : The Second Attack

The 9th of May dawned warm and sunny; a marvellous Sunday – no, a bloody Sunday.

History of the 55th Regiment

Thus, about 6 am, twenty minutes after zero hour, both the First Army's attacks had been stopped in their tracks. On the southern sector it had been a bloody fiasco with nine battalions suffering frightful loss and no gains to show for it. There were not even any modest lodgements which might be reinforced. On the northern sector fierce fighting was still going on in the four breaches that had been made in the German front line but a grievous price had been paid for them. In both sectors of the First Army's assault the front-line trenches were an appalling sight, filled with dead and wounded, with stretcher parties, leaderless men and all the débris of attack. The narrow stretch of no-man's-land was strewn with the bodies of the dead while the survivors sought what little cover the ground and the shell-holes provided. During any brief lull in the tumult moans and piteous cries for help could be heard from the wounded lying out beyond our breastworks.

In his headquarters in the Rue du Bois General Haking had been unable to follow the progress of the slaughter on the 1st Division's front. Peering through the sandbagged loopholes, he could see little because of the smoke and dust. He was considerably disappointed, though far from downcast, when he learned of the fate of the first assault and he determined to press the attack. Brigadier Davies (3rd Brigade) asked for a further fifteen-minute bombardment, but Brigadier Thesiger of the sorely stricken 2nd Brigade told Haking he did not think this was long enough. He had already received several pleas for increased artillery support from his battalion commanders, together with reports that the enemy wire had not been satisfactorily cut. Haking quickly made up his mind. He told Fanshawe to renew the bombardment for a further forty-five minutes and ordered his two brigade commanders to mount a fresh attack at 7 am. He also got in touch with the commander of the Meerut Division, General Anderson, and explained that his initial assault had failed and that he was preparing to renew it at 7 am. He asked if the Dehra Dun brigade would co-operate on his left flank, and to this Anderson agreed.

Fanshawe had specifically instructed the artillery to concentrate on cutting the enemy wire. Yet lying out in no-man's-land at varying distances from the wire were hundreds of men, most of them wounded, and they suffered further torment as a torrent of shrapnel suddenly broke over the wire. The unreliability of our ammunition and the inexperience of our gunners caused much of the shelling to fall short. Devoid of cover, our men could only press their bodies closer into the earth as the shrapnel tore and flayed the ground around them. Those already wounded were further mangled or killed outright, while many unwounded were soon to become casualties of our gunfire.

Our heavy losses in the first attack and the confusion and congestion in the trenches made it extremely difficult to reorganize our troops for another assault in such a short time. Despite lack of numbers and the problems of regrouping, the two brigades did their best, but with results that were obvious in advance to all except the Divisional Commander.

It is difficult to discover from existing records what the detailed response was to Haking's order. The Official History simply states that the second attempt 'consisted of a series of individual efforts' and leaves it at that. This does less than justice to the efforts of men attempting to carry out orders under the most thankless conditions. To give an example of the confusion: at 6.30 am those men of the 2/Royal Sussex who could move were instructed to crawl back and retire behind our breastworks, shambles that it was, under cover of the fresh bombardment. Although D Company received this order, C Company did not and was left marooned out in no-man's-land for several hours. The 1/5th Royal Sussex, who were inextricably mingled with men of the regular battalion, received similar orders a little later, thanks to the bravery of Sergeant Roberts who went out three times to the firing line under heavy shell and small-arms fire to carry wounded comrades in.

In the 2nd Brigade, in view of the losses sustained by the four assaulting battalions, the response was made by the reserve battalion, the 1/Loyal North Lancashires. As the remains of the two Sussex battalions were slowly making their way back to the front-line breastworks, the 1/Loyal North Lancashires arrived. They had been in position behind the Rue du Bois and when ordered forward they had advanced with little difficulty and with only a few casualties, partly in the open and partly through the communication trenches. They found they had to crowd into the front trench filled with the dead and wounded of the Sussex battalions. They were faced with the unenviable task of having to advance across a no-man's-land strewn with the bodies of the two battalions. Undaunted, three companies of the Loyals climbed over the parapet shortly after 7 am and moved forward at the double. Captain W.H. Roy was one of the company officers and he wrote later:

> They were met with a very hot fire from the front and from the left flank which ultimately checked the line about 100 yards in front of our breastworks. Every officer in front was hit, and the casualties in the other ranks were very heavy. Our machine guns then opened fire from the breastworks and, later, in accordance with instructions from 2nd Brigade Headquarters received about 7.50 am, as many men as possible were withdrawn behind the front parapet. Previous to this a message had been sent to the 2nd Brigade that the enemy's wire to our front had not been successfully cut.

Captain Roy was badly wounded by a bullet which smashed his right shoulder. Later, in hospital at Boulogne, he commented succinctly: 'It was a horribly bloodthirsty affair.'

It is not clear if Haking fully realized the extent of the losses in the 2nd and 3rd Brigades or the situation in his front line, though this would probably have made little difference to his orders. It is hard to believe that he expected the remains of these battalions to reorganize under fire, then attack and penetrate the enemy defences in strength. It is even harder to endorse his decision to throw in a single fresh battalion (the 1/Loyal North Lancashires) in these circumstances to support a disorganized and desultory assault.

Between 9 am and 10 am, after being relieved by a battalion from the 1st Brigade, the North Lancashires made their way back

to the house in the Rue du Bois where Dr Nangle had been waiting since dawn to receive the wounded, not knowing what was
happening to the men of his battalion. The house came under
shellfire, like the other buildings in the Rue du Bois, and the
ground trembled under the impact of the British bombardment.
At length the wounded began to arrive. In his letter Dr Nangle
continued:

> They came on, one after the other, some being carried,
> others hobbling along as best they could, and I didn't have a
> moment to spare until noon. By that time the regiment had
> come to form up behind my dressing station minus 13 offi-
> cers and 250 men, most of whom were lying out between the
> two lines unable to move. Of my particular friends two were
> killed and two died of wounds during the day . . . My house
> bore a charmed life and escaped more or less intact,
> although those on either side were hit.

It is not easy to determine what Brigadier Davies did on behalf of
the 3rd Brigade to give substance to his Divisional Commander's
order. He was a realist who had already drawn Haking's attention
to the need for a further bombardment. One senses that he did
not strive assiduously to withdraw and regroup his battered battalions in order to send them out again to face the German
machine guns. In any case, the remains of his companies, like
those of the 2nd Brigade, were lying out in no-man's-land under
heavy artillery fire, scarcely able to move. The supporting battalion of Territorials, the 1/4th Royal Welch Fusiliers, had moved up
to the front-line breastwork after the initial assault had ground to
a halt, losing six officers and sixty-five men in the process. Their
function in the battle was to act as 'mopping-up battalion' to the
brigade. Brigadier Davies sensibly decided not to commit them to
the attack under such circumstances. He also told his two battalions in reserve, 1/South Wales Borderers and 1/Gloucestershires,
not to move up to the front-line trenches at this point. Their fate
was to be decided later in the day.

In the confusion that cloaks this unhappy episode, it seems that
individual officers did gather together the remains of their broken
companies and lead them forward again in a forlorn attack against
a waiting enemy. One survivor recalled that several small groups
attempted to push forward, but, as they grew closer to the
German line, they found the enemy 'standing three and four deep

in their breastworks and fighting like demons'. The men of the 3rd Brigade were now forced to flatten themselves to the earth as our guns showered shrapnel over the crowded German trenches. The enemy infantry suffered heavily, but the machine-gun crews in their heavily protected emplacements remained untouched. In the face of such fire, no further advance could be contemplated.

Back at Violaines, Major Castendyk had heard the artillery of Haking's 1st Division begin their second bombardment of his 3rd Battalion's front. A little after 7 am, when the second attack by the 1st Division had been easily dealt with, he received a telephone call from Major Wülfing. It is interesting, in view of what happened later in the afternoon, that the battalion commander stressed that in his opinion the battle was now over. Wülfing's view was confirmed by the German walking wounded passing by on their way back to La Bassée. They shouted to Castendyk that the Tommies had had a bellyful of it that morning – *die Nase für heute voll hätte.*

Meanwhile, on the left of the 1st Division, Brigadier Jacob did his best to carry out Anderson's promise to Haking. He called upon the Seaforths to attack again, the survivors of the original assaulting companies being reinforced by platoons from the other two companies. After the renewed bombardment, they made not one, but two further attempts to advance; in each case they were stopped in their tracks by machine-gun fire and suffered further casualties. The other two battalions in the brigade, the 1/4th Seaforths and the 2/2nd Gurkhas, were in no position to help. They had been disorganized by the loss of their officers, had taken heavy casualties and were trying to regroup. The survivors were taking cover in no-man's-land, watching apprehensively as our artillery again pounded the German parapet. When the shelling ceased, they saw the Highlanders make their brave attempt to reach the German line. The men of the Dehra Dun Brigade, like their comrades in the other brigades, were now forced to remain in the open, unable either to advance or retire.

Thus the second, rather fitful, attack by the southern pincer died away with nothing to show for it other than further losses to the three brigades which bore the main burden of the assault.

Back at 1st Division headquarters in the Rue du Bois, General Haking telephoned his Corps Commander, General Monro, at Essars at 7.20 am, with the unpleasant and embarrassing news that his second attack had failed as completely as his first. Nothing daunted, however, Haking went on to ask Monro if he could bring up his reserve brigade, the 1st (Guards), and send them into the attack. He added, 'If the wire is cut by deliberate fire and more of the enemy's machine guns are knocked out, the assault can be delivered again after midday.' Monro curtly told him that he should do no such thing without further orders. He then pressed Haking for further details of what had happened to his two brigades and how he viewed the situation on his front. Reluctantly, the aggressive Haking replied that, even if the entire 2nd Division were flung into the battle, it would have little chance of success. Noting that several of Haking's battalions had virtually been destroyed, Monro told him that he should order the 1st Brigade forward to hold the line while the remains of those battalions of the 2nd and 3rd Brigades were withdrawn to the rear.

Meanwhile, on the Indian Corps front, General Anderson had to report to General Willcocks a similar sad lack of success with his second attack. After a brief conversation, the Corps Commander sanctioned yet a third attack and General Anderson ordered another artillery bombardment lasting forty minutes – later prolonged by twenty minutes – to start at 7.45 am. The intention was for our howitzers to pound the enemy trenches opposite the 2/2nd Gurkhas and 1/4th Seaforths who were to form the attacking force. About this time the OC 1/4th Seaforths reported to brigade headquarters that the enemy opposite was being reinforced and appeared to be mounting a counter-attack. Brigadier Jacob therefore sent up two companies of the 1/9th Gurkhas to help the 1/Seaforths, who had suffered severe losses after taking part in both attacks, and ordered the OC 1/9th Gurkhas to support the 1/4th Seaforths with the remainder of his battalion. However, owing to the congested state of the communication trenches, only 200 men of the battalion could get up to the front. The difficulties they encountered were graphically described by General Willcocks:

These trenches, difficult to pass through even when occupied only by the ordinary traffic, were now in a state which beggars description. The German guns had been pouring high explosive and shrapnel into them all the morning; in many places the parapet had been blown in, blocking the way, while numbers of dead and wounded were lying at the bottom of the trenches. The direction boards had in many cases been destroyed, and men were wandering about, vainly attempting to find the nearest way to their units or to the aid posts. The nearer one got to the front, the more of a shambles the trenches became; wounded men creeping and crawling along amidst the mud and débris of the parapet, many of them, unable to extricate themselves, dying alone and unattended, while, amidst this infernal scene the German shells were continually bursting.

Like our earlier bombardment, this new one did little damage but it had the unfortunate effect of galvanizing the German artillery, hitherto fairly quiet on this part of the battlefield, into action. The enemy guns opened a heavy fire upon the British and Indian breastworks, support trenches and communication trenches. This caused losses in the supporting companies of the Dehra Dun Brigade and in Drake-Brockman's force (which had not even been able to begin to carry out its role in the action) and shells also fell upon advanced units of the Bareilly Brigade, especially the 41st Dogras, in their assembly area behind the Rue du Bois.

At 8 am, a short while after General Anderson had issued orders for the extension of the bombardment, he received a telephone call from 1st Division headquarters. He was informed that the attack of the 2nd and 3rd Brigades had failed and that the situation on their front was so confused and desperate that they would need a good two hours to reorganize before they could resume the offensive. General Anderson relayed this message to his Corps Commander. Willcocks was naturally unwilling to attack without any support on his right and he sensibly cancelled the proposed attack by Jacob's brigade at 8.45 am. He told Anderson to organize another assault in the meantime to coincide with that of the 1st Division when it was finally ready to proceed.

This decision left most of Anderson's attacking force still pinned down in no-man's-land under small-arms and artillery fire. Unfortunately, the order stopping the attack failed to reach the 2/2nd Gurkhas, who were attempting to dig in as best they could. At 8.40 am Major Rooke led part of his company, which had been in reserve, over the parapet; they rushed forward and crossed the ditch, where they were joined by more of their unwounded comrades. Although Major Rooke was shot almost at once, his men doubled across no-man's-land under intense fire. A small party of Gurkhas got within about twenty yards of the German trenches; some of them actually climbed into the enemy line, only to be dispatched there. Of the remainder, some were forced to lie out close to the German wire, where they became the target for enemy grenades. Here they had to stay until nightfall. This gallant little episode is confirmed by the German war diary which records that a small, determined group of Gurkhas did in fact reach their wire. They had discarded all their equipment, including their rifles, but, 'running like cats' along the wire, they saw a gap, went through it, clambered over the breastworks and attacked the defenders with their kukris. Their bravery was of no avail. They were all shot or bayoneted and in the evening the Germans buried their bodies in a communal unmarked grave.

Noticing signs of disorganization and incipient withdrawal among the enemy opposite, Major Boileau made his way along the line to see Lieut-Colonel Prothero of the 2/Welsh and asked him if he was game to take advantage of the situation and join in storming the trenches with the rest of the Gurkhas. Prothero demurred, explaining he had been ordered not to advance and that, because of heavy casualties, his battalion was being relieved.

At his headquarters in Merville Haig waited for news of his attack. Would he achieve the kind of breakthrough he had seen at Neuve Chapelle? This time he had no doubt that his reserve divisions would be in a position to follow up and exploit the gaps and that the arms of his pincers would envelop a large number of the enemy. The prize of Aubers Ridge would then be in his grasp.

The early news Haig received from his corps commanders, confirmed by more detailed reports from his divisional liaison officers, was disquieting. Apparently the main southern thrust had run into difficulties, though there had been some success in the northern sector. Haig did not realize the extent to which his initial attack had failed nor was he aware at this stage of how heavy his losses had been in officers and men. He was reluctant to believe that such a meticulously planned offensive, enjoying numerical superiority and the element of surprise, could have been seriously thwarted. Confident that his troops had met only a temporary setback, Haig's natural optimism, and his determination not to fail again with this, his second battle, urged him to continue the assault. Like his corps commanders, Haig was unaware of the near-chaotic situation in the First Army's front-line trenches after the repulse of the first attack. His prime concern was to renew the attack and maintain the momentum of the offensive, and he made this very clear to his staff.

The morning wore on. Haig's uneasiness increased, though he showed little sign of it, even when news was brought to him just before 8 am that the second attack by the 2nd and 3rd Brigades and the Dehra Dun Brigade had collapsed without any progress being made. Half an hour later he heard from Rawlinson at IV Corps Headquarters that the attack of his 8th Division had come to a standstill, although certain lodgements had been made in the enemy line. At 8.45 am he sent instructions to Rawlinson to renew his attack as soon as possible. His actual words were, 'press the attack vigorously and without delay'. Shortly afterwards Haig received the encouraging but embarrassing news that the French offensive in the south had made an excellent start. The French Tenth Army had breached the German defences on a wide front and had made considerable gains of ground. This further strengthened Haig's resolve to do all in his power to assist his ally and to demonstrate that his First Army was lacking in neither courage nor determination. He therefore ordered the 1st Division and the Meerut Division to reorganize and prepare to make a third attempt on the German line at 12 noon after a forty-minute bombardment.

Back on Haking's 1st Division front, the shattered battalions of his 2nd and 3rd Brigades were slowly being withdrawn to the rear to regroup while the 1st (Guards) Brigade took over their stretch of line. Any relief carried out in broad daylight is hazardous and there was to be no respite for our troops in this case. About 9.30 am, as soon as the German artillery observers detected some movement along our trenches, they directed heavy and continuous shellfire from both field and large-calibre guns upon our lines. For an hour they bombarded the front and support breastworks, the communication trenches, and the buildings in the Rue du Bois from Chocolat Menier Corner to Port Arthur. Thus the relief had to be effected under a barrage of high explosive and shrapnel from guns which our batteries had been unable to locate and silence. The troops found the communication trenches almost impassable; enemy shelling had also blown in parts of the parapet of the front breastworks and dead and wounded men lay in the bottom of the trenches among a wilderness of broken scaling-ladders and smashed bridges.

Matters were no better with the stricken Dehra Dun Brigade on the left, where the remains of three attacking battalions, the Gurkhas and the Seaforths, were lying out in no-man's-land under fire. Eventually Lieut-Colonel Ritchie of the 1/Seaforths, knowing that most of his officers had been shot and his men were pinned down by the enemy fire, ordered all those who were able to move to return to their own lines whenever they could. Some succeeded in doing so, but many, like the Gurkhas and the 1/4th Seaforths, had to stay out in the open until they could crawl back either under cover of a later attack in the afternoon by the Bareilly Brigade or in the friendly darkness. They were hardly better off in their own breastworks because the front and support trenches were under heavy shrapnel and high-explosive fire all day.

About this time Captain S.H.C. Woolrych of the Intelligence Corps, who was attached to the Indian Corps, made his way towards the front line. He wrote later:

> I went down again to the Meerut HQ near Croix Barbée on the Rue du Bacquerot and, as I could get no information, I decided to go down to the trenches. As I neared the end of the second block of land, I met hundreds of wounded straggling along with plentiful evidence of their wounds. At the Rue des Berceaux I halted for some little time, for it was here that the communication trench started. To the right was the 'tramway' up which came native bearers carrying the most severe cases, whom they deposited under a haystack just in front of me.

Following Haig's orders to reorganize for a third assault at 12 noon, General Anderson now instructed the Dehra Dun Brigade to withdraw and the Bareilly Brigade under Brigadier Southey to relieve them and carry out the attack.

Disturbed by the turn events were taking and anxious to expedite the progress of his offensive, Haig left Merville and drove the short distance to Lestrem to see General Willcocks at Indian Corps headquarters. As usual, he left his Chief General Staff Officer, Brigadier R.H.K. Butler, in charge. Haig did not think highly of Willcocks. He had been unimpressed by his first visit to the Indian Corps front earlier in the year and Willcocks had not improved matters by his conduct at Neuve Chapelle. Ordered by Haig to make a night attack over unreconnoitred ground, he had responded to appeals from his disenchanted commanders. First, he agreed to delay the attack and then, eventually, he decided to countermand Haig's instruction. It was not an auspicious beginning.

Haig arrived at Lestrem expecting to find a reflection of his own confidence and final preparations being made for the attack at midday. Instead, he was greeted by a less than buoyant Willcocks, who had to explain that he had just heard from

General Anderson that the Dehra Dun Brigade had been so badly cut-up that it was in no condition to renew the attack and that it was being relieved by the Bareilly Brigade. Anderson had added that, because of the difficulties on his front, the Bareilly Brigade would not be ready to join in the southern pincer attack at 12 noon. Indeed, it seemed as though Brigadier Southey would need at least another two hours. Already Haig knew that, despite General Haking making aggressive noises, the 1st Division would not be ready itself to attack at noon. Accepting the situation with rather bad grace, he agreed to postpone the attack until 2.40 pm, with the same preliminary bombardment starting at 2 pm.

Haig next drove to the headquarters of I Corps near Essars where he found General Monro engaged in organizing the attack for the new time of 2.40 pm. Haig emphasized that, as well as the howitzers, all available 18pdrs should be used with HE shell against the German parapet – even though the 18pdrs appeared to have little effect on the enemy breastworks.

As soon as he received his fresh orders from General Monro, General Haking instructed the commanders of the 2nd and 3rd Brigades to send their supporting battalions forward to the front line and prepare for the assault at 2.40 pm. He also asked his Corps Commander for two battalions from the 1st (Guards) Brigade. This time Monro reluctantly agreed; he already distrusted Haking's handling of his troops in battle but he knew that Haig approved of Haking's zeal for attack. He therefore assigned the 1/Black Watch and the 1/Cameron Highlanders to him, a decision he would live to regret.

Brigadier Southey found exactly the same problems in carrying out the relief of the Dehra Dun Brigade as General Haking was encountering on the 1st Division front. His situation was, if anything, even worse and he soon realized that it would be impossible to organize the relief and also mount an attack by 2.40 pm. At 11.20 am he reported this depressing news to General Anderson. Haig by this time had returned to Lestrem and, when Willcocks passed on this unpalatable report, he had no alternative but to put back once again the attack by the 1st and Meerut Divisions, this time until 4 pm. He was far from pleased.

By 11.30 am Haig had still received no news about the progress of the renewed attack by the 8th Division which he had ordered. Thus an increasingly irritable Haig repeated to Rawlinson at 11.45 am his urgent order of 8.45 am to press home the attack with vigour and he demanded to know what was happening on the northern front. Haig took his lunch with Willcocks in the Indian mess but it was a subdued affair. As usual at meal times, Haig remained inscrutable and uncommunicative – and even more so on this occasion.

8. Zero hour at Aubers Ridge. A sapper, in a support trench near
Cellar Farm with men of the 2/Scottish Rifles, is about to detonate a
mine under the German trenches. The explosion was followed by the
charge of the Kensingtons. (*Liddle Collection*)

9. Men of the 2/Lincolnshires passing through the mine crater. Note the German prisoners and the wounded of both sides. (*Imperial War Museum*)

10. Men of 1 Battalion, 16 Bavarian Reserve Infantry Regiment, waiting in the park of the château at Fournes to move forward.

11. After the battle, looking back at the British parapet. Twenty-three bodies of the 1/Cameronians lie within forty feet. (*Imperial War Museum*)

12. British prisoners being escorted to the rear.

13. 'The Iron Harvest.'

14. The Indian Memorial to the Missing, opposite Port Arthur.

CHAPTER TEN

Battle : Failure on the Left

In peaceful thought the field of death survey'd,
  To fainting squadrons sent the timely aid,
Inspir'd repuls'd Battalions to engage,
  And taught the doubtful battle where to rage.
Joseph Addison, 'The Campaign' (on Marlborough)

Rawlinson had received Haig's order sent at 8.45 am, spurring him on to press the attack, and attempted to carry it out. However, the Corps Commander had little idea of the confused and desperate situation in his sector following the repulse of the opening assault. This is epitomized by a conversation recorded between Rawlinson and Brigadier Oxley when the latter reported the failure of the attack:

General Rawlinson: 'This is most unsatisfactory. Where are the Sherwood Foresters? Where are the East Lancashires on the right?'
Brigadier Oxley: 'They are lying out in no-man's-land, sir, and most of them will never stand again.'

He discussed the situation with a concerned General Davies, who tried to convey something of the conditions along the 8th Division's front. Davies told him that his division would be unable to organize a fresh attack as quickly as Haig had stressed and Rawlinson wanted. The latter, unwilling to accept the reasons for the delay, urged upon Davies his plans for the renewed assault. Rawlinson's plan of attack was unrealistic to say the least. He wanted a general bombardment, with the fire of our guns east of the Sailly–Fromelles road directed upon the German second line to avoid causing casualties among our troops lodged in the enemy's front line. Then Brigadier Oxley's 24th Brigade would attack once again on the right, while the recently arrived Brigadier Pinney would attempt to push forward troops from the 25th Brigade to reinforce those engaged in fierce hand-to-hand fighting in parts of the German defences. Davies agreed to do his best to attack as soon as he could and again checked on the progress of his two brigades.

Brigadier Oxley's Brigade had already suffered shocking losses in the original assault. The survivors, crowded into the front-line breastworks which had been badly damaged by shellfire, were now cruelly exposed to shrapnel and were taking further casualties. His reserves had been reduced to one battalion, the 1/Worcestershires, and further movement along the choked and broken communication trenches was extremely difficult. His brigade was therefore quite unable to renew the assault at this time or to contemplate reinforcing the 2/Northamptonshires on the extreme right.

On his left, Brigadier Pinney was attempting to bring some kind of order into a difficult situation. Elements of four of his battalions were fighting in the enemy line and it was imperative that reinforcements be sent forward without delay if the breaches in the German defences were to be consolidated and then exploited. This was never going to be an easy task, with the narrow strip of no-man's-land being heavily shelled and raked with small-arms fire. Organizing reinforcements, given the state of the front-line trenches, was something of a nightmare. The survivors of the attacking battalions had become intermingled with the supporting companies, while the leading elements of the reserve battalions had had to battle their way forward against the flow of stretcher parties and hundreds of wounded making their way slowly towards the rear.

If the Germans had been shaken by the detonation of our mines and the opening of our offensive, they responded to the threat, as we have seen, with their customary speed and skill. Because our shelling had destroyed the telephone lines (laid in triplicate) between 3rd Battalion HQ at Fromelles and the front, Major von Lüneschloss had been unable to get in touch with his reserve company (11) occupying a defensive position some 400 yards behind the front line. When Brigadier Kiefhaber, commanding the 16 RIR, heard about this at his headquarters in the Château at Fournes, he ordered 3rd Battalion HQ to move up to Turk's Corner (*Türkenecke*) to be closer to the action. As soon as Major von Lüneschloss had established his HQ there, he sent up two platoons from 11 Company to help Lieutenant Schmitt and 12 Company on the right of his front.

Brigadier Pinney had made a start on the problems on his front when he received a message from the Kensingtons on the extreme left around Delangre Farm that they were under heavy fire, continuing to suffer casualties and were running short of bombs. Such was the intensity of the machine-gun and artillery fire in this sector that it was only possible to cross the short distance to the German line by crawling in single file up the narrow sap to the mine craters. Shortly after 11 am a party of some 200 men of the 2/Royal Berkshires, who had been sorted out and reorganized from the wreckage of the front-line breastworks, were led forward up the sap by Captain C. Nugent. They kept their heads well down as they crawled towards the craters with machine-gun bullets grazing the ground just above them. Once among the ruins of the enemy line, men of the two battalions held on, defying the Germans to drive them out.

What had seemed painfully clear at 9 am now became blindingly obvious to General Davies and his two brigadiers by mid-morning. It was plainly quite impossible to prepare an attack for several hours, given that the remains of the assaulting battalions were still in the crowded front trenches. It would take a considerable time to extricate the two shattered brigades to an already congested rear and replace them with fresh troops. This was still not appreciated by Rawlinson and certainly not by Haig who was becoming impatient with the seeming lack of response by IV Corps to his orders. As we saw in the last chapter, this resulted in Haig repeating his original order to IV Corps at 11.45 am.

Circumstances now forced Rawlinson to alter his plan. Because of the difficulty of knowing exactly which sections of the German front defences our troops were holding, the Corps Commander decided to concentrate his artillery fire on the 400 yards of trench west of the Sailly–Fromelles road. The defenders of this stretch had so far remained largely unaffected by the battle, having dealt with the original attack by the 2/East Lancashires and 1/Sherwood Foresters. And this was where Oxley's fresh battalions were to attack. Rawlinson's decision involved another frontal assault against a confident and alert enemy, rather than attempting to reinforce on a larger scale the lodgement already made in the German defences at such cost.

After a rapid consultation with Oxley and with Pinney, the latter repeating his inability to mount a properly co-ordinated attack,

General Davies told Oxley to attack 'with what men you can muster'. To allow time for reorganization, he agreed to the attack taking place at 1.30 pm. Brigadier Oxley sent instructions to his two reserve battalions, the 1/Worcestershire (Lieut-Colonel Grogan) and the 1/5th Black Watch, who were to attack side by side, to move up to the forward assembly trenches. They were to be supported by the 2/Queen's (Major H.R. Bottomley), brought across from General Gough's 7th Division. In reserve were two battalions from the 23rd Brigade, the 2/Middlesex and the 1/7th Middlesex, which had not even been included in the original plans for the offensive. Their task had been to hold the line, which they had already been doing for twelve days, and they now found they might be called upon to play a more active role.

It was 12.50 pm when Lieut-Colonel Grogan received the order for his battalion to attack. While making what preparations he could, he told Brigadier Oxley that in his opinion the assault could not possibly succeed. The confusion among the two battalions in front of him made any organized and rapid advance over the breastworks quite out of the question. The British artillery now opened fire and many shells, falling short, caused casualties among his men and those of the 1/5th Black Watch. A few minutes later the enemy artillery redoubled its efforts, shelling the assembly trenches just behind the front line heavily and accurately. The men huddled in their shallow trenches, seeking what cover they could find. They could find very little, and several companies were reduced by more than half as they waited for our own rather sketchy bombardment to lift. Lieut-Colonel Grogan realized the futility of attempting to assault untouched enemy defences under these conditions and, on his own responsibility, cancelled the attack – an action which his superiors later approved. Thus the 24th Brigade's assault was abandoned. In this brief period the 1/Worcestershires and 1/5th Black Watch had lost 235 and 146 men respectively.

In reserve behind the 8th Division, Major-General Gough had become restless at the lack of accurate information about the progress of the offensive. He could get little from Rawlinson's headquarters at Laventie and even General Davies, whose headquarters were close to his own in the Rue du Bacquerot, was unable to clarify the confused position on the 8th Division's front. As usual, Gough decided to visit the forward units to find out at first hand what was happening. Early in the afternoon he found Brigadier Oxley:

His headquarters were in a tiny cellar of a ruined building with little more than a sheet of tin roofing above him; considering the shells bursting all round, I thought this most unpleasantly insufficient as head cover!

I walked past rows of small narrow trenches which were crowded with men, many of whom were dead or wounded. These trenches had been dug for assembly purposes, to cover the attacking troops. They were quite insufficient for that function, as they were not very deep, were cramped and narrow, and all too close together. The Germans had spotted them from the air and shelled them heavily, making them into death traps rather than cover. I saw some shells land among them as I passed, and the proximity of these did not fail to bring home sharply to my mind that our situation was not a happy one.

After a further brief reconnaissance, Gough made his way back to the Rue du Bacquerot, knowing that the latest attack had failed. Here he found a message telling him to place his 21st Brigade at his Corps Commander's disposal. He at once telephoned Rawlinson, explained what he had seen on the 8th Division's front and stressed the futility of further attacks. He had no wish to see one of his own brigades pointlessly sacrificed. Gough's visit to the front line proved invaluable; first-hand knowledge of battlefield conditions by senior commanders became even rarer as the war wore on.

Haig sat in the mess after lunch waiting for news of the 8th Division's attack. A little before 2 pm a dispatch rider arrived with a message from Rawlinson: the belated attack by Davies's 8th Division had been an utter failure. The 25th Brigade had found it impossible to take part, while the assault planned by the 24th Brigade had failed to materialize. Even Haig's usual imperturbability could not conceal his feelings. An observer noted:

> The Chief took it very hard. We had been getting reports all morning of how well the French were doing and he must have felt that they would be laughing at our efforts, as they did in December. He wrote something in pencil and handed it to the DR and left the Indian Corps mess without another word.

What Haig had written was a terse instruction again urging Rawlinson to launch another and this time more effective assault and placing the 21st Brigade from General Gough's 7th Division at Rawlinson's disposal. Haig felt that the response by the 24th Brigade had been most unsatisfactory. He realized only too clearly that, unless the northern attack were successful, his plan of encircling the enemy would fail and he would be left with a single unsupported thrust south of Neuve Chapelle angled away from Aubers Ridge – and this thrust itself had already run into serious difficulties.

When Haig eventually arrived back at his headquarters he found a most disturbing development. A sombre Brigadier Butler handed him another message from Rawlinson reporting that General Gough had visited the front-line trenches and the situation he found there had convinced him it would be futile to put in the 21st Brigade. Gough had stressed that any further attempt to attack there in daylight would only result in another bloody failure. This report appeared to end Haig's hopes of prosecuting the northern thrust with success. He felt that IV Corps had failed him in, shall we say, its disinclination to press home the second attack. Although Haig's fears about what would follow the collapse of the northern pincer now looked like being realized, he had no intention of giving up yet. In any case to give up at this stage ran counter to his stubborn nature. Unwilling to believe that his troops could not breach the German defences and fearing French reaction, Haig now rested his hopes on the resumption of the offensive at 4 pm by his southern pincer.

After the abortive attack at 1.30 by the 24th Brigade, Brigadiers Oxley and Pinney faced difficult problems. There was no question of their battered brigades being required to mount another offensive. They were quite incapable of doing so; they were more than fully occupied in regrouping, evacuating the wounded, clearing and repairing the parapet as best they could under harassing shellfire. At the same time fighting still raged in the four lodgements made in the German trenches, where our men were desperately holding out against enemy counter-attacks. It was normal German policy to mount immediate counter-attacks to secure lost positions and they were adept at preparing and carrying them out quickly. They had two immediate aims: to support any sections of the defeated garrison who were still resisting and to catch an exhausted and depleted enemy in smashed trenches, exposed and unprepared for defence. As their attacks grew in strength, so our numbers diminished; hand-to-hand fighting with bayonet and bomb steadily took its toll.

In the interests of clarity it will be convenient now to deal with the fortunes of the various lodgements. In doing so, it should be remembered that small-scale savage conflicts were going on there all day long and in one sector would continue into the night. Even when their battalions were being relieved and the wounded brought in, these gallant troops fought on, the battle flaring up irregularly and in different degrees of intensity along the whole of the 8th Division's front.

On the extreme right of Brigadier Oxley's 24th Brigade we have seen how Lieutenant Parker and his men of the 2/Northamptonshires had fought grimly to maintain their hold on a section of the German salient. But they were too few to consolidate their gains and they were eventually forced out of the enemy front line by a series of German counter-attacks. As the men of D Company tried to withdraw over the breastworks several were shot down, but Lieutenant Parker immediately occupied shell craters just outside the German parapet and, though heavily bombed, clung on with great determination. Oxley reluctantly recognized that there was little chance of, and less point in, trying to hold this isolated position. He therefore ordered Lieutenant Parker to withdraw what was left of D Company under cover of dusk. At 8 pm Lieutenant Parker managed to extricate and bring back with him twenty-four men, including ten wounded. It was later discovered that this determined group had at one time narrowly escaped being wiped out by fire from a British 9.2-inch howitzer. An order had been given to bombard the actual section of the trench they were occupying but they were saved by the caution of the artillery commander, who dropped shells either side of them and broke up an impending counter-attack. For his gallantry throughout the day, Lieutenant Parker was awarded the Military Cross. A little later the battalion's stretcher-bearers went out to collect the many wounded who had been sheltering in no-man's-land as best they could throughout the day, but the enemy fire was so heavy that they had to stay out there all night. Those of the battalion who had regained the trenches had to stay there under shellfire until the following morning.

The situation on the front of the 24th Brigade remained unchanged all the afternoon. It proved impossible to withdraw our men from the smashed breastworks because the stretch of open ground behind the front line was being heavily shelled. Later in the afternoon the remnants of the 2/East Lancashires were moved along the front-line breastworks towards the orchard where the 2/Northamptonshires had originally sheltered. This enabled the 1/Worcestershires to reach the front line at long last. There they had to stay, crowded among the dead and wounded, under a continual bombardment. Eventually darkness fell and the survivors of the 24th Brigade were withdrawn, leaving the 1/Worcestershires to hold the line, rebuild the battered breastworks and give what help they could to the many wounded and dying.

On the 25th Brigade's front Brigadier Pinney was trying during the later part of the morning to carry out his promise to reinforce the three groups fighting in the German trenches. On the right, just east of the Sailly–Fromelles road, the mixed garrison of the 2/Rifle Brigade and 1/Royal Irish Rifles under Lieut-Colonel Stephens still held a stretch of enemy trenches. 2nd Lieutenant Gray collected fifty men from the 2/Rifle Brigade, brought them forward and formed them up in an abandoned trench. Then, when he gave the signal, his men leapt up and dashed across no-man's-land despite a hail of bullets. More than half the party were shot down before they could reach the German line but Lieutenant Gray and twenty men joined Lieut-Colonel Stephens in the captured trench. There, despite heavy shelling, they consolidated their position and waited for reinforcements. These did not arrive. Stephens and Gray saw the collapse of the attack at 1.30 pm across the other side of the Rue Delvas and their hope of being able to advance on the back of this assault rapidly faded. After the failure of this attack, the Germans were able to concentrate their energies on the irritating lodgements in their lines. A series of counter-attacks punctuated the afternoon but all were beaten off, though by this time Lieut-Colonel Stephens's men were running dangerously short of bombs, ammunition and weapons.

During a brief lull in the fighting Stephens handed over command to Lieutenant Newport of the 1/Royal Irish Rifles and made his way back to the British lines to take over the 25th Brigade from Brigadier Pinney. Once there he quickly collected about seventy men of the 2/Rifle Brigade with two machine guns and at 5.45 pm sent them back across no-man's-land, together with two bombing parties from the 2/Royal Berkshires, to strengthen Lieutenant Newport's small garrison. After several further enemy counter-attacks, Stephens made another effort to send up reinforcements. The 15th Field Company, under Major P.K. Batty, started to dig a communication trench across no-man's-land. The intention was for the 2/Queen's of the 22nd Brigade to use this as soon as it was dusk to reach Lieutenant Newport and his force. In fact D Company was ordered forward to do so, but such was the chaotic state of our front trenches that Stephens was forced to send them back. At 7.50 pm the Germans launched yet another counter-attack, but fortunately Lieutenant Gray had managed to put a captured machine gun into working order and with its help the enemy attack was broken up. For his part in the day's action Lieutenant Gray received the Military Cross.

Dusk fell, but fighting in this sector still continued during the night. During the later afternoon three companies of the 1st Battalion, 16 RIR, under Major Arnold, had been moved across to the rear of Rouges Bancs. It was decided that Major Arnold and his men should mount a night attack at 9.15 pm to recapture their lost front line, moving up to their attack line from the trench between Rouges Bancs and the 'House with the White Fence'. Dead on time the three companies pushed forward independently in the darkness with the result that one company strayed badly off course and suffered heavy losses, including its company commander, from our artillery fire. Eventually the three companies arrived at their jumping-off point at 10.30 pm, but their attack had to be postponed because it was far from clear which stretches of their old front line were occupied by Lieutenant Newport's small force. Major Arnold sent out patrols to mark the boundaries of the British position and then ordered the attack to go in at 1.30 am. This attack was disrupted by our shellfire before it had got under way and it was a somewhat chastened Major Arnold who, after a hurried meeting with his company commanders, gave instructions for a fresh and more vigorous effort at 2.45 am. This assault by 1 and 3 Companies again achieved very little until 4 Company was put in on the left flank under its dashing leader, Lieutenant Gebhardt. What happened next is vividly described in the Regimental History:

Cheering and shouting, our men advanced into the enemy's relentless fire; Lieutenant Keller collapses, badly wounded in the stomach. Two enemy machine guns stop the frontal attack of 1 and 3 Companies. It is vital that they are put out of action. Lieutenant Gebhardt urges a section of his company to use hand-grenades as they fight their way up the trench and orders the rest of his men to assist from outside the trench. At that moment, brave Lieutenant Hock plunges into the trench and with hand-grenades pushes the enemy back step by step. The dark figures of the English are clearly visible in the background and provide an easy target for our riflemen. A lull in the English machine-gun fire gives Lieutenant Gebhardt the opportunity to leap into the trench himself and press home the attack.

Despite the blocks we had built in the captured trenches, our flanks were slowly driven in. By now our stock of bombs was exhausted and the position had become untenable; the order to withdraw was given. As the enemy overran our defences, those who did not surrender were 'finished off', in the German phrase, with hand-grenades or bayonet. The survivors and the lightly wounded made their way back in the darkness to the safety of our breastworks.

Some idea of the ferocity of the fighting and the losses suffered by the two battalions can be gained from the fact that not a single officer of the 1/Royal Irish Rifles survived unwounded. The battalion had lost 477 officers and men and, when it marched back to its billets later in the morning, it did so under the Regimental Sergeant-Major. The 2/Rifle Brigade had suffered even more heavily; their casualties amounted to twenty-one officers and 632 men. When they finally assembled at 5 am to march off to their billets near Sailly, they could only muster three officers and 195 men.

Some distance from Lieutenant Newport's combined force, men of the 2/Lincolnshires under Captain Thruston still held a stretch of captured trenches. Despite continuous enemy pressure, they held out until early evening when Rawlinson decided that no further reinforcement should be attempted since the 7th Division was now going to relieve the 8th and renew the attack in the morning. Brigadier Pinney therefore decided to withdraw Captain Thruston and his troops after dusk and sent a runner across with orders to this effect. Shortly afterwards, about 8 pm, the Germans launched yet another bombing attack and came crowding in from both flanks. With no bombs or machine guns left, Captain Thruston gave the order to retire. His men, numbering some 200, fought their way out in the darkness and managed to cross no-man's-land and reach our lines. The desperate nature of the fighting at this critical moment is illustrated by the award of the Distinguished Conduct Medal to Private W. Cowling. When the order to retire was given, Private Cowling covered the retreat by holding up a number of the enemy in hand-to-hand fighting. He killed several of them and, though his rifle and bayonet were eventually torn from his grasp, he still succeeded in making his escape.

It should be noted that the 2/Lincolnshires and the 2/Royal Berkshires each lost almost 300 officers and men in the action, even though they were not among the original assaulting battalions.

Lastly we come to the 1/13th Kensingtons on the far left of the 25th Brigade. Reinforced by the party of the 2/Royal Berkshires at 11 am, they were still holding on in the face of frequent counter-attacks in parts of the German front line and deep inside their defences. Private J.H. Wood twice went across between the captured trenches and the British front line under fire carrying messages. The second time he brought back with him a party with sorely needed boxes of ammunition. He received the Distinguished Conduct Medal, as did Sergeant G.R. Pike who, after clearing a hundred yards of enemy trench, found he had few bombs left and crossed no-man's-land to bring a fresh supply. Fierce fighting raged all morning along the Kensingtons' sector.

Towards midday Lieutenant Schmitt and his augmented defenders were able to take the offensive and they began attacking the left flank of the Kensingtons with hand-grenades. Under cover of a mortar bombardment they rushed their position and forced groups of Kensingtons out of their hard-won ground and back towards the German front line. In one group there was only one survivor, Private V.E. Cohen, who, though wounded, 'continued to throw bombs with great courage and coolness until too exhausted to move'. He also received the Distinguished Conduct Medal.

After two hours of fighting, Delangre Farm was retaken and the Kensingtons, exhausted and running short of grenades, were being pushed back to the mine craters and were in danger of being cut off. All the time the Germans were creeping in closer and the Kensingtons were in many cases reduced to using the rifles of dead Germans. At this moment the Germans launched yet another counter-attack from the right flank and this proved decisive. Our men were forced to give ground, suffering heavy losses. About 2.45 pm their numbers were no longer sufficient to defend their position and, before they could be overwhelmed, Brigadier Pinney ordered these gallant Territorials and their comrades from the 1/Royal Berkshires to retire to our breastworks.

Meanwhile German reinforcements were on their way. The recently relieved 1st Battalion (Major Arnold) had been roused from its billets in Fournes and from 6.30 am placed on stand-by. They spent the morning resting under the trees in the grounds of the Château, but at 2 pm the battalion received orders to march to Fromelles. On arrival, 2 Company was at once ordered to recapture the area west of Delangre Farm, where isolated groups of our troops were still continuing to fight on with great courage, while the CO led the other three companies, as we have seen, across towards Rouges Bancs. Advancing at the double, 2 Company encountered some eighty men of the Kensingtons. Unable to break out back to their line, they made a gallant last stand but after a brief struggle they were all either killed or captured. This was the fate of other smaller parties as the Germans relentlessly mopped up the remaining attackers.

Some of our men succeeded in reaching the British line, but many were taken prisoner. Among them was Private Anderton of B Company. Nothing was known of his fate, like that of so many others in the battalion, and he was posted as missing. A friend of his, Private Yeardye, wrote to Anderton's mother a week after the battle:

> All we know is that our regiment took three lines of German trenches on May 9th and that the few brave chaps who reached the third line (Andy included) were cut off from the rest of the brigade by heavy machine-gun and enfilade fire. Reinforcements were killed on their way to the rescue, and the 13th/London, who were overwhelmed by superior numbers, had the order to retire. A few succeeded in getting out, but many were captured.

Six weeks later an anxious but still hopeful Mrs Anderton received a letter, dated 15 May, 1915, from her son, a prisoner of war in Germany. He wrote:

> I consider myself fortunate in having survived practically unharmed (I have a mere scratch on my left hand) an action so terrible as that in which I was engaged last Sunday. I am not alone here; Private England and a few more friends having escaped with me.

One of the surviving officers, Captain Kimber, described in a letter to his parents, later published in *The Times*, his hazardous attempts to extricate his party from deep in the German position near Delangre Farm.

We crawled for hours above our waists in the mud and foul water of the German trenches, isolated and cut off by an enemy we could not see, but who was steadily reducing our numbers by very excellent sniping. We were four subalterns in command of thirty to forty men. Two of the officers were killed. The other man and myself determined to wait until darkness and then try to get through the German lines to our own. It was a risk, but everything was a risk that day.

It was not till 8.15 pm that the exhausted survivors scrambled over the British parapet to safety. Not only for his courage and determination in extricating the remains of his company but for 'conspicuous ability and coolness in leading his company and getting it into position under a heavy fire south of Delangre Farm', Captain Kimber received the Military Cross.

Lieut-Colonel F.G. Lewis, who led the attack and had to return to hospital as soon as he had seen the survivors of his battalion back to their billets, was made a CMG in the King's Birthday Honours the following month. Of the seventeen company officers of the Kensingtons who charged that morning, eight were dead, four wounded and one was missing. Of the other ranks, 423 were killed, wounded, missing or taken prisoner. Thus the battalion had lost about 70 per cent of its effectives. The Corps Commander wrote a generous epitaph; Rawlinson described their part in the attack as 'a feat of arms unsurpassed by any battalion in this great war'.

A German officer who witnessed the retirement of the battalions of the 25th Brigade generously referred to the men who had attacked so bravely, held on so staunchly and had eventually been forced to retire exhausted, outnumbered and about to be overrun, as 'These God-like fools'.

CHAPTER ELEVEN

Battle : The Third Attack : 'At all costs'

From the fabled vase the genie in his shattering horror came.
Edmund Blunden, 'Trench Nomenclature'

We must now return to the southern sector where we left Generals
Haking and Anderson trying to withdraw their shattered battalions
and to organize fresh troops for the new joint attack ordered by
Haig for 4 pm. Their efforts were making slow progress under most
difficult conditions. By midday it became obvious that those battalions of Haking's 2nd and 3rd Brigades which had been
concerned in the earlier attacks would be quite unable to take any
further part in the battle. Haking therefore ordered up to the front
line the two battalions he had borrowed from the 1st Brigade and
the two battalions of the 3rd Brigade which had been in reserve.

The third major attack was thus to be delivered by the 1/Black
Watch and the 1/Camerons on the right of the cinder track and, on
the left, by the 1/South Wales Borderers and the 1/Gloucestershires
from the 3rd Brigade. It was to be preceded by a forty-minute bombardment. If this sounds all too familiar, it is because the plan was,
in effect, a copy of the original disastrous attack made by the 1st
Division. The attack was also to be made over exactly the same
ground where the first and second assaults in the morning had been
destroyed. During the afternoon, General Horne, the phlegmatic
Scottish gunner commanding the 2nd Division in reserve two miles
away, arranged with Haking for his division to move up and
leapfrog through the 1st Division, if the attack at 4 pm proved successful. In view of the events of the morning, this seems an
unnaturally optimistic appreciation of the situation.

There was hardly the same spirit of optimism and determination
among the Bareilly Brigade of the Meerut Division, who were to

advance on the left of the 1st Division. Brigadier Southey had been in touch with Brigadier Jacob during the protracted relief of the Dehra Dun Brigade. He had no wish to see his brigade similarly slaughtered, so he reported to his Divisional Commander that, in Jacob's opinion, the enemy defences had in no way been weakened and that the machine-gun fire which had decimated his own brigade was as intense and well-directed as ever. Southey added for good measure that, although the German parapets had been slightly damaged by our shelling, this had been more than compensated for by the arrival of reinforcements. His three attacking battalions had already been exposed to shellfire while moving slowly and painfully up to the front line and he wanted General Anderson to be aware of this before his attack started – that is, assuming he could get his troops into position in time.

General Anderson passed on the gist of this unwelcome report to his Corps Commander, yet emphasized to Southey that the attack must proceed as ordered. General Willcocks concurred. He later recalled that, no matter what the circumstance, 'I considered it imperative to carry out this assault and sent instructions that it was to be pressed *at all costs*'. This phrase reminds one of Haig's 'regardless of loss'; obviously Haig's visit to Willcocks had served to stiffen his sinews. The Corps Commander justified himself on the grounds that Haig's orders were quite distinct and that the progress of the 1st Division on his right depended on the success of his own attack. 'I therefore felt bound to do all in my power to comply with the Army orders.' Anderson passed this on to Southey, adding his own gloss that the attack was to be 'carried on into the night if necessary'. This fatuous instruction was only one of several fatuous orders given on 9 May.

During the action in the morning, the source of the machine-gun fire that caused such terrible losses among the 1/Seaforths on the left had eventually been located in the south-west corner of the Bois du Biez. The building of this strongpoint, you will remember, had been reported earlier by Military Intelligence. General Anderson now arranged for artillery fire to destroy this position during the bombardment timed to start at 3.20 pm. He also warned Brigadier Southey not to make any attack east of the Estaires–La Bassée road. The left of the 41st Dogras, now taking over the role of the 1/Seaforths, was instructed to keep close to the west edge of the road which, being a low embankment, gave them some slight (very slight as it turned out) protection from fire from the east and north-east. The relief of the Dehra Dun Brigade continued maddeningly slowly; when finally completed, it had taken over five hours starting from 10.30 am.

By 3.50 pm the Bareilly Brigade were at last in position – in the middle of our preliminary bombardment – but they had lost over two hundred men in the process. Some idea of the severity of the shelling to which the brigade had been subjected on their slow and tortuous way forward is illustrated by the fact that No. 3 Company of the 58th Vaughan's Rifles lost one British and two Indian officers killed and had forty-five casualties among the other ranks. As a result, the company had to be reinforced by a company from the supporting battalion, the 1/4th Black Watch.

The battalions were now formed up in the front-line breastworks with the 2/Black Watch on the right, the 58th Vaughan's Rifles in the centre and the 41st Dogras on the left. The 1/4th Black Watch and the machine guns of the 125th Napier's Rifles were left in brigade reserve. As the Highlanders and the Indians looked over the parapet they could see the ground in front of them covered with the bodies of the dead and wounded of the Dehra Dun Brigade. They could also see large numbers of Germans filing down their communications trenches and spreading out along the front line, apparently little incommoded by our shelling.

This was a reflection of the German command's decision to re-inforce their defenders. The 55th Infantry Regiment had suffered some 400 casualties in the morning's fighting mainly from shellfire. But these were more than made good during the course of the morning by the arrival of the supporting companies. Thus the Germans now had more troops holding the front line in this sector than they had at the start of the battle. Later on in the morning the RFC spotted reinforcements in the shape of three more companies moving from their rest billets to take the place of the original supporting companies. The defenders continued to sweep the hundreds of men lying out in no-man's-land with machine-gun fire. Later, after the battle, several officers reported that they had seen German marksmen confidently standing up behind their breast-works during our feeble bombardment and picking off our troops while they were forming up for the assault.

Preparations for the third attack against the German defences on the southern front were now virtually complete – except for yet another frustrating delay on the right. Of the four fresh battalions of the 1st Division, three were in position on time but the 1/Camerons were still trying to reach the front line. It was not their fault. First, they had been sent back at 10.30 am to man a third-line trench; then, when they were ordered to move up towards the front line, they found their way obstructed by the survivors of the Royal Sussex battalions who were being withdrawn to the rear. The Commanding Officer of the 1/Camerons, Major E. Craig Brown, had already warned Brigadier Lowther at 1st (Guards) Brigade Headquarters that he might be unable to be in position to attack at 4 pm. At 3.45 pm he telephoned again to confirm that his leading companies would not be ready in time. With the preliminary bombardment in full swing, Brigadier Lowther ordered the 1/Black Watch (Lieut-Colonel C.E. Stewart) to attack as arranged and told Major Brown to follow as soon after zero hour as possible.

Thus the attack of these two battalions on the right was a disjointed affair from the start. Yet, as our preliminary bombardment approached its climax, there was a certain degree of optimism (optimism was part of our generals' stock-in trade) felt by General Haking and, to a much lesser extent, by his brigadiers. The artillery preparation appeared rather more effective than that of the morning. Certainly towards the right of their front, where the 1/Black Watch were to attack, the enemy parapet seemed to have been partially demolished and there were several stretches where the wire had been properly cut.

A few minutes before our barrage lifted, A and B Companies of the 1/Black Watch scrambled out of the breastworks, formed up, and to the skirl of the pipes went forward at the double across the 300 yards that lay between them and the enemy trenches. They were quickly followed by two platoons each from C and D Companies. The men of the Black Watch were played into action by Lance-Corporal Stuart who started playing his pipes the moment he left the parapet and, although badly wounded, continued playing all the way to the German line. For this he was awarded the Distinguished Conduct Medal. As the Highlanders in their hodden kilts advanced across no-man's-land, a number of men from both battalions of the Royal Sussex, who had been lying out there since early morning now got to their feet and joined in the charge.

It seems that the Germans, perhaps a little complacent and off-guard, having already destroyed two attacks over this stretch of ground, were initially taken somewhat by surprise. They had been keeping their heads down as our barrage, more accurate than earlier in the day, fell upon their breastworks. When our bombardment lifted and the dust and smoke had cleared, they found that the first wave of the Black Watch was already threading its way through their wire. Behind them no-man's-land was filled with threatening waves of Highlanders. On the right the Black Watch spotted several gaps in the wire, and a party of over forty men from A Company swarmed into the German front line through breaches in the parapet and began to clear the trenches in hand-to-hand fighting. The first man to climb onto their parapet was Corporal John Ripley and from there he directed those following him to the gaps in the German wire. He then led his section to the enemy's support trench, which had earlier been designated as their final objective, and established himself there with seven or eight men, blocking both flanks and organizing a fire position. He continued to defend this until all his men had fallen and he himself had been badly wounded in the head.

Behind him the Germans in the front line retreated down the communication trenches only to collide with reinforcements coming up it. In the confusion the Black Watch were able to account for many of the enemy, mainly by turning captured machine guns on them. Yet once more it was the same story of there being too few men left to exploit early success. They could expect no help from B Company on their immediate left who had met determined resistance and had been virtually destroyed. Urgent requests for support were sent back to Colonel Stewart, but to no avail. The Germans may not have been prepared for the attack but they quickly recovered their balance and soon made it impossible for reinforcements to cross a no-man's-land swept by machine-gun fire. The supporting waves of the Black Watch were mown down by enfilade fire from three machine guns on the left flank and rifle fire from the right of I Battalion. Heavy shellfire from the 43rd Field Artillery and from two batteries of the 7th Foot Artillery Regiments now descended upon that part of no-man's-land occupied by the stricken battalion.

The small group of Highlanders in the enemy defences now found itself being attacked from three sides as the Germans mounted a counter-attack. By working round the flanks via other communication trenches, the enemy finally surrounded and destroyed almost the whole party with grenades and small-arms fire after an hour's bitter fighting. One of the few survivors was Corporal Ripley who managed to make his way back to his own line. For his outstanding bravery and leadership he received the Victoria Cross. He survived this battle and the war, finishing as a sergeant in his battalion.

Meanwhile, on the battalion left, Lieutenant Scott of C

Company had also managed to break into the enemy line but he and all the men with him were killed as they attempted to advance further. The remaining two platoons of C Company were sent forward to support their comrades but were swept away by machine-gun fire.

When Brigadier Lowther heard that the Black Watch had penetrated the German defences on the right, he ordered the 1st Loyal North Lancashires, who were already holding the front-line breastworks, to support them. But before its companies could leave their trench the order was countermanded because the 3rd Brigade on their left had been unable to make any progress. The survivors of the Black Watch were now ordered to withdraw from the German line. The battalion had lost fourteen officers and 461 other ranks; it was to prove a black day for the regiment. One of the survivors from the slaughter was a certain Captain Miller who, according to Robert Graves, escaped 'the Rue du Bois massacre by swimming down a flooded trench'. Certain survivors had great reputations. Miller used to be pointed at in the streets when the battalion was in reserve billets. 'See that fellow? That's Jock Miller. Out from the start and hasn't got it yet.'

On the left of the Black Watch two and a half companies of the 1/Cameron Highlanders had managed to force their way through the communication trenches and into the front line and were ready to attack a few minutes after 4 pm. They advanced at the same time as the supporting platoons of the Black Watch and they met a similar fate at the hands of the German machine gunners now fully alerted to the threat. Bullets tore into the ranks of the Cameronians; of the 350 men who went over the top, 180 became casualties before they were half-way across no-man's-land; the total loss to the battalion in the action was nine officers and 240 other ranks. The rest of the battalion was still held up in the communication trenches. When they finally reached the front line about 4.40 pm they saw the bodies of their comrades scattered over the first hundred yards of no-man's-land with the survivors seeking what cover they could in the ditches and from any slight undulations in the ground. Mercifully, they were not ordered to advance.

Any optimism felt by Brigadier Davies of the 3rd Brigade on the other side of the cinder track evaporated swiftly after 4 pm. As soon as the 1/South Wales Borderers and the 1/Gloucesters left the protection of the breastworks on a front of some 800 yards, they were met by furious machine-gun fire. Both battalions bravely advanced into the face of this fire but a hundred yards into no-man's-land the merciless fire stopped the attack and drove the men to seek cover, like the Cameron Highlanders on their right. In this brief advance the 1/South Wales Borderers lost nine officers and 224 other ranks, while the 1/Gloucesters' casualties were ten officers and 252 other ranks.

By 4.20 it was patently clear that this third attack by the 1st Division had also failed. Brigadiers Lowther and Davies informed General Haking of the result of Haig's directive and stressed the size of the losses incurred by their troops. Haking's reaction was typical. Undeterred by the casualties among these regular battalions, he issued instructions for a further ten-minute bombardment of the German front line, to be followed by yet another assault – the fourth of the day – by the same troops over the same ground as soon as their officers could withdraw and reorganize them. It was a callous, despicable order. The brief bombardment went ahead; it seemed to have no significant effect. By this time both Haking's brigadiers had had enough of this reckless waste of life. They felt that to send troops forward yet again into the teeth of such machine-gun fire would be a criminal squandering of brave men and they told Haking so in blunt terms. They emphasized that another attempt to storm the enemy line would be pointless and disastrous. Haking backed down. He ordered the survivors of his various battalions, many of whom had been lying out in no-man's-land under artillery and small-arms fire since the opening assault, to withdraw as best they could to the front-line breastworks under cover of another barrage.

In this ill-starred battle it is perhaps invidious to single out a particular battalion for the part it played. Yet one cannot help remarking on the dash and determination of the 1/Black Watch. Even if by 4 pm one or two factors were slightly, very slightly, in their favour, their renowned fighting qualities achieved more in terms of penetration of the German defences than almost any other battalion in the 1st Division or the Meerut Division during the day.

About this time one of our 15-inch shells hit a large ammunition dump in the enemy rear at Herlies. There was a tremendous, earth-shaking explosion and a great cloud of smoke erupted over the plateau ahead. It hung over the area for some time before it began to drift slowly westwards as a pinkish mist over Aubers Ridge. As it crossed our lines there were excited cries of 'Gas!' from men who had suffered enough and feared another nightmare. Our troops had been issued with a primitive form of mask, though none so far had experienced gas in action. However, bad news travels fast and they were quite aware of the horrors inflicted on unprepared troops by the German gas attack at Ypres a couple of weeks earlier. Fortunately they were to be spared on this occasion. There had already been a minor alarm at the end of April when observers noticed what seemed to be pipes protruding over the edge of the enemy parapet in several places. Luckily these did not turn out to be the iron pipes that led gas from German gas cylinders out into no-man's-land. It appears from examination of prisoners taken during the battle that the Germans had made no preparations for the use of gas. They had issued improvised respirators to their men, but the prisoners had been told that this was because the German Staff anticipated that we would use gas after what had taken place at Ypres.

It is now time to examine what happened to the Bareilly Brigade on the left of the attack. As the men waited for the signal to advance, they knew that the enemy were unshaken, the wire not properly cut, the enemy parapet largely intact, and that there was every likelihood of what happened to the Dehra Dun Brigade happening to them. A few minutes before 4 pm they were ordered to climb out over the parapet and form up. They immediately came under murderous machine-gun fire, even heavier than that faced by the Dehra Dun in the morning. Some thirty bridges were supposed to have been made for crossing the dyke on the brigade's front but few were actually in position when the attack began. Hundreds of men were mown down and fell across the parapet or on the few yards of ground between the parapet and the dyke.

The 2/Black Watch on the right and the right-hand company of the 58th Rifles met such fire from their left front and left flank that only very few succeeded in crossing the dyke. Among these was Lance-Corporal David Finlay of the Black Watch, who was to be awarded the Victoria Cross for his bravery. He coolly led a bombing party of twelve men across the dyke. Two men were shot dead while crossing it but the others advanced by rushes from one shell hole to another towards the German line, eight more of them being killed or wounded. Finlay told the two survivors to crawl back and then went over to one of his wounded men and carried him a hundred yards back to safety across a bullet-swept no-man's-land. Lance-Corporal Finlay survived the battle but died in early 1916 in the campaign in Mesopotamia.

In the centre the supporting companies of the 58th Rifles managed to advance for a hundred yards despite the heavy fire. Here they were checked and pinned down by our own artillery barrage, which was not only pounding the enemy front line but also, it appears, an area about 130 yards in front of it.

On the left by the road two and a half companies of the 41st Dogras crossed the parapet. They had been shelled early in the morning in their assembly area and they had been shelled during the long time it had taken them to reach the front, one company being reduced to twenty-eight men. Now watched by the Commanding Officer, Lieut-Colonel W. Tribe, from over the parapet, they aligned themselves with the 58th Rifles and attempted to advance. Like the other two battalions, they were brought to an abrupt halt, their officers being shot down almost at once. The only unwounded officer sent back word that he was still ready and willing to continue but Tribe told him to cancel the attack and wait for darkness before trying to get his men back to their trench. Lieut-Colonel Harvey of the 2/Black Watch also realized that any further attempt to advance would be suicidal and he ordered his supporting companies to remain behind the breastworks.

The whole brigade was now forced to go to ground and seek what cover it could. Casualties, among both the attackers and the supporting companies sheltering in the front trenches, were so serious that any thought of the brigade resuming the attack had to be abandoned. Brigadier Southey recognized this and a little after 4 pm he issued orders for his battalions to reorganize and prepare for a fresh assault, if ordered.

He now had the unpleasant task of reporting to his Divisional Commander that his attack had come to a bloody halt with heavy losses. Southey told General Anderson it would be useless to send forward the remainder of his brigade. Anderson could do little but agree with him, and then gave instructions for the remaining brigade of the Meerut Division, the Garhwal Brigade, to take over the front line from Southey's troops.

The situation the Garhwal Brigade found in the front line as they moved up and began the slow and wearisome task of relieving their comrades is vividly illustrated in an account by Captain W.G. Bagot-Chester MC, of the 2/3 Gurkha Rifles. His battalion had been waiting in reserve in a redoubt until being ordered forward:

We had to advance about two thousand yards across open country to start with, but we were not fired on until we reached a long communication trench leading up to the front trench-line. Of course we advanced in artillery formation. Toward the last hundred yards or so German 'Woolly Bears' [shrapnel shells which burst with a cloudlike effect] began to burst overhead, and 'Jack Johnsons' close by, but I had only one man hit at this point. We then got into a long communication trench leading up from Lansdowne Post to the Gridiron Trenches. Here we were blocked for a long time, shelling increasing every moment, wounded trying to get by us. After a time we got into the Gridiron where it was absolute hell. Hun shells, large and small, bursting everywhere, blowing the parapet here and there, and knocking tree branches off. Here there was fearful confusion. No one knew the way to anywhere. There was such a maze of trenches, and such a crowd of people, many wounded, all wanting to go in different directions, one regiment going back, ours trying to go forward, wounded and stretcher-bearers going back, etc. I presently went on to a trench called the Pioneer Trench. There I had twenty-six casualties from shell. Halvidar Manbir had his leg blown off, and was in such agony that he asked to be shot.

As one got further to the front trench, the place got more of a shambles, wounded and dead everywhere. Those who could creep or walk were trying to get back; others were simply lying and waiting. The ground in front was littered with Seaforth bodies and 41st Dogras. From the Pioneer Trench I went on to the front trench, occupied by the 41st Dogras, who, however, had very few men left, so heavily had they suffered. One of the British officers had completely lost his nerve and was rather a pitiable sight. I tried to comfort him a bit. We had to set to work at once to try to clean up the trench. It was full of killed and wounded, equipment of all sorts, and the ground in front was strewn with dead Seaforths, who made the charge this morning at 5.40 am from this trench, also 41st Dogras, who made a second attempt.

This brief, abortive attack by the Bareilly Brigade brought their casualties for the day to over 1000 officers and men. The 2/Black Watch had lost 265 men (or 50 per cent of those who went over the top), the 58th Rifles over 250, the 1/4th Black Watch 173, while the 41st Dogras had by now lost 400 out of their rifle strength of 650. Colonel Tribe was himself wounded in the chest by a shell splinter; he recovered, only to be killed in action later in the war.

So ended the third assault on the German line by the 1st and Meerut Divisions. Though delivered with great bravery, it proved

131

another costly failure in a series of disastrous attacks. The afternoon sun now began to sink in the sky and shadows crept across the scarred and pitted battlefield. As the fighting died away, so the drifts of dust and smoke in no-man's-land slowly dispersed to reveal a landscape of horrifying aspect.

Watching the course of the battle from the gun lines with some foreboding was a regular Indian Army officer, Captain Hobart ('Hobo') of the 1st Bengal Sappers and Miners. He was later to become famous as Major-General Sir Percy Hobart, the outspoken and controversial expert on armoured warfare and the development of specialized armour. Determined to get into the thick of the action, he had won a well-deserved MC at Neuve Chapelle, but, as a valuable specialist, he had been ordered to stay out of the front line during the attack on Aubers Ridge. He was already becoming angry and sickened at the reckless waste of trained soldiers as a result of the tactics employed by our leading generals. He confided to his diary after the battle:

'All that courage and endurance. All that forethought and organization. All those gallant lives, given – to crack the shell of the German line. And didn't.'

CHAPTER TWELVE

Battle : Last Post

'So many good men gone and no gain whatever.'
Dr Nangle

A few minutes before 5 pm Haig received the news that the third assault in the southern sector had utterly failed. He took it with little change of expression, but disappointment bit deep. He was unwilling to admit defeat, to accept that his troops had been decisively repulsed yet again and that his cherished offensive lay in ruins. He was determined, however, to make one last effort later in the day; surely, he thought, the weight of his repeated bombardments and attacks must have sapped the enemy's strength and resolve.

After a brief exchange with his staff, he issued instructions that no further reinforcements should be sent to support attacks which had already failed and that any captured ground (of which there was, in truth, virtually none) was to be held. Next he ordered that the three divisions were to be reorganized and, with the addition of fresh battalions, were to prepare to deliver a bayonet attack about 8 pm as dusk fell. This late attack was to be preceded by a short, intensive bombardment. Haig also gave instructions that in the meantime those strong points and machine-gun positions which had caused such heavy losses in the earlier attacks were to be systematically shelled. To improve the chances of success of his proposed attack, Haig placed the 141st Brigade, a Territorial unit from First Army Reserve, at the disposal of I Corps.

Once again Haig was overtaken by events. At 6 pm, before the staff had completed the arrangements for an assault at 8 pm, his liaison officers reported that the roads and communication trenches leading to the front line were so damaged and congested that the fresh battalions detailed for the attack could not possibly be in position in time. There was no chance of their attempting to save time by advancing across the open because this was dominated and raked by the enemy artillery. Any movements by large bodies of men would be almost certain to bring prolonged shelling down upon them. They did not tell Haig that his senior commanders were less than optimistic about the chances of success of yet another attack. It would not be unnatural for them to use the shocking conditions behind the front as an excuse for not being able to reach the front line.

Haig was infuriated by the further delay as he saw his plans for one last attack before nightfall, an assault which just might yield him the success he had striven for all day, again disrupted. Faced by these difficulties, he was reluctantly forced to postpone his attack. Having issued orders to this effect, he arranged for his Corps Commanders and senior staff officers to meet him at the Indian Corps headquarters at 7 pm to discuss the situation and decide upon their course of action.

It was a much chastened group of senior officers who assembled at Lestrem a little later. At this time the troops in the four lodgements on the northern front were still holding out but their efforts were shortly to draw to a close. No impression at all had been made on the enemy's defences in the southern sector. Haig and his Corps Commanders still had no real idea of the enormity of their losses. Gone were the optimism and heady expectations of the previous day. Haig, bitterly disappointed and frustrated, opened the conference by stating baldly that he thought the lack of progress of the offensive so far was 'regrettable'. His cold blue eyes surveyed the faces in front of him, no doubt resting momentarily on Rawlinson. Briefly, he outlined the situation as he saw it. In his view the First Army had two options, either to proceed with the night bayonet assault when the fresh troops eventually reached the front, or to wait until daylight the next day, Monday, and attack after another artillery bombardment. He asked for comments and he quickly found there was opposition to his first option. His Corps Commanders had had time to confer and they pointed out to Haig that fresh battalions attacking in the dark over difficult ground against still relatively undamaged enemy defences would meet considerable problems. This was something of an understatement. Haig did not press the first option too vigorously. After a short discussion, there was general agreement that the offensive should be postponed until daylight the next morning – much to the relief of those concerned. At 7.30 pm the meeting broke up. Haig ordered the 7th Division to relieve the 8th during the night and to resume the attack on Monday, using a plan similar to Sunday's. His Corps Commanders returned to their headquarters to issue detailed orders for the renewal of the offensive at dawn.

One artillery officer confided to his diary:

> I think it is just as well for our infantry that it was put off, for of all the bloody jobs, an assault at night on unbroken infantry with machine guns in well-wired trenches and ruined houses must be the worst and most futile.

When Gough received orders to relieve the 8th Division and to renew the attack the next morning, he at once told his three brigadiers to see their opposite numbers in the 8th Division as quickly as possible and report back to him at 8 pm at a rendezvous near Petillon. Meanwhile, he would discuss the situation with Major-General Davies. They met later in a cottage by the roadside and sat crowded round a small table in the light of candles and electric torches. Their conversation was punctuated by the explosion of shells falling along the road and among the fields nearby. As the candles flickered and the puffs of dust drifted down from the ceiling, the brigadiers reported that the support trenches were full of unwounded, wounded and dead, inextricably mixed up and still being subjected to shellfire. In the front line, confusion, if possible, was even worse. Above all, the forming-up trenches had been so battered during the battle by enemy artillery that the assaulting battalions of the 7th Division would be cruelly exposed to accurate shellfire while waiting to attack. It was, they emphasized, quite impractical to attempt the relief by night and quite impossible under the circumstances to mount an assault at dawn the next day. They waited for Gough's reaction. He paused and then said, 'Well, that is it, then. It cannot be done. Go back and stand your brigades down. I shall return to my headquarters to tell Corps that I have cancelled the operation in view of conditions here.'

This was a bold and brave decision by Gough, and one flying in the face of Haig's orders. Yet it was accepted without much discussion by Rawlinson as both Davies and Gough emphasized that the attack envisaged by Haig would have virtually no chance of success. Gough went on to suggest to Rawlinson that it would be much more sensible if the 7th Division were to be moved during the night and put in south of Neuve Chapelle towards Festubert. Rawlinson telephoned Haig at GHQ, explained the situation facing IV Corps and put forward Gough's idea. Haig accepted what Rawlinson said and at once countermanded his orders for the attack by the 7th Division; he noted Gough's idea but took no further action at that time.

Further telephone conversations between GHQ and the Corps Commanders over their organizational problems resulted in the time of the offensive on Monday being altered again. At 11.30 pm it was finally agreed that I Corps should now make the main thrust at 4 pm after a four-hour bombardment of the German defences, mainly by 6-inch and 9.2-inch howitzers. The Indian Corps, with fresh battalions in its front line, was to be ready to advance if the I Corps assault was successful. IV Corps would take no part in this action unless the Germans provoked a response; the 8th Division was to continue to man the front line as best it could.

Then, some time after midnight, disturbing reports began to reach Haig's headquarters. Stocks of artillery shells were running low and details of the huge losses suffered by the infantry at last became known. Haig decided he must have much more information before committing his troops to the afternoon attack and he therefore arranged for his Corps Commanders to meet him at 9 am at I Corps Headquarters.

Monday proved another warm sunny day after an uncertain start. Willcocks and Rawlinson joined Monro in his room; they formed a glum and slightly apprehensive group as they waited for Haig to arrive. The Commander of the First Army entered with his staff, sat down at the table and came straight to the point. He told them there was not enough ammunition to maintain attacks on both the northern and the southern sectors – attacks which might last for several days. Moreover, the shells for the 4.7-inch batteries in the northern sector had proved so defective that the guns there were virtually useless for counter-battery work. This news did not seem to distress the Corps Commanders unduly. In the discussion that followed, Haig and his generals quickly agreed that the German defences had been so much stronger than anticipated that no infantry assault would stand any chance of success until they had been systematically pounded and destroyed – as the French had already realized. Haig had little difficulty in taking the sense of the meeting; he decided to abandon the attack. His Corps Commanders breathed a little more easily. It may have suited the *amour propre* of Haig and his generals to seize upon these reasons for calling off the offensive; but the decision was a damning indictment of their tactics. It is particularly disturbing that there seems to have been no real discussion of one major objection to an immediate resumption of the offensive: that the three attacking divisions had suffered terrible losses and that the survivors were exhausted and disorganized.

Haig now cancelled the assault arranged for 4 pm on the grounds that he no longer had the men or the ammunition to maintain the momentum of attacks on both fronts. He also decided to write off his northern attack and to concentrate all his forces south of Neuve Chapelle, happy in the knowledge that Sir John French had originally ordered the main effort to be made there, and he now took up Gough's suggestion that the 7th Division should move to the Festubert area. Haig thus abandoned his original battle-plan, but he continued to argue strongly that it was still vital to help the French Tenth Army at Vimy Ridge. To this end he proposed that the 7th Division and the 2nd Division should launch another offensive against the Ridge as soon as possible. The meeting ended. Haig contacted his C in C at Hazebrouck, reported on the situation facing the First Army and put forward his new plan. Sir John French, shocked and disappointed by the First Army's failure on Sunday, felt he had little option but to agree to the postponement of further operations until Haig had completed preparations for his revised offensive.

The battle of Aubers Ridge was over. During the night the dying embers of our lodgements had been snuffed out by German counter-attacks. By 3 am the last survivors had crawled back into our front line. The Germans had recaptured all the small pockets of ground, which had been taken at such cost and held with such courage. We were back exactly where we started.

During the late afternoon on Sunday and continuing into the night, officers began the task of extricating the survivors of those battalions which had been relieved and returning them to their billets in the rear areas. Disentangling the various companies was a difficult task, made more difficult by the condition of the communication trenches and by the large number of walking wounded making their way back while the enemy artillery was silent.

On the 1st Division front, once the exhausted men were clear of the Rue du Bois, they were formed up and marched wearily back to their billets. One Territorial battalion, the 1/5th Royal Sussex, consisting of men drawn from the Cinque Ports, received orders at 6 pm to move back via Le Touret to their billets at Gonnehem. Their CO (Colonel F. Langham) recorded in the War Diary:

We formed up in a field behind Chocolat Menier Corner, told the men off and marched down in fours through a considerably disorganized mob of men from other regiments.

Langham's phrase 'considerably disorganized mob' is instructive and illuminates the situation behind the lines. Led by their CO, the battalion marched away singing 'Sussex by the Sea'. Langham wrote later:

No end of brave things were done, and our men were splendid but helpless. They advanced with the utmost steadiness as if on parade and, when they lay down to take cover, were aligned as though on a field day. A very small proportion of those who went over the parapet succeeded in getting back unwounded.

When they met their regular battalion, the 2/Royal Sussex, three days later, they were greeted with shouts of 'Good Old Fifth!' – approval enough.

There was no singing from the 1/Seaforths as they returned to their billets. Observers remarked that it was most pathetic to watch this splendid battalion, before the action nearly 1000 strong with twenty-six officers, marching off with a solitary piper at its head, having lost over 500 men.

We have seen how Churchill watched the earlier stages of the battle from the same vantage point as Sir John French. As the battle developed during the morning, Churchill became impatient at being unable to see very much of what was going on. Excusing himself, he left Sir John, climbed down from the tower and, in true Churchillian fashion, attempted to get nearer to the action. To his chagrin he found that as he made his way forward the flatness of the ground and the smoke billowing across the battle area made it impossible to follow what was happening. Eventually he turned back and later that afternoon made his way to Haig's HQ at Merville where a major Casualty Clearing Station had been set up in the Convent not far away.

Here Churchill witnessed the gruesome spectacle of a large Casualty Clearing Station towards the end of a day's fighting. He found more than 1000 wounded men, many horribly mangled and torn, being sorted out for treatment. As a procession of motor ambulances unloaded their bloody cargoes at the entrance, so at the back of the Convent a succession of corpses was being brought out to the burial detail.

Inside the Convent rooms were filled with walking wounded, most of them in pain but determinedly cheerful. After a cup of tea and a cigarette these would be sent by ambulance down the line to a Base Hospital. One large room was overflowing with hopeless cases who were too far gone for surgery. Priority was given to an unending line of urgent cases being carried towards the operating room which now resembled a butcher's shop with blood, limbs and filthy dressings everywhere. The door was wide open and as Churchill passed by he saw 'the terrible spectacle of a man being trepanned'. Meanwhile, from outside came the unceasing thunder of the guns; as Churchill observed: 'The process of death and mutilation was still at its height'.

As the light faded and the dust began to settle over the battlefield, no-man's-land appeared to come to a curious life. The torn earth around the swathes and piles of dead was suddenly alive with dark forms, crawling and limping, as hundreds of men began to drag themselves back to the British front line. Muddy, bloodied, with haggard faces, worn out by the stress of battle and by unrelenting shelling and machine gun fire, they struggled towards the parapet and with a last convulsive effort slithered over the breastworks into the safety of the trench. Stretcher-bearers went out to bring in those too badly wounded to move; many of them had remained out all day in the sun, suffering agonies of thirst, amid the tumult and the terror which raged around them.

For the troops of the Dehra Dun and Bareilly Brigades withdrawal was a long, laborious and painful process. The survivors were not extricated and passed to the rear until well after midnight. In the battle the two understrength brigades had suffered over 2000 casualties or 45 per cent of their number.

Elsewhere more wounded now began to filter back to the Regimental Aid Posts. Dr Nangle of the 1/Loyal North Lancs recorded the return of the wounded men in his battalion to his dressing station in the Rue du Bois. His house had survived the shelling more or less intact; Nangle himself had a narrow escape when two men he was talking to were hit by shrapnel.

In the evening the wounded, removed from the front, began to come in in a continuous stream. I went up at 9 pm and we got in one officer and a few men. The Germans had shelled us heavily in the afternoon and in many places the breastwork was battered in; there were many horrible sights, and outside the ground was strewn with bodies.

We were relieved at 2 am but I did not get away until 5 am when I rejoined the regiment. The whole day long the guns were banging away and the noise went on throughout the night. A very, very trying time; so many good men gone and no gain whatever. We have been a gloomy party lately; only nine officers left out of thirteen, but eight were killed or died shortly afterwards and all my particular friends have gone. Such a war!

The same painful scenes were to be enacted all along the front. Beyond the breastworks now occupied by the 23rd Brigade and the 1/Worcestershires the open ground was thickly strewn with the dead and wounded of the 2/East Lancashires and the 1/Sherwood Foresters. The wounded were in a desperate plight because the firing which went on until dusk made it impossible for any help to reach them. Even after nightfall bursts of fire continued intermittently from an enemy still on the alert for a fresh attack and this made the work of the rescue parties dangerous. Many of the wounded were brought in before dawn but daylight revealed many more still lying out in no-man's-land and signalling pitifully for help. Volunteers crawled out again and again into no-man's-land under heavy fire and dragged back as many as they could reach into the shelter of the breastworks.

The battle was to leave indelible impressions upon those battalions who had suffered grievous losses. Men of the 2/East Lancs were in future to compare all hazardous situations with their experience at Aubers Ridge. There was general agreement that nothing could ever again be 'as bad as the ninth of May'.

On the German side, as darkness descended, the defenders took stock of their position beneath the Ridge. Stretches of their breastworks were a sorry sight, particularly towards the right of their line in the northern sector where parts had been pulverized leaving only a series of shell-holes in their place. Dead and wounded lay amid the tangled wreckage of the dug-outs and in the damaged communication trenches. Rescue work continued far into the night. In the absence of any ambulance wagons, collecting the wounded and bringing them to the rear was an exhausting job for the stretcher-bearers. The Germans admit that their transport and medical tents could not cope with the number of wounded. Doctors and orderlies cared for them as best they could; all available dug-outs and *Wohngraben* were used to shelter those who needed urgent attention. The dead, too, were collected, identified and carried to the rear for burial. All this difficult work had to be carried out on top of the ground because of the state of the communication trenches.

At Army Headquarters the staff congratulated themselves on defeating the First Army's assault at such relatively low cost. But there was no room for complacency because they felt the British would be likely to renew their offensive almost immediately and they feared a night attack. Orders were issued for extra sentries to be posted and for work to begin as soon as practicable on repairing the damage to their defences. Thus the troops holding the front line had little rest.

During the night the firing died down, though there was still the whine and explosion of a random shell and sporadic bursts of small-arms fire, dying away almost as soon as they had started. This lull was used to reorganize units, relieve exhausted companies and to bring some semblance of order to the front line. But the sentries remained watchful and alert, looking out into the darkness towards the British lines. Every now and then they were blinded by the sudden brilliance of flares which hung in the sky and illuminated the corpse-strewn battlefield below.

The night passed slowly. As soon as it was light the Germans in both sectors began urgent repairs to the breastworks and communications trenches. Telephone lines were relaid, food and water brought up to the troops holding the line, as well as fresh supplies of ammunition and grenades. Brigadier Kiefhaber was able to report to Lieut-General von Ditfurth, his Divisional Commander, that the German front line held by the 16 RIR was back in his possession and that all enemy troops had been cleared out of the ruined houses behind the line. Numerous British dead were lying inside the German lines where they had been killed in the savage counter-attacks of the previous day. In front of him no-man's-land was strewn with hundreds of British dead. Kiefhaber stressed the courage and determination of his troops in the face of vastly superior enemy numbers and praised the artillery for its effective disruption of the attacks of the supporting battalions and the movement of reserves. Von Ditfurth was only too happy to pass the gist of this on to Army Headquarters.

Meanwhile, in the southern sector soon after dawn, the band of the 55th Regiment gathered by a large pit behind the lines. Around it, bareheaded in the early morning light, stood many of the weary and blood-stained survivors of the I and III Battalions. All around, the horizon was lit up by occasional flashes from the guns of both sides and there was the steady rumble of the batteries to the south of La Bassée. Against this backcloth, the band began the service for the dead by playing the solemn hymn: *Es ist bestimmt in Gottes Rat* ('God in his wisdom has decreed'). In the pale light cast by the flares, some 230 of the Regiment's dead were lowered into the mass grave. The voices of the soldiers drifted out across the battered German trenches, grew fainter and died away amidst the desolation of no-man's-land.

On Saturday, 16 May, 1915, a night attack, preceded by a two-day bombardment, opened the Battle of Festubert. Fought over part of the same ground, it lasted ten days, gained 600 yards and cost Haig's First Army another 17,000 casualties.

CHAPTER THIRTEEN

Envoi

In a few years' time, when this war is a romance in memory, the soldier looking for his battlefield will find his marks gone, Centre Way, Peel Trench, Munster Alley, and all these other paths to glory will be deep under the corn, and gleaners will sing at Dead Mule Corner.

John Masefield, *The Old Front Line*

The British dead were left where they fell. It had to be so. With no advance made, it was not possible to collect and bury the several thousand corpses with which the two strips of no-man's-land were strewn. They were left to swell and blacken in the summer sun and slowly decompose. The tunics of those men caught in the German wire lifted and flapped at first in the breeze; within a few months, rags fluttered along the entanglements. During the next three years autumn rains, frosts and winter snows were to speed the disintegration of the dead.

Owen Buckmaster was a company commander in the 7th Battalion of the Duke of Cornwall's Light Infantry. In August, 1915, he found himself in the line in front of the Rue du Bois which was now tolerably peaceful. In his memoirs, *Roundabout*, he wrote:

Outside the trenches it was another story. Just over the parapet were the bodies of many of the 2nd Battalion of the Sussex Regiment, killed in the attack on Aubers Ridge on the 9th May, 1915. There they lay, facing the enemy, mummified, packs squared, bayonets fixed as if on parade, shot down and wiped out before they had hardly been able to get through our own wire; their lives squandered by the folly and incompetence of the staff. Anyone with any commonsense could have

143

seen that no man could have done what they were asked to do. In front of the trenches the terrain was flat, without a particle of cover. In the spring only the blades of young corn would have been growing on it. To reach the German lines the men would have had to cross several hundred yards of this ground in the face of withering fire from the machine guns concealed in deep emplacements, and skilfully sited so as to support each other and rake every yard of ground with fire.

After the Battle of Festubert the Bois Grenier/La Bassée front became a quiet sector for the rest of the war, primarily because of the difficult terrain. This *soi-disant* calm was broken only by two small-scale diversionary attacks on the first day of the Battle of Loos on 25 September and by the disastrous and politically damaging assault upon Fromelles in July, 1916, by the 4th Australian and 46th Midland Division of Haking's XI Corps. By the time the Australians entered this sector the story of the Battle of Aubers Ridge had been almost wholly forgotten. It remained only a vague rumour among the troops that certain famous English regiments spoke of that particular day with dreadful memories of a futile and tragic attack. Now more corpses were added to those slowly rotting away in front of the German line.

Major P.H. Pilditch, RFA, visited the area on 10 October, 1918, to find the grave of a close friend who had been killed in the early fighting in October, 1914. In his diary he gives a chilling description of the Aubers Ridge battlefield as it appeared just before the armistice which ended the war:

On the way back we spent some time in the old no-man's-land of four years' duration, round about Fauquissart and Aubers. It was a morbid but intensely interesting occupation tracing the various battles among the hundreds of skulls, bones and remains scattered thickly about. The progress of our successive attacks could be clearly seen from the types of equipment on the skeletons, soft caps denoting 1914 and early 1915, then respirators, then steel helmets marking attacks in 1916. Also Australian slouch hats, used in the costly and abortive attack in 1916. There were many of these poor remains all along the German wire.

On the actual day of the armistice an Australian soldier returned to the area of the Sugar-loaf salient where his battalion had attacked

– the same ground where Oxley's 24th Brigade had suffered such heavy casualties:

> We found the old no-man's-land simply full of our dead. In the narrow sector west of the Laies River and east of the Sugar-loaf salient, the skulls and bones and torn uniforms were lying about everywhere. I found a bit of Australian kit lying fifty yards from the corner of the salient, and the bones of an Australian officer and several men within 100 yards of it. Farther round, immediately on their flank, were a few British – you can tell them by their leather equipment. And within 100 yards of the west corner of the Sugar-loaf salient there was lying a small party of English too – also with an officer – you could tell by the cloth of his coat.

For the Germans Sunday, 9 May was a day not to be forgotten either, certainly not by Lieutenant Huls and the survivors of 9 Company, 57th Regiment. By the time of the armistice in 1918 there were very few of them left, but they still had vivid memories of that day. It was, as one of their riflemen summed it up after the war, 'A nasty business. Yes, comrades, it was a nasty business. Bloody nasty!'

Today the battlefield is still rural, a wide belt of unspoilt farmland between the Ridge and the industrial area running north-west from La Bassée and Béthune. It is given over to arable farming, though there are some cattle, and fields of wheat, maize, sugar-beet and potatoes flourish.

On the crest of Aubers Ridge, along its slopes and dotted among the fields behind the old German lines, the remains of cunningly sited concrete strongpoints are very visible. They are still there because they are too difficult and too expensive to demolish. However, it should be emphasized that these strongpoints did not exist in May, 1915; they were built later in the war. They now vary from the ruined to the menacing, with their sinister slits grinning fixedly at potential attackers from the west. If you push through the nettles, rank grass and bushes around the entrances, the unappetizing interiors yield little today apart from bits of rubbish floating in several inches of scummy water.

But there is hardly any evidence left of the savage conflict on 9 May. Shallow trenches have long ago been filled in, sandbag breastworks have rotted and disintegrated and seventy years of ploughing and cultivation have removed virtually all signs of the original trench system. The Rivière des Laies is a good marker for those traces that do remain, while the lines of the German communication trenches can still be seen running north from la Quinque Rue near La Tourelle towards the old front line.

The few houses, hamlets and farms within the narrow confines of the battlefield were either destroyed by artillery fire or so badly damaged they had to be virtually rebuilt. All that remains of Delangre Farm, for example, is a pockmarked and uneven field, studded with brambles and given over to rough grazing in the Rue de la Cordonnerie.

On the site of Port Arthur stands La Bombe café-bar, a rather depressing establishment that few of the cars and heavy lorries roaring along the main road choose to visit. Opposite it, on land where so many men of the Dehra Dun and Bareilly Brigades were killed, is the splendid and imaginative Indian Memorial to the Missing, designed by Sir Herbert Baker. In the various British cemeteries in the area there are, for obvious reasons, very few headstones relating to soldiers killed on 9 May. The names of those who fell in the battle and have no known grave are among those recorded by regiments on the endless stone panels of the cemetery at Le Touret.

One particular grave deserves mention. The gallant commander of the 25th Brigade, Brigadier-General A.W.G. Lowry Cole, CB, DSO, lies buried in the small square cemetery of Le Trou Aid Post, situated in the Petit Rue de Petillon behind the Rivière des Laies. This beautifully kept cemetery is protected by deep drainage ditches and shaded by willow trees. When I visited it on a hot day in early September butterflies fluttered in the sunshine among the dark red roses planted on the graves.

Ploughing continues to turn up quantities of unexploded shells and mortar and shell fragments, called by the farmers 'the iron harvest'. These are cautiously removed and heaped by the roadside for collection. Everywhere along the front, rusty old iron picquets have been removed and re-used to support fences of barbed wire, but today these are harmless barriers which simply mark field boundaries.

On a May morning the sun smiles down upon the peaceful fields stretching out into the distance below the quiet villages on the Ridge. To the rare traveller passing through this unexceptionable landscape there is little to suggest the slaughter on a Sunday in early summer eighty years ago.

CHAPTER FOURTEEN

Repercussions : The Munitions Scandal

> What is best to be done for the country? How can the
> Government be carried on?
>
> The Duke of Wellington

Although the battle had been swiftly brought to a bloody conclusion, this was not to be the end of the matter. There was to be an
unexpected and momentous sequel. For some months there had
been growing dissatisfaction throughout the country with the conduct of the war, fuelled by lengthening casualty lists in the
newspapers. There was an uneasy feeling that those in charge of the
nation's affairs had not been prosecuting the war with sufficient
energy and determination. From the outset the Press had consistently supported the Government; news of the battles on the
Western Front had been presented to an innocent and gullible public in the most favourable light; small gains were inflated into
significant advances and setbacks were few. However, even the
Press became a little restive after Neuve Chapelle when rumours
began to circulate about a shortage of shells for the guns. Lord
Northcliffe, proprietor of *The Times* and the *Daily Mail*, had been
receiving detailed complaints for some time from both officers and
men at the front about conditions in the trenches, including comments from a number of members of Parliament who had been
commissioned soon after the outbreak of war. The censor had
repeatedly refused to let him publish them. Public disquiet was now
heightened by the return of the wounded from Neuve Chapelle and
Second Ypres with stories of delays, bungled attacks and a de-
moralizing shortage of shells. Some hints of these criticisms at last
began to find their way into the local and national papers.

For a little while it was possible for the Cabinet to maintain the line taken by Asquith and Newcastle. The disaster at Aubers Ridge on 9 May received little attention from the Press, and that little was hopelessly inaccurate and misleading. But within days echoes of the fiasco quickly began to reverberate down the corridors of Westminster and around the clubs in Pall Mall. With the arrival of the wounded and men on leave, stories started to circulate in London about another failed offensive by the First Army accompanied by heavy casualties. It was an explosive situation and it only needed a spark to set it off.

The spark was Colonel Repington. He was already aware that Sir John, incensed by the continuing failure of Kitchener and the War Office to respond to his demands for more ammunition, was considering going over their heads and appealing directly to leading politicians and the Press. As we have seen, he had watched the battle with the Commander-in-Chief, though it is difficult to reconcile this with his distorted piece published in *The Times* on 12 May. (His report, the usual euphoric nonsense, is given in full on pp. 173, 174.)

French had left the Aubers Ridge battlefield early and returned, accompanied by Repington, to his headquarters. Here he found a telegram from the War Office instructing him to send 2000 rounds of 4.5-inch and 20,000 rounds of 18pdr ammunition from his scanty reserves to Marseilles for shipment to the Dardanelles. This was the last straw. If Sir John had harboured any doubts about the consequences of his proposed course of action, this order dispelled them. The combined effects of his next actions were to have far-reaching consequences for the Government, for Kitchener and in due course for himself. In his memoirs, entitled *1914*, he describes what he did:

I immediately gave instructions that evidence should be furnished to Colonel Repington, military correspondent of *The Times*, who happened to be then at Headquarters, that the vital need of high-explosive shells had been a fatal bar to our Army's success on that day [Repington could hardly have asked for more explosive copy!]. I directed that copies of all the correspondence which had taken place between myself and the Government on the question of the supply of ammunition be made at once, and I sent my Secretary, Brinsley FitzGerald, with Captain Frederick Guest, one of my ADCs, to England with instructions that these proofs should be laid before Mr Lloyd George (the Chancellor of the Exchequer), who had already shown me, by his special interest in this subject, that he grasped the deadly nature of our necessities. I

148

instructed also that they should be laid before Mr Arthur J. Balfour and Mr Bonar Law [senior Conservative politicians who were also coopted members of Asquith's War Council], whose sympathetic understanding of my difficulties, when they visited me in France, had led me to expect that they would take the action that this grave exigency demanded.

FitzGerald also carried with him the following memorandum marked 'Secret':

Memorandum from Sir John French: 'Information Regarding Ammunition'

INFORMATION REGARDING AMMUNITION

1. Large quantities of high-explosive shells for field guns have become essential owing to the form of warfare in which the Army is engaged. The enemy is entrenched from the sea to the Swiss frontier. There is no flank in his position that can be turned. It is necessary, therefore, for all offensive operations to start by breaking the enemy's line, which presupposes the attack of formidable field entrenchments. Shrapnel, being the man-killing projectile which is used against troops in the open, is primarily used in defence. In offensive operations it is used for searching communication trenches, preventing the enemy's reinforcements intervening in the fight, repelling counter-attacks and, as an alternative for high-explosive shell for cutting wire entanglements. It is, however, ineffective against the occupants of the trenches, breastworks or buildings. It is, therefore, necessary to have high-explosive shell to destroy parapets, obstacles, buildings and many forms of fortified localities that the enemy constructs, more particularly his machine-gun emplacements. Without an adequate supply the attack is impotent against the defenders of field fortifications, as the first step cannot be taken. Guns require 50 per cent of HE shell. Howitzers use high-explosive shell almost exclusively.
2. We have found by experience that the field guns actually engaged in offensive operations, such as Neuve Chapelle, fire about 120 rounds per gun per day.
   Heavy guns and howitzers, according to their calibre, fire less in proportion. The guns of the whole Army are of course

149

never equally heavily engaged at the same time, but the number of guns available and the amount of ammunition are the limiting factors when a plan of attack is being considered. There is, therefore, scarcely any limit to the supply of ammunition that could be usefully employed. The more ammunition, the bigger the scale on which the attack can be delivered, and the more persistently it can be pressed.

Demands must, however, be reasonable, and our position would be very greatly improved if our supply reached the figures in the attached Table A within three months. Up to the present it has been below these figures.

WANTED THREE MONTHS HENCE, SAY, AUGUST IST

TABLE A

Nature	Guns now in country	Rounds per gun per day		Total rounds required daily*	
		Shrapnel	HE	Shrapnel	HE
18-pdr	700	12	12	8500	8500
13-pdr	125	12	12	1500	1500
15-pdr BLC	200	12	12	2500	2500
4.7-in. gun	80	8	8	650	650
60-pdr	28	8	8	250	250
5-in. howitzer	50	–	15	–	750
4.5-in. howitzer	130	4	16	500	2000
6-in. howitzer	40	–	12	–	500
9.2-in. howitzer	12	–	12	–	150
				13,900	16,800
			Total	30,700 daily	
			Grand Total	921,000 monthly	

* Round numbers are given. Expansion must be provided for at a similar rate. We need more guns and a correspondingly larger amount of ammunition.

3. Table B shows the percentage of high explosive of certain natures received since application for increased quantities was made between September and December last.

PERCENTAGE OF HIGH EXPLOSIVE RECEIVED SINCE FIRST APPLICATION FOR IT IN INCREASED QUANTITIES

TABLE B

Nature of Gun	Dec.	Jan.	Feb.	March	April	May
	Per Cent	Per Cent	Per Cent	Per Cent	Per Cent	Per Cent
13-pdr	Nil	Nil	Nil	Nil	Nil	Nil
18-pdr	3.8	6.8	8.3	8.2	6.1	8
4.5-in. howitzer	44.4	68.5	88	75	59	65
60-pdr	-	66	60	56	53	50
6-in. howitzer	55	59	51	77	69	50

The two men saw Lloyd George on 12 May, who commented later that this was the first communication on the shell question he had received from the Commander-in-Chief. Significantly, Lloyd George made no reference to the propriety of Sir John French's action. FitzGerald and Guest later went to see Balfour and Bonar Law and laid the facts before them, as ordered. While they were doing this, Repington was busy composing a considered report for *The Times* using the material French had given him. It appeared on 14 May and created an immediate furore. This was the first time that the British public had been plainly told about the shell shortage on the Western Front, its gravity and the effect it was having on our troops and upon our offensive operations. Equally damaging, politically, was the fact that Repington's article bluntly contradicted what the Prime Minister had said at Newcastle the previous month. Asquith found it hard to forgive Kitchener and their relationship deteriorated.

The Times, 14 May, 1915

NEED FOR SHELLS
British Attacks Checked
Limited Supply The Cause
A Lesson from France

'The want of an unlimited supply of high explosive was a total bar to our success.' It is to this need that our Military Correspondent, in the message we print below, attributes largely the disappointing results of the British attacks in the districts of Fromelles and Richebourg on Sunday. By way of contrast, he records the fact that the French, in cooperation with whom we made our movement upon the German lines, fired 276 rounds of high explosive per gun in one day and levelled the enemy's defences with the ground.

From our Military Correspondent,
Northern France, 12 May

It is important for an understanding of the British share in the operations of this week, to realize that we are suffering from certain disadvantages which make striking successes difficult to achieve.

In the mists of winter, at the time of my previous visit to the Army, it was not easy to see the German positions. During the clear days of the past week it has been possible to reconnoitre more closely the German line and to observe what a great advantage the enemy gained before his initial offensive was finally brought to an end in the battles of October and November last.

From a point north-eastward of Ypres, right down to the south where the British right rests, the Germans hold almost all the undulating but clearly marked heights, dominating the positions where we stood at the close of the autumn fighting, and still stand, at Ypres, at St Eloi, around our Armentières Salient, along the Aubers Ridge and, further to the south, on the Vimy Heights. Opposite the French, the Germans hold the high ground and almost everywhere look down on to our positions.

FORMIDABLE DEFENCES

To assail these ridges, with their command over our lines, their superior facilities for observation, and their numerous lines of trenches, which have hardened week by week, and are provided with every scientific and clever device for arresting an attack, is no light task.

The two armies of the Crown Prince of Bavaria and the Duke of Württemberg are still in our front, and at full strength. There are not many points where an attack can be attempted, and at these points the enemy has accumulated defences, has brought into them hundreds of machine guns, which are skilfully concealed, and has covered the front of every successive line of trenches by barbed-wire entanglements. Supported by formidable artillery, and held by good troops, these German lines are not easily to be taken.

Secondly, we are still suffering from the aftermath of the first gas attack at Ypres. That attack drove back our allies on our left and uncovered our position. The consolidation of our near position east of Ypres took time, and cost many lives. It was not only the victims of the German poison that we had to deplore, but the heavy casualties which the surprise cost us. These matters have had their influence upon our arrangements for supporting our Allies in their offensive from Arras which has been pushed forward with so much gallantry and perseverance.

LACK OF HIGH EXPLOSIVE

The results of our attacks on Sunday last in the districts of Fromelles and Richebourg were disappointing. We found the enemy much more strongly posted than we expected. We had not sufficient high explosive to level his parapets to the ground after the French practice and, when our infantry gallantly stormed the trenches, as they did in both attacks, they found a garrison undismayed, many entanglements still intact and Maxims on all sides ready to pour in streams of bullets. We could not maintain ourselves in the trenches won, and our reserves were not thrown in because the conditions for success in an assault were not present.

The attacks were well-planned and valiantly conducted. The infantry did splendidly, but the conditions were too hard.

The want of an unlimited supply of high explosive was a fatal bar to our success.

We have had many casualties this week but, if we have not won all we hoped, we have detained in our front a force equivalent to our own, and have greatly facilitated the French offensive on our right. This offensive swept on towards the Arras-Lens road like a flood. It gained the heights of Notre Dame de Lorette and the hills west of it, flowed round the villages of Ablain, Carency, Souchez and Neuville St Vaast, and almost isolated them and their German garrisons.

By dint of the expenditure of 276 rounds of high explosive per gun in one day, all the German defences, except the villages, were levelled with the ground and, though we must expect that German reinforcements will be sent from other parts of the long Western line, we have good hope that the Freiburg Army Corps and other German troops will be destroyed and that the gallant French Generals who are leading this powerful and valiant attack will gain a great success.

OUR URGENT NEEDS

On our side we have easily defeated all attacks on Ypres. The value of German troops in the attack has greatly deteriorated, and we can deal easily with them in the open. But until we are thoroughly equipped for this trench warfare, we attack under grave disadvantages. The men are in high spirits, taking their cue from the ever-confident and resolute attitude of the Commander-in-Chief.

If we can break through this hard outer crust of the German defences, we believe that we can scatter the German Armies, whose offensive causes us no concern at all. But to break this hard crust we need more high explosive, more heavy howitzers, and more men. This special form of warfare has no precedent in history.

It is certain that we can smash the German crust if we have the means. So the means we must have, and as quickly as possible.

In political life it is rare for a single issue to bring about a great upheaval. Usually this is caused by several factors combining to create a situation where one further incident – a scandal, a resignation or a piece of ill-considered legislation – is sufficient to cause a violent reaction. Thus it was not the shell shortage at Aubers

Ridge revealed by Repington that by itself brought down Asquith's Government. His article simply served to focus the disappointment caused by the failure of the Aubers Ridge offensive, by the anger over the gas attack at Ypres which had caught our troops unprepared, the disquiet over the Dardanelles adventure, and by growing public concern at the leisurely and ineffective way the war was being conducted by the Liberal Government. All these matters now came together to create a volatile situation where one more blow might bring disaster down upon the Government. That critical blow, untimely and unexpected, was struck the very next day after Repington's article.

It had not been easy for Asquith's Cabinet to conceal the differences over the Dardanelles campaign between Churchill, the First Lord of the Admiralty, and the First Sea Lord, Lord Fisher, his senior naval adviser. 'Jackie' Fisher, the creator of the modern navy, pugnacious, outspoken and 'the darling of the Conservatives' in Beaverbrook's phrase, had made little secret of his opposition to the attempt to force the Dardanelles employing the Navy alone. He was even more hostile to later developments involving a military expedition and further demands upon the Royal Navy. Finally he could contain himself no longer and on Saturday, 15 May he resigned in protest against the Dardanelles 'foolishness'.

This was the immediate cause of the downfall of the Liberal Government. In the next few days the political crisis came to a head. Fisher's intemperate action led to a flurry of activity. It cast a shadow over the integrity and actions of the First Lord of the Admiralty, Winston Churchill, who at once saw Asquith and offered to resign. His offer was refused. At the same time, Fisher resisted all attempts by powerful friends, such as Churchill, Lloyd George and even the Prime Minister himself, to make him reconsider his decision and embarked on a bizarre course of behaviour that made his return to office out of the question. Bonar Law discussed the serious political situation with Lloyd George; they agreed it made a coalition government necessary and that Lloyd George should suggest this to Asquith. Such a proposal now suited Bonar Law and Balfour, while Lloyd George saw it as his chance to take a major, and more aggressive, part in the conduct of the war.

Meanwhile, Asquith was left in no doubt by the outcry from the Conservative party at this turn of events that to preserve national unity and present a harmonious parliamentary front he would have to form a coalition government and reconstruct his Cabinet.

Balfour had made it clear that under no circumstances would the Conservatives stomach Churchill – who was anathema to his party – continuing in high office following Fisher's departure. Asquith not unwillingly gave way and announced his intention to reconstruct his government to a tense House on 19 May. The Prime Minister moved swiftly to appoint leading Conservatives to his Cabinet, but it involved some painful decisions. In the reshuffle he removed Churchill from the Admiralty and made him Chancellor of the Duchy of Lancaster, a post usually reserved, as Lloyd George commented, 'either for beginners in the Cabinet or for distinguished politicians who had reached the first stages of unmistakable decrepitude'. He was also forced to sacrifice Lord Haldane, to whom the country owed so much. Many in the House expected Kitchener to follow him but Asquith realized that Kitchener's continuing reputation and popularity among the public made this impossible. Others were not so deterred.

Lloyd George had naturally been intimately involved in the reconstruction process. All the time, however, he had been seething with anger at his realization that Kitchener had withheld Sir John French's memos and letters about the shell shortage not only from the original Cabinet 'Shells' Committee of which Kitchener himself had been the reluctant chairman, but also from the Munitions of War Committee. Lloyd George saw his opportunity and he took it. On 19 May he wrote a lengthy letter to the Prime Minister stressing the points that had been made so forcefully to him by French in his report. He went on to complain about the way this information had been withheld from the Munitions Committee by the War Office (i.e. Kitchener) and stated that he would no longer preside over such a farce.

Two days later Lord Northcliffe re-entered the fray. He was no friend of Kitchener and he put the blame for the shell shortage firmly upon him. When he heard that Kitchener was to continue as Secretary of State for War in the reconstructed government he published a bitter personal attack upon him in the *Daily Mail* on 21 May under the headline: 'The Shells Scandal: Lord Kitchener's Tragic Blunder'. Many were upset by this attack upon a national institution, but there was scant sympathy for Kitchener among the Cabinet. He had upset too many people and made too many enemies; they had been intimidated too long by the stern, imposing figure of England's most famous soldier and by the impact of his powerful personality.

Northcliffe followed up this attack on Kitchener by running a campaign for the next ten days on the theme of the shells 'scandal'. If this had any effect at all, it was to strengthen Lloyd George's hand in talks with the Prime Minister about the most effective way of settling the munitions problem. It was no surprise then that, when Asquith announced details of his new Cabinet to the House on 26 May, he also announced the most significant decision of all – his invitation to Lloyd George to form a Ministry of Munitions charged with the task of mobilizing the nation's resources for armament production. The new Ministry would embody the functions of the former Munitions of War Committee, but with this crucial difference: it possessed the executive authority and the power that Lloyd George had been seeking for months. Lloyd George willingly gave up the Treasury, recruited 'men of push and go' and set off on the mission that was to contribute largely to the winning of the war and lead him to the premiership.

It is not within the compass of this book to deal with Lloyd George's success in harnessing and expanding the engineering capacity of the nation. One might simply illustrate his achievements by comparing the brief bombardments and lengthy recriminations of the first half of 1915 with the intensity, weight and duration of the bombardment that opened the Battle of the Somme a year later.

If Lloyd George had been infuriated by Kitchener's behaviour, Kitchener in his turn was very angry with French. He had endured for months a wrangle with his Commander-in-Chief over the supply of guns and shells to the Western Front. In the last few weeks he had had to contend with the Second Battle of Ypres and the offensive against Aubers Ridge, while at the same time being embroiled in Churchill's scheme to force the Dardanelles and having to find men, guns and shells for it. He bitterly resented French going behind his back to stir up the Press and leading politicians against him. Sir John French had knowingly tempted the wrath of Achilles and in due course it was to descend upon him. His cause was not helped by the failure of Haig's third attempt to make progress against Aubers Ridge; the Battle of Festubert had opened on 16 May and was now grinding to an expensive and inglorious halt. In September would come an even more disastrous offensive at Loos leading to calls for his resignation as Commander-in-Chief. Sir John's reactions after the débâcle of 9 May proved a potent factor in his removal.

Kitchener was to soldier on in the Coalition Government until his tragic death the following summer, but his reputation had suffered a severe blow. The idol was seen to have feet of clay, and from this point his dominant role in the Cabinet and his influence over the conduct of the war began to wane.

CHAPTER FIFTEEN

Epilogue

'. . . a serious disappointment' : Official History

QUESTIONS AND SOME ANSWERS

Were the aims of the offensive achieved?

No. The attack was a bloody fiasco. Though the enemy's line was breached in several places in the northern sector, no breakthrough was achieved, no ground was gained and secured, and nearly 12,000 men were killed and wounded in a space of hours. The Official History, lapsing for once from its usual sympathetic, pro-Establishment stance, concludes that 'the results of the offensive of the 9th May were a serious disappointment'. No doubt those battalion commanders fortunate enough to survive considered that this verdict was something of an understatement, as they contemplated the remnants of their shattered battalions.

One of the supposed advantages or, indeed, reasons for the joint attack with the French Tenth Army was that the British assault would suck in the German reserves and stop them being moved south to strengthen the German defences at Vimy Ridge. This simply did not happen. Reports from the Royal Flying Corps during the battle indicated that only units in local reserve were being moved towards the firing line. This is confirmed by the History of the 16 RIR which records, as we have seen, that only the 17th and 21st Regiments sent troops to help the 16 RIR during the battle on the northern sector. The same was true on the 14th Division's front to the south. Thus our offensive failed to prevent reserves from the German Sixth Army being moved south from Roubaix and Tournai to counter the French advance.

Yet our senior commanders, concerned to save something from the wreckage of their hopes, clung doggedly to the belief, with no evidence to support it, that their attack had at least prevented enemy reserves from being used against the French at Vimy. For example, Sir Henry Rawlinson spoke to the survivors of the Kensingtons soon after they had been extricated from the battle. Besides pointing out that they had succeeded in relieving the pressure on Ypres at a critical moment (a dubious point since the battle there ebbed to a close on 10 May) he stressed that they had helped the French advance by drawing off German reinforcements which were moving to the support of their troops to the south of La Bassée. The Kensingtons had no means of knowing whether this was true or not; it was not, of course, but, apart from congratulating them on their gallant charge and their conduct in the action, it was all the encouragement he could offer them.

Rawlinson's view of the proceedings was reinforced by a special order issued by Haig the day after the battle. It stated that 'the attacks made all along our line proved of great assistance to our allies on the right'. This comforting and sedulously cultivated conclusion by the High Command percolated rapidly down through the First Army. Thus we find 2nd Lieutenant Moore writing in his letter of 17 May:

> Although from one point of view the attack was a failure, it drew the enormous German reinforcements up and so enabled the French to get through lower down the line so was by no means in vain.

The only real consolation Haig and his commanders could extract from the débâcle was that it confirmed the impression of Neuve Chapelle that the men of the First Army, despite the long winter months in the trenches under arduous conditions, had not lost their attacking spirit and that morale remained high. It was not adequately appreciated, or perhaps there was little wish to recognize the fact, that there is a limit to a battalion's or a brigade's élan, stamina and appetite for attack. As in the case of the individual soldier, its reservoir of courage and endurance is also finite and cannot be endlessly drawn upon.

Years after the war Haig must have been pleased and relieved by the verdict on the battle in the Official History. He was happy to settle for the authorized, sanitized version in which the aggressive commander sees his meticulously planned offensive jeopardized by lack of guns and shells and by the disappointing performance of certain senior officers in the action. (No one had the gall to place any blame upon the infantry.) Perhaps Haig was not entirely surprised by the outcome, because the draft of the two chapters dealing with the battle in the Official History had been sent to him for his comments. This also applied to other sectors of the work dealing with the battles on the Western Front, and there is no doubt that in a number of cases Haig's criticisms and suggestions influenced the final version.

Haig returned the chapters on Aubers Ridge commenting:

> I think you have brought out very well the terrible [sic] conditions under which the First Army had to carry out the C. in C.'s orders 'to support the French at all costs'. The ammunition was very bad: fuzes inefficient, and a great shortage of all kinds of shell. So the means for a real bombardment were lacking.

Something must be said about Haig's conduct of the battle. Perhaps I should emphasize that I am concerned here with the Haig who was Commander of the First Army in 1915 and not with Haig the Commander-in-Chief from 1916. I wish to deal with those aspects arising from his conduct of the battle that throw light upon the Battle of Loos and on his subsequent great offensives after he succeeded French as Commander-in-Chief.

It is unfortunate that Haig did not feel it necessary to intervene at certain points in the battle. He was ready enough on occasions to reject or alter the plans of his subordinates if he thought these were either faulty or did not suit him, but already he seemed reluctant to interfere with, or override, their decisions during the actual fighting. He tended to limit himself to urging his senior commanders remorselessly forward. He did not see the Army Commander's role as a particularly active one once the plans had been made and the offensive set in motion. After all, there were corps commanders and divisional generals to attend to the broad direction of the battle and the actual mechanics of the fighting. Yet at Aubers Ridge he could have intervened to ensure that what little success had been achieved in the northern sector was reinforced. And much as he wanted both arms of his pincer-attack to penetrate the German defences, he could and should have prevented futile and wasteful frontal assaults being made by I Corps when the day was already lost. As we have seen, he was prepared to go on attacking with exhausted and demoralized troops and it was primarily pressure from his senior commanders that forced him to call off his offensive.

Haig was a complex character, a difficult man to understand, and his psychology is a fascinating field for those interested in the battles on the Western Front. It can be enjoyably pursued in Norman Dixon's *On the Psychology of Military Incompetence* where he examines Haig's personality in detail and provides many insights into his behaviour. He seeks to show that Haig's defects as a commander sprang from personality flaws stemming from his background and training. This, however, is a seductive path along which a layman must tread warily.

Dixon lists the four factors which he claims have led historically to the downfall of the great captains:

1. Wastage of man-power
2. Over-confidence
3. Underestimation of the enemy
4. Ignoring intelligence reports

and it is instructive to examine Haig's early command performance against them.

His willingness to countenance what was virtually the final destruction of many of his regular battalions in repeated assaults on the enemy line reveals a poverty of imagination as well as suggesting a lack of compassion for his troops. It also discloses something of his stubborn nature.

After the initial success at Neuve Chapelle Haig was certainly over-confident about his ability to break through the German lines – that 'crust,' as both he and Sir John French referred to the enemy defences. But 'crust' is an inaccurate and misleading term when applied to later and more complex German trench-systems. Haig's belief in the correctness of his judgement, based on his training and military experience, was absolute.

He was not the man to underestimate the fighting qualities of the German infantryman though he was perhaps surprised at their stubbornness in defence. He did underestimate the effect of their machine guns and their skill in regrouping and mounting rapid counter-attacks.

Haig was certainly at fault in ignoring the warnings he received from Military Intelligence about the increasing strength of the German defences. His attitude reflected a reluctance to accept facts or situations which did not accord with his ideas or preconceptions.

Thus we are already seeing in 1915 aspects of Haig's leadership and conduct that would be observed more clearly and on a much greater scale from the Battle of Loos onwards.

What were the lessons?
At this stage you may exclaim with Hamlet's friend, Horatio: 'It needs no ghost come from the grave to tell us this'. Although the following sections may seem self-evident, the lessons need to be stated because of their relevance to later offensives carried out by the British Army under Haig.

1. A stubborn and brave enemy in a strongly fortified trench system cannot be overwhelmed by the weight of a purely infantry assault.
2. Such a trench system can only be captured if the artillery bombardment is heavy enough and sustained sufficiently to demolish the enemy parapet and trenches, destroy his machine-gun strongpoints within and behind his defences, neutralize his batteries and cut his barbed-wire entanglements. Heavy howitzers and plenty of ammunition must be available for this purpose.
3. Counter-battery fire must be improved.
4. The vulnerability of attacking infantry, even regular battalions, to machine-gun fire cannot be over emphasized.
5. The wire must be cut to enable the assaulting troops to carry the enemy's front line.
6. The folly of repeating frontal attacks which have already failed, instead of reinforcing any successes – though, in truth, there were few enough of these at Aubers Ridge. Repetition in such circumstances merely results in further heavy casualties and loss of morale.
7. The great difficulty experienced in moving up supporting troops and reinforcements along smashed and congested communication trenches.

In this action the communication problems mentioned earlier in the book were not particularly significant since the attack made such little progress.

To what extent were the lessons learned?

Sir John French had watched the progress of the battle from the tower in Laventie and had seen his regular battalions slaughtered by the German machine guns. Shortly afterwards he wrote to a friend, 'It's simple murder to send infantry against these powerfully fortified entrenchments until they've been heavily hammered.' Later in his book, *1914*, he commented:

> Nothing since the Battle of Aisne had ever impressed me so deeply with the terrible shortage of artillery and ammunition as did the events of that day. As I watched the Aubers Ridge, I clearly saw the great inequality of the artillery duel and, as attack after attack failed, I could see the absence of sufficient artillery support was doubling and trebling our losses in men.

In a few brief hours Haig had also experienced enough of the altered conditions at Aubers Ridge to make him modify his ideas. He recorded in his diary on 10 May:

i. The defences on our front are so carefully and strongly made, and mutual support with the machine guns is so complete, that in order to demolish them a *long methodical bombardment* will be necessary by heavy artillery (guns and howitzers) before Infantry are sent forward to attack.

ii. To destroy the enemy's *matériel*, 60pdr *guns* will be tried, as well as the 15-in., 9.2 and 6-in. siege hows. Accurate observation of *each shot* will be arranged so as to make sure of flattening out the enemy's 'strongpoints' of support before the Infantry is launched.

French and Haig now realized as never before that, if they were to smash the enemy defences and enable their troops to make the cherished breakthrough for the cavalry to exploit, they needed many more guns and vastly more ammunition. They rapidly became converts to the French view, stemming from bitter experience, of the need for a heavy and methodical bombardment lasting several days to precede any major offensive. Thus weight of metal became the key phrase among the High Command. Artillery would in future become the main instrument of attack and the role of the infantry would be to mop up and occupy the resulting desolation.

Haig recognized that by adopting a policy of lengthy and heavy bombardments he abandoned the element of surprise, that most valuable of qualities in an attack. But he hoped that surprise could still be achieved by other means. One way was the night attack, considered but properly rejected towards the end of the Aubers débâcle. Haig employed it to good effect a few days later to open the Battle of Festubert. Another was his decision to use chlorine gas in conjunction with the initial assault at Loos in September. This was not very successful because the weather conditions for the discharge of gas from canisters turned out to be unfavourable – like the weather for most of our attacks during the war. Thus Aubers Ridge and Festubert became the last battles on the Western Front to be conducted without using gas or gas shells.

In connection with Loos, perhaps it should be emphasized that French and Haig were forced to attack there by combined pressure from Kitchener and Joffre. It is much to Haig's credit that he protested strongly against being asked to attack on such a bare and exposed front, which could be swept by machine-gun and rifle fire from an enemy entrenched behind belts of wire and occupying heavily defended ruined houses and strongpoints. His argument was rejected. One doubts if this can be construed as evidence that Haig and his corps commanders had realized the vulnerability of infantry to machine-gun fire in view of their conduct of the battle and of Haig's subsequent offensives during the Somme campaign of 1916. Both on the Somme and at Passchendaele the following year, his stubborn nature resulted in attack after attack being made on defences where previous attempts had been murderously repulsed. Again, many of the minor unsung attacks were made without the benefit of any artillery support and, in some cases, in broad daylight as well. No doubt it was considered necessary to accept heavy casualties in order to break the enemy's defences. The assumption was that, no matter how strong they were or how furious the enemy fire, some of the attackers would always get through. This was usually true; the only problem was that so often the number who penetrated the enemy line were so pitifully few that they tended to be overwhelmed by the German counter-attacks.

Rawlinson was another who appeared to have learned something from the events of 9 May and he offered a more sober assessment when he wrote to Major Wigram, the King's Assistant Private Secretary, on 11 May:

165

Before you receive this you will have heard that the result of our attacks the day before yesterday has not been satisfactory. The Ist, IVth and Indian Corps were all repulsed, and we stand today just where we did three days ago, except that we have lost 10,000 officers and men in the First Army, and expended a very large amount of ammunition. But we have, at least, learned that the policy of 'storm and follow on' cannot be successfully conducted unless the front of the attack is wide, and the bombardment is continued for considerably longer than half an hour.

In a later letter to Colonel FitzGerald, Private Secretary to Lord Kitchener (who was to be drowned with his chief in June, 1916, when HMS *Hampshire*, in which they were travelling to Russia, was sunk by a mine off the Orkneys) he added:

The true cause of our failure is that our tactics have been faulty, and that we have misconceived the strength and resisting power of the enemy . . . It is a shortage of heavy guns and howitzers that we suffer from. Most of the casualties have occurred, not in taking the first trenches, but in assaulting the keeps behind the front line, where the Germans have been dug in with their machine guns cunningly concealed.

There was to be no solution at this stage of the war to the problem of finding an effective way of breaking right through the enemy's defences in strength on a wide front. Mass infantry attacks would therefore continue, and continue to result in appalling losses, no matter how methodically or ingeniously delivered, and despite monumental bombardments. This would be the case until November, 1917, when the element of surprise would come together with the defence-breaking weapon, the tank. Then, without any preliminary bombardment, the massed tank attack at Cambrai tore a great hole in the German defences and a new dimension of warfare came into being.

But this was over two years in the future. Meanwhile, French and Haig had still not realized that the day of the cavalry was over and that the machine gun had claimed yet another victim. Both were to cling tenaciously to the mystique of the *arme blanche* and to the theory of its traditional exploitation of the gap and breakthrough. French, in particular, found it difficult to appreciate the problems presented by the new siege warfare. He continued to feel that, if only he had possessed sufficient shells at Aubers Ridge (and at Neuve Chapelle), he could have pulled it off. On 24 May, 1915, he wrote to Winifred Bennett saying how much he wanted to:

> break thro' this tremendous *crust* of defence which has been forming and consolidating throughout the winter: once we have done, I think we may get the Devils on the run. How I should love to have a real good 'go' at them in the open with lots of cavalry and horse artillery and run them to earth. Well! It may come.

This was certainly Haig's view, too, and he was Commander-in-Chief when the wish was eventually realized in the summer and autumn of 1918. It was to be achieved in ways undreamed of in early 1915, with hundreds of tanks and aircraft, improved communications, new infantry tactics and vast quantities of guns and ammunition.

CASUALTIES

It is never easy to arrive at accurate figures for casualties in the battles on the Western Front, even for a battle that only lasted for one day. The initial losses were given early on Monday, 10 May as 145 officers and 9400 other ranks. The Official History gives the total casualties for Aubers Ridge as 458 officers and 11,161 other ranks. I have checked divisional and regimental histories, war diaries and other sources and give below the losses suffered by those battalions from the three divisions actually engaged in the battle as accurately as I have been able to ascertain them. My estimate of the losses of the three divisions, including a conservative allowance for the casualties suffered by the Garhwal Brigade, is 10,500. If I add to that total the casualty returns for 9 May from the 2nd, 7th, Lahore, 47th and 49th Divisions, amounting to 340 (twelve officers and 328 other ranks), it brings my overall total for the losses suffered by Haig's First Army at Aubers Ridge to 10,840: 412 officers and 10,428 other ranks.

It has not been possible to break down all the casualty returns into killed, wounded and missing. I suggest that a ratio of one killed to three wounded would not be unreasonable. Usually about two-thirds of the wounded were able to return to duty after treatment at a dressing station or in hospital.

The battalions involved at Aubers Ridge did not suffer the

terrible losses experienced at 1st Ypres, the Somme and Passchendaele, although, with casualty rates ranging from 25 per cent to well over 50 per cent and, in one case, up to 70 per cent, these were appalling enough in all conscience. Traditionally, a casualty rate of 30 per cent was regarded as exceptionally heavy, very severe, unacceptable, or at the limit of tolerance. It could be argued that the casualties suffered in one day by the three divisions at Aubers Ridge were almost commensurate with those sustained by the thirteen divisions on the first day of the Battle of the Somme.

1st Division

1st (Guards) Brigade	Officers	ORs	Total
1/Black Watch	14	461	475
1/Camerons	9	240	249
2nd Brigade			
2/Royal Sussex	14	537	551
1/Northamptonshire	17	543	560
1/Loyal North Lancashire	13	226	239
2/KRRC	11	240	251
1/5th Royal Sussex (TF)	11	191	202
3rd Brigade			
1/Gloucestershire	10	252	262
1/South Wales Borderers	9	224	233
2/Welsh	11	245	256
2/Royal Munster Fusiliers	19	379	398
1/4th R.W. Fusiliers (TW)	6	65	71
Total	144	3603	3747

N.B. The Official History gives casualty figures for the 1st Division as 160 officers and 3808 other ranks, a total of 3968.

Meerut Division

Dehra Dun Brigade	Officer	ORs	Total
2/2nd Gurkhas	8	93	101
1/Seaforths	21	488	509
6th Jats	2	52	54
1/4th Seaforths (TF)	8	216	224
1/9th Gurkhas	-	127	127

Bareilly Brigade

2/Black Watch	8	262	270
41st Dogras	12	399	411
58th Vaughan's Rifles	10	242	252
1/4th Black Watch (TF)	7	167	174
Total	**76**	**2046**	**2122**

N.B. These figures differ considerably from those given in the Official History (94 officers and 2535 other ranks, a total of 2629), but they do not include any losses suffered by the Garhwal Brigade.

8th Division
23rd Brigade

2/Scottish Rifles	12	156	168
2/Devons	7	234	241

24th Brigade

1/Worcestershire	5	224	229
2/East Lancashire	19	435	454
1/Sherwood Foresters	16	343	359
2/Northamptonshire	12	414	426
1/5th Black Watch (TF)	8	137	145

25th Brigade

2/Lincolnshire	7	277	284
2/Royal Berkshire	18	276	294
1/Royal Irish Rifles	23	454	477
2/Rifle Brigade	21	632	653
1/13th London (TF)	13	423	436
1/1st London (TF)	5	194	199
Total	**166**	**4199**	**4365**

N.B. My figures here are largely supported by *The History of the 8th Division*. The figures given by the Official History are 192 officers and 4490 other ranks, a total of 4682.

Sadly, the battle marked the beginning of the end for the Indian Corps. On top of the casualties suffered by the Meerut Division at Aubers Ridge, the other division in the Indian Corps, the Lahore, was to incur substantial losses during the Battle of Festubert a few days later. It is not always appreciated how severe their losses were. For example, in a year's service on the Western Front Vaughan's Rifles lost thirty-three British and thirty-one Indian officers and more than 1500 other ranks – in effect, wiping it out twice. Because of the difficulty over obtaining suitable reinforcements for its two battered and shrunken divisions, the Indian Corps was eventually withdrawn from France in November, 1915, and broken up, with various units being sent to Egypt, Mesopotamia and East Africa. In these theatres, in less hostile climates, the Indian regiments performed with much credit. Their contribution to the early part of the war should not be underestimated or forgotten. General Willcocks later published a book, *The Indian Corps in France*, and he asked Lord Curzon, the Viceroy, to write an introduction. Curzon struck an accurate and properly elegiac note:

Neither should we forget the conditions under which Indian soldiers served. They came to a country where the climate, the language, the people, the customs, were entirely different from any of which they had knowledge. They were presently faced with the sharp severity of a Northern winter. They, who had never suffered heavy shellfire, who had no experience of high-explosive, who had never seen warfare in the air, who were totally ignorant of modern trench fighting, were exposed to all the latest and most scientific developments of the art of destruction .. . . They were plunged in surroundings which must have been intensely depressing to the spirit of man. Almost from the start they suffered shattering losses. In the face of these trials and difficulties, the cheerfulness, loyalty, the good discipline, the intrepid courage of these denizens of another clime, cannot be too highly praised.

The two British divisions involved in the Battle of Aubers Ridge, the 1st and the 8th, had already suffered terrible casualties in previous actions, especially the 1st. They had both now lost another 4000 men in a few hours. So grievous were their losses that they had to be withdrawn and reorganized. Following their casualties at Aubers Ridge these divisions were never quite the same. Although their losses were quickly made good by fresh drafts, there could be no question of these troops replacing the seasoned experienced regulars of the BEF. In his fascinating and moving book, *Morale: A Study of Men of Courage*, John Baynes emphasizes this point in a most telling way. He describes in detail the background of the 2nd Scottish Rifles, as the second battalion of the Cameronians were known, and how they were destroyed at Neuve Chapelle. This was a splendid regular battalion, where nearly every man had a minimum of five years' service and where most of them were mature men in their twenties, nearly all unmarried. Proud of their regiment and its traditions, they formed a tough, efficient battalion. After the losses sustained at Neuve Chapelle, it never regained the spirit and élan of the original battalion.

The offensive qualities of individual divisions were rarely debated in public, although, after the war, reports that certain battalions, brigades or divisions had performed less than creditably, either in attack or defence, emerged in memoirs and narratives. In private, of course, comments and comparisons were frequent. In 1917 Robert Graves was an instructor for a time at the notorious Bull Ring at Etaples. In the Instructors' Mess they talked freely about the reliability of various divisions in battle. Their short list of the best of the BEF divisions at this time comprised the 2nd, 7th, 29th and the Guards Division.

This view is corroborated by that experienced and cynical observer, C.E. Montague, who, in his bitter and scathing book, *Disenchantment*, published in 1922, commented that 'out of all of us sorry home troops, only the Guards division, two kilted divisions and three English ones could be said to know how to fight'.

It is fair to point out that it is highly unlikely that the 2nd and the 7th Divisions, had they been called upon, would have made any greater impact on the German defences at Aubers Ridge.

It is interesting, though depressing, to compare the results of the four British offensives in 1915 in terms of casualties and ground gained:

BATTLE	No of Divisions actually involved	Duration of battle (days)	Casualties	Ground gained
Neuve Chapelle March	4	3	12,892	1000 yards on front of 3000 yards
Aubers Ridge May	3	1	10,840	nil
Festubert May	6	10	16,648	600 yards on a front of 4000 yards
Loos Sept/October	10	19	60,000 (approx)	maximum penetration of 1½ miles; Loos captured and 8000 yards of enemy trenches seized

GERMAN CASUALTIES

As far as can be ascertained, the German casualties at Aubers Ridge were as follows:

Southern Sector

55 Regiment lost 611: 230 dead, 372 wounded and 9 missing out of a total strength of about 2500

57 Regiment lost 300 approx

Northern sector

The 6th Bavarian Reserve Infantry Division lost approximately 640: 294 dead and 246 wounded or missing. Of this total, 46 were from the 21 RIR and the remainder from the 16 RIR

Total German losses: 1551

PRESS COVERAGE

It is instructive to examine how the press reported the battle.

On Monday, 10 May *The Times* printed a brief communiqué from Sir John French:

> Our First Army attacked the enemy's lines between Bois Grenier and Festubert and gained the ground south-east of Festubert.

This is a paltry report of our first joint offensive with the French designed to achieve a major breakthrough, though its brevity is perhaps understandable given what happened on the day. The reference to ground being captured is illuminating. In fact, *The Times* had been concentrating quite properly on the Second Battle of Ypres still raging in the north. Yet even this desperate struggle was overshadowed on 10 May by the report of the sinking of the *Lusitania*. Torpedoed off the south-east coast of Ireland on 7 May by a German submarine, the liner sank with the loss of most of its 2000 passengers. A number of American citizens were drowned and the sinking was an emotional factor contributing to the decision of the United States to enter the war.

On the following day (11 May) *The Times* carried a brief item stating that there had been no further advance on Monday on the First Army front and that the fighting had been confined to artillery action. It was not until 12 May that Repington's account of the battle appeared.

The Times, 12 May 1915
From our Special Correspondent

The Fight for Aubers Ridge
Northern France, May 12th

. . . sufficient details of the action have now filtered through to give an idea in broad outline of the course of the battle. Our attack began on Saturday with a terrific bombardment of the German trenches on the hills. Then our whole line advanced, from Festubert and Neuve Chapelle to the Bois Grenier, with its centre in Laventie.

The right and the centre stormed the Aubers ridge, the left

made a direct advance on Haubourdin, the south-western suburb of Lille. The right and the centre carried the first line of the enemy's trenches without serious opposition. They had been pounded to a shapeless mass by our artillery fire and practically abandoned by the enemy.

The villages of Fromelles and Aubers fells into our hands. Our troops, amongst whom were the Indians, pressed on to the second line. They came under a withering fire from rifles and machine guns.

The enemy's infantry was massed in great force on their second line and had suffered little from our shells. These trenches were deep and reinforced with concrete, with underground galleries, giving almost complete immunity from shell fire. When our bombardment ceased and our infantry began the advance the enemy issued from these subterranean shelters, manned their battered surface trenches, and turned upon our advancing troops the concentrated fire of massed machine guns.

Our men fought like heroes in face of tremendous odds.

On the left our troops were successful. They almost reached Haubourdin. Then the enemy's counter-attack was launched upon them. A fresh force in great numbers debouched from Lille and stayed their progress. Slowly, and fighting hard, we were driven back.

But we retained a footing on the Aubers ridge and hold it still. Yesterday there was nothing but artillery fire.

This largely fictitious piece bore almost no relation to the course of the battle or its results. No doubt it cheered up the public, who were gratified to learn that our troops had managed to retain the footing gained on Aubers Ridge! Some perceptive readers, however, might have contrasted our total lack of penetration with the genuine initial success of the French offensive at Vimy Ridge, where our ally advanced south of Carency some three miles on a five-mile front on the first day.

The only mention in the popular press came a few days later with an evocative and fairly accurate piece in the *Daily Mail*. This dealt with the opening assault and would have brought little comfort to those grieving for the dead or to the close relatives of the survivors.

APPOINTMENTS AND DISAPPOINTMENTS

Subsequent careers of the senior commanders (British Army)

After yet another expensive failure at the Battle of Loos by the First Army in September, 1915, Sir John French's part in the offensive was strongly criticized. Criticism was intensified after the publication of his less than accurate dispatch in early November and it led to his leadership being finally discredited. Following intrigues by Haig and others who wished to see him go, French was eventually forced to resign in December. As from 1 January, 1916, he was officially succeeded as Commander-in-Chief of the Forces in France by General Sir Douglas Haig. As a sop, French was appointed to the undemanding post of Commander-in-Chief of Home Forces. From 1918 to 1921 he was an unsuccessful Lord Lieutenant of Ireland. In 1919 he published his unreliable memoirs, entitled *1914*, which only served to underline the maxim, *qui s'excuse, s'accuse*.

Of the three corps commanders:

Lieut-General Sir Henry Rawlinson Bt (1864–1925) was recommended by Haig as his successor as GOC, First Army, but the post went to Sir Charles Munro (see below). Rawlinson became commander of the Fourth Army and was responsible for the conduct of the Battle of the Somme (1916) and the Battle of Passchendaele (1917). After the war he was Commander-in-Chief, India.

Lieut-General Sir Charles Monro (1860–1929) was sent by Kitchener to report on the situation in the Dardanelles. After a lightning tour of the Gallipoli peninsula, he sensibly advised immediate evacuation, thus earning Churchill's jibe: 'He came, he saw, he capitulated'. He became commander of the First Army in 1916 and was later Commander-in-Chief, India from 1916 to 1920.

Lieut-General Sir J. Willcocks (1857–1926) was, much to his surprise, abruptly and unkindly dismissed by Haig for, so he gathered, 'lack of initiative and tactical skill'. He was replaced as commander of the Indian corps before the Battle of Loos by Lieut-General Sir C.A. Anderson, who had commanded the Meerut Division at Aubers Ridge.

Of the divisional commanders:

Lieut-General Sir C.A. Anderson (1857–1940), following the dissolution of the Indian Corps, was appointed in 1917 to command the Southern Army in India.

Major-General F.J. Davies (1864–1948) was replaced as commander of the 8th Division. There seems little doubt that Haig welcomed the opportunity of getting rid of Davies on the grounds of his division's supposed reluctance to pile fruitless attack upon fruitless attack. In the face of mishaps and disasters, Haig seems to have been a little too ready to look for scapegoats and to shift the blame for failure on to either the shoulders of his subordinates or inadequacies of supply. Two months before, he had been quick to blame Davies for his failure to advance at a critical point in the Battle of Neuve Chapelle, but had been forced to withdraw when Rawlinson, Davies's Corps Commander, admitted that the responsibility for this was his alone. General Davies returned to London and served as Military Secretary at the War Office from 1916 to 1919.

Major-General R.C.B. Haking (1862–1945) was not noted for his care of, or loyalty to, the troops under him and he received scant praise for his handling of the 1st Division in the battle. Haig, however, was impressed by his 'attacking spirit' and Haking was promoted to the command of XI Corps which he held until 1918. As a corps commander, his less attractive characteristics would be displayed on a larger and even more disastrous canvas a few months later at Loos. Here, in an infamous attack, he sent two inexperienced 'New Army' divisions into uncut wire and German machine guns in broad daylight. They suffered over 8000 casualties in three and a half hours.

Robert Graves has a pertinent story about his divisional commander in *Goodbye To All That*:

> Haking commands this division. He's the author of our standard text book, *Company Training*. The last shows have not been suitable ones for company commanders to profit by his directions. He came round this morning to an informal inspection of the battalion, and shook hands with the survivors (of Aubers Ridge). There were tears in his eyes. Sergeant Smith swore, half aloud: 'Bloody lot of use that is: busts up his bloody division, and then weeps over what's bloody left . . .'. It's said here that Haking told General French that the division's morale had gone completely. So far as I can see that is inaccurate; the division will fight all right, but with little enthusiasm.

Haking, who backed Haig in his manoeuvring to oust Sir John French, would have been given command of an army later in the war, but fortunately this proposal was vetoed by the War Office.

After Aubers Ridge, Loos and another attack at Fromelles in 1916 involving the 4th Australian Division, Haking was given the nickname 'Butcher'. Any hopes that he may have cherished of further promotion were not to be realized. Quite the opposite. Minutes of a meeting of the War Cabinet held on 11 April, 1918, reveal the following, under the heading of 'Retention of Incompetent Officers':

> The Prime Minister said that he had that afternoon received a deputation from the Liberal War Committee, who had been firm supporters of the war, during the previous and present Administrations. They had made very serious protests against the retention of officers whom they considered incompetent, and had particularly named General Gough and General Haking. The latter, he understood, commanded the Army Corps in the region of Béthune, which was now in retreat.

Major-General H. de la P. Gough (1870–1963) was promoted to the command of I Corps in 1916 and later commanded the Fifth Army from 1916 to 1918. His army was overwhelmed by the German onslaught in March, 1918, and he was relieved of his command by Haig.

Major-General H.S. Horne (1861–1929), after service in Egypt defending the Suez Canal, returned to the Western Front in 1916 to command XV Corps. During the Battle of the Somme he gained a reputation as a hard-driving commander and a few months later, in October, he was given command of the First Army.

Of the brigade commanders directly involved:
None was to have such a glittering career as *Brigadier C.W. Jacob* (1863–1948) of the Dehra Dun Brigade. He took over the Meerut Division from Anderson and Haig later promoted him to command II Corps from 1916 until 1919. Enjoying the confidence of his men, unafraid to speak his mind and receptive to new ideas, Field Marshal Sir Claud Jacob succeeded Rawlinson as Commander-in-Chief, India in 1925.

Brigadier G.H. Thesiger (1868–1915) (2nd Brigade) was promoted to command the 9th (Scottish) Division, but was killed on the second day of the offensive at Loos.

Brigadier H.R. Davies (1865–1950) (3rd Brigade) later commanded the 11th Division. He was the brother of Major-General F.J. Davies, 8th Division.

Brigadier R.J. Pinney (1863–1943) (23rd Brigade) later commanded the 33rd Division.

Brigadier R.S. Oxley (1863–1951) (24th Brigade) was sent home in July, 1916, during the Battle of the Somme for the alleged failure of his brigade to hold Contalmaison on 7 July when its ammunition and grenades ran out and it was bombed out by the Germans, suffering 800 casualties in the process. There may have been an element of personal antagonism in his dismissal, stemming from earlier rivalry with Haig at the Staff College. Oxley served as DA and QMG from 1916 to 1919.

Appendices

1. Extract from the Order of the Battle of the First Army: Aubers Ridge, 1915
2. Extract from the German Order of Battle: Aubers Ridge, 1915
3. I Corps Operation Order No. 79 of 7 May, 1915
4. Extracts from the War Diary of the 2nd Battalion, Royal Sussex Regiment for May, 1915
5. The War Diary of the 2/2nd Gurkhas for 9 May, 1915
6. The war establishment of an infantry division in April, 1915

Appendix 1

Extract from:
ORDER OF BATTLE
FIRST ARMY
AUBERS RIDGE 1915

Commander	General Sir D. Haig KCB KCIE KCVO ADC
Br.-[Major-]General, General Staff	Br.-[Major-]General R.H.K. Butler
D A and Q M G	Br.-[Major-]General P.E.F. Hobbs CB CMG
Major-General, Royal Artillery	Major-General H.F. Mercer CB ADC
Chief Engineer	Major-General S.R. Rice CB

I CORPS

Commander	Lieut.-Gen. Sir C.C. Monro KCB
Br.-General, General Staff	Br.-Gen. R.D. Whigham CB DSO
D A and Q M G	Br.-Gen. H.N. Sargent DSO
Br.-General, Royal Artillery	Br.-Gen. R.A.K. Montgomery CB DSO
Chief Engineer	Br.-Gen. C. Godby

1ST DIVISION: Major-Gen. R.C.B. Haking
1st (Guards) Brigade: Br.-Gen. H.C. Lowther
1/Coldstream Gds   1/Black Watch   1/14th London (London Scottish) (TF)
1/Scots Gds   1/Camerons
2nd Brigade: Br.-Gen. G.H. Thesiger
2/R. Sussex   1/L.N. Lancs.   1/9th King's (TF)
1/Northamptonshire   2/KRRC   1/5th R. Sussex (TF)
3rd Brigade: Br.-Gen. H.R. Davies
1/SWB   2/Welsh   1/4th R. Welch Fus. (TF)
1/Gloucestershire   2/R. Mun. Fus.
RFA Bdes
XXV (118, 114, 115 Btys)   XXXIX (46, 51, 54 Btys)
XXVI (116, 117 Btys)
Field Coys, RE: 23, 26 & 1/1st Lowland (TF)
Mtd Troops: B Sqdn, Northumberland Hrs (Yeo.) Cyclist Coy

2ND DIVISION: Major-Gen. H.S. Horne

IV CORPS

Commander	Lieut.-Gen. Sir H.S. Rawlinson Bt KCB CVO
D A and Q M G	Br.-Gen. A.G. Dallas CB
Br.-General, Royal Artillery	Br.-Gen. A.H. Hussey CB
Chief Engineer	Br.-Gen. R.U.H. Buckland CB ADC

7TH DIVISION: Major-Gen. H. de la P. Gough

20th Brigade: Br.Gen. F.J. Heyworth
1/Grenadier Gds   2/Border   1/6th Gordons (TF)
2/Scots Gds   2/Gordons
21st Brigade: Br.-Gen. G.E. Watts
2/Bedfordshire   2/R. Scots Fus.   1/4th Camerons (TF)
2/Green Howards   2/Wiltshire
22nd Brigade: Br.-Gen. S.T.B. Lawford
2/Queen's   1/R. Welch Fus.   1/8th R. Scots (TF)
2/R. Warwickshire   1/S. Staffordshire
RHA Bde: XIV (F & T Btys)
RFA Bdes
XXII (104, 105, 106 Btys)   55th Bty of
XXXV (12, 25, 58 Btys)   XXXVII (How.) Bde
Field Coys, RE: 54, 55 & 1/2nd Highland (TF)
Mtd Troops: H Q & A Sqdn, Northumberland Hrs (Yeo.), Cyclist Coy

8TH DIVISION: Major-Gen. F.J. Davies

23rd Brigade: Br.-Gen. R.J. Pinney
2/Devonshire   2/Scottish Rifles   1/6th Scottish Rifles (TF)
2/W. Yorkshire   2 Middlesex   1/7th Middlesex (TF)
24th Brigade: Br.-Gen. R.S. Oxley
1/Worcestershire   1/Sherwood Foresters   1/5th Black Watch (TF)
2/E. Lancashire   2/Northamptonshire
25th Brigade: Br.-Gen. A.W.G. Lowry Cole
2/Lincolnshire   1/R. Irish Rifles   1/1st London (TF)
2/R. Berkshire   2/Rifle Brigade   1/13th London (TF)
RHA Bde: V (O & Z Btys)
RFA Bdes
XXXIII (32, 33, 36 Btys) XXXVII (How.) 31 & 35 Btys
XLV (1, 3, 5 Btys)
Field Coys, RE: 2, 15 & 1/1st Home Counties (TF)
Mtd Troops: C Sqdn, Northumberland Hrs (Yeo.), Cyclist Coy

INDIAN CORPS

Commander	Lieut.-Gen. Sir J. Willcocks KCB KCSI KCMG DSO
Br.-General, General Staff	Br.-Gen. H. Hudson, CB CIE
D A and Q M G	Br.-Gen. A.S. Cobbe VC DSO
Br.-General, Royal Artillery	Br.-Gen. A.B. Scott CB DSO
Chief Engineer	Br.-Gen. H.C. Nanton CB

MEERUT DIVISION: Lieut.-Gen. Sir C.A. Anderson KCB
Dehra Dun Brigade: Br.-Gen C.W. Jacob

181

1/Seaforths	2/2nd Gurkhas	1/4th Seaforths (TF)
6th Jats	1/9th Gurkhas	

Garhwal Brigade: Br.-Gen. C.G. Blackader

2/Leicestershire	2/3rd Gurkhas	1/3rd London (TF)
39th Garhwalis	2/8th Gurkhas	

Bareilly Brigade: Br.-Gen. W.M. Southey

2/Black Watch	58th Vaughan's Rifles	1/4th Black Watch (TF)
41st Dogras	125th Napier's Rifles	

RFA Bdes

IV (7, 14, 66 Btys)	XIII (2, 8, 44 Btys)
IX (19, 20, 28 Btys)	30th Bty of XLIII (How.) Bde

Engineers: 3 & 4 Coys, 1st Sappers and Miners

Pioneers: 107th Pioneers

Mtd Troops: 4th Cavalry

LAHORE DIVISION: Major-Gen. H.D'U. Keary

ROYAL FLYING CORPS

1st Wing: Lieut.-Colonel H.M Trenchard

Nos. 2, 3, 16 Squadrons

Appendix 2

GERMAN ORDER OF BATTLE
AUBERS RIDGE 1915
Sixth Army (part of)

Commander: Crown Prince Rupprecht of Bavaria
Chief of the Staff: Major-General Krafft von Dellmensingen
VII Corps (General von Claer):
13th Division (Lieut-General von dem Borne):
    25th Brigade: 13th and 158th Regiments
    26th Brigade: 15th and 55th Regiments

14th Division (Lieut-General von Ditfurth):
    27th Brigade: 16th and 53rd Regiments
    79th Brigade: 56th and 57th Regiments

Corps Troops: 11th Jäger Battalion
6th Bavarian Reserve Division (Lieut-General von Scanzoni):
    12th Bavarian Reserve Brigade: 16th and 17th Bavarian Res.
    Regts
    14th Bavarian Reserve Brigade: 20th, 21st and 9th Bavarian Res.
    Regts

Appendix 3

I CORPS OPERATION ORDER No. 79

7th May 1915

1. The First Army will advance tomorrow with the object of breaking through the enemy's line and gaining the La Bassée–Lille road between La Bassée and Fournes.

Its further advance will be directed on the line Bauvin-Don.

Two Cavalry Corps and three divisions are being held in readiness as a general reserve under the orders of the Field Marshal Commanding-in-Chief to exploit any success.

2. The I Corps is to attack from the Rue du Bois and advance on Rue du Marais-Illies, maintaining its right at Givenchy and Cuinchy.

3. The Indian Corps is to attack on the left of the I Corps and is to capture the Distillery and the Ferme du Biez. Its subsequent advance will be directed on Ligny le Grand-La Cliqueterie Farm.

The road Ferme du Biez–Ligny le Petit–Ligny le Grand is assigned to the Indian Corps.

4. The 1st Division will attack from its breastworks in front of the Rue du Bois.

Its first objectives are:

Hostile trenches P8–P10, the road junction P15 and the road thence to La Tourelle.

Its subsequent advance will be directed on Rue du Marais–Lorgies, a defensive flank being organized from P4 by La Quinque Rue to Rue du Marais.

Touch will be maintained with the Indian Corps throughout.

5. The infantry under GOC London Division holding the defen-

sive front north of Festubert will be prepared to relieve the infantry of the 1st Division at P4 La Quinque Rue and Rue du Marais, when those points have been secured, and to take advantage of any weakening of the enemy about the Rue d'Ouvert to occupy that locality.

6. The 2nd Division (less 4th Guards Brigade) with Motor Machine Gun Battery attached, will be in Corps Reserve in the area Loisne-Le Touret-Le Hamel in readiness to continue to advance. The troops of 1st Division must be clear of above area by 3.30 am.

7. The 5th London Brigade will be in First Army Reserve, about Essars and Les Choquaux (1 mile SW of Locon), from 5 am.

8. The 1st Battn Queen's Regt (less two companies) will be under the direct orders of the Corps Commander north of Béthune.

9. The artillery will complete such registration as may be necessary by 5 am at which hour the preliminary bombardment will begin in accordance with special instructions already issued as to times and objectives.

GOC London Division will arrange for wire-cutting batteries and machine guns to open fire on enemy's wire opposite Festubert and Cuinchy at 4.45 am.

10. At 5.40 am the infantry of the 1st Division will assault. The troops under GOC London Division will at the same time open a vigorous fire attack along their entire front.

11. Advanced I Corps HQ will be established at W.30.a.7.8 (on the Locon Road 1½ miles from Béthune) at 4 pm today.

R. WHIGHAM, Br.-General
General Staff, I Corps

Issued at 11.30 am

Appendix 4

Extracts from the War Diary of 2nd Battalion,
Royal Sussex Regiment

7th May
LES FACONS
Received orders for an assault on the German lines opposite
RICHEBOURG L'AVOUE to take place on the morning of the 8th.
Remained in LES FACONS making necessary arrangements for the
next day. 7 pm just as we were moving off to RICHEBOURG received
orders that the attack had been postponed 24 hours and we were
to remain where we were for that night.

8th May
LES FACONS – RICHEBOURG L'AVOUE
Remained at LES FACONS all day and moved up to RICHEBOURG
L'AVOUE in the evening. On arrival took over breastworks from
BLACK WATCH. During the night, bombs and wooden bridges were
drawn for crossing the stream in front of our line. 5 Sappers
(Mining experts) joined our two companies which were going to
lead the attack in order to cut the wires of any mines in German
lines, when we had captured them.

Capts Villiers and St Croix were wounded in the RUE DU BOIS
on the way up.

9th May
RICHEBOURG L'AVOUE
The day started with an issue of tea and rum at 3.30 am.
Battalion limits with regard to enemy's first line trenches, R8 to VI.
Frontage of Bn about 400 yards. Bn left on Cinder track.

Bombardment commenced at 5 am. At this hour the Battalion was distributed as follows:

1st Line of Breastworks –	C Company right
	D Company left
2nd Line of Breastworks –	A Company right
	B Company left
	(less 1 platoon, No.8)

No. 8 platoon under 2nd Lt. F.T. Goring attached to Lowland Coy RE in breastworks immediately behind the RUE DU BOIS.
Machine-guns were distributed as follows:
2 on extreme left of Bn line. One of these guns remained in this position throughout. 2 guns about 100 yards to the left of Bn right. Battn Headquarters at telephone near right flank of Battalion, in front breastwork. At 5.30 am an intense bombardment commenced and two platoons of C and D Coys respectively advanced over the parapet.

First line from right to left being formed by No.9 Platoon (2nd Lt. Fewtrell), 11 Platoon (Sgt Reeves), 15 Platoon (2nd Lt. Roberts), 16 Platoon (Sgt Dray), and were closely followed by the second line formed by 10 Platoon (Sgt Startup), 12 Platoon (2nd Lt. Taylor), 13 Platoon (2nd Lt. Child), 14 Platoon (Sgt Lower). The advance over the parapet was made in line except by 15 and 13 Platoons which crossed the parapet at a particular spot which afforded some cover.

At the same time A Coy advanced from second line of breastworks on the top of the ground, the two platoons in front being No. 3 (2nd Lt. Shaw) right, and No. 2 Platoon (Sgt Catchpole) left, followed respectively by No. 4 Platoon (Lt. Dicker) and No. 1 Platoon (2nd Lt. Talbot) at a distance of about 50 yards.

A Coy's advance was in column of sections to a flank at deploying interval. When 3 and 2 Platoons left the rear breastwork, the outer platoons filed inwards behind the breastwork, thus getting into position behind the leading platoons before they advanced. Meanwhile, B Coy's three platoons, advancing from the 2nd-line breastworks to the first line by the left communication trench having started two minutes before the advertised time (5.28 am) in order to allow of their reaching the first line at the same time as A Company.

Of these companies, the whole of A followed C over the breastworks, and two platoons of B Coy followed D Coy. These were No.

6 Platoon (2nd Lt. Miller) right, and No. 5 Platoon (2nd Lt. Juckes) left.

No. 7 Platoon (2nd Lt. Wallington) was ordered to remain behind the front breastworks by OC B Coy (Capt. C E Bond DSO). The Machine Gun Officer had given orders for two machine guns to go forward with the leading Coys' line, one from each flank, and the other two guns were to advance in a similar manner with the supporting Coy's 2nd line. Both guns were only to move if substantial progress was being made. The two right guns actually went forward, but the two left guns remained in their original position except that one of these was moved about 15 yards to the left front, to a listening post. This gun was withdrawn to its original position after firing for about a quarter of an hour.

No. 8 Platoon advancing with a section of Lowland Coy RE on the top of the ground reached the left portion of the first-line breastworks just after No. 7 Platoon. It appears that through some misunderstanding an order was passed that the sappers should advance over the breastworks. Many did so, being shortly afterwards recalled, but not before they had suffered several casualties. No. 8 Platoon carried sand bags, barbed wire for making good the enemy's position if taken.

Before our supporting companies were clear of the first-line breastworks, the 5th Bn Royal Sussex Regt arrived, many of them going straight over the breastworks and becoming mingled with our men.

The following arrangements had been made with regard to Bombers by 2nd Lt. Austin, commdg D Company – Bombers of 14 and 15 Platoons were to collect at V1 when enemy's first line was reached with the intention to bomb the enemy out of the communication trench in rear. C Coy's bombers were distributed, one with each of sections. Sgt Startup having orders to supervise the work of these bombers as occasion offered on arriving at enemy's first line. B Coy's bombers were with their platoons except those of No. 8 (attached to RE) who were attached to No. 6 Platoon (2nd Lt. Miller). A Coy's bombers were grouped near their respective Platoon commanders. The leading Coys, C and D, carried bridges and ladders. C Coy 5 bridges and 2 ladders. D Coy 6 bridges and 2 ladders.

From information collected it appears that on the right Capt. R.F. Finke, C Coy was hit early in the action but continued to lead his men. The same is also reported of 2nd Lt. Taylor, C Coy, who was leading C Coy's 2nd line. 2nd Lt. Fewtrell, leading C Coy's first line, advanced to within about 40 yards of the enemy's wire. Capt. Finch, Commdg A Coy, also reached this line.

2nd Lt. Shaw was wounded whilst leading his platoon and was subsequently killed whilst endeavours were being made to bring him back.

Lieut. Dicker and 2nd Lt. Talbot were both wounded.

The right of our line was subjected to enfilade fire from Machine Guns.

On the left 2nd Lt. Austin, D Coy appears to have been hit early in the engagement, leaving 2nd Lt. Roberts in command of D Coy's first line – 2nd Lt. Roberts was wounded and 2nd Lt. Child, in command of D Coy's 2nd line, was killed. Coy Sgt Major Butcher assumed command and ordered the first line to dig themselves in. Of B Coy, 2nd Lt. Miller and 2 Lt. Juckes were both hit.

The left suffered very severely from enfilade fire from an angle in the German trench opposite the Munster Fusiliers, the early retirement of this Bn leaving our left flank in the air, in general the centre of gravity of the assaulting troops did not get much more than 150 yards, or about half way to the German breastworks, though a portion succeeded in getting within about 40 yards of it, and one man appears to have reached the parapet itself.

Flags were carried to denote the position of Companies.

The German fired from loopholes low down in the parapet.

At 6.30 am orders were given to withdraw behind our first breastworks, under cover of reopened bombardment. D Coy's first line seems to have received this order, but not C Coy's. Several men managed to get back during the day but some remained till dark, a few joining in the assault by the 1st Brigade delivered in the afternoon.

The two machine guns on the right were got back and three out of the four machine guns and what remained of the Battalion were returned to a line of breastworks behind the Rue du Bois, the fourth Machine Gun by request remained up in the first line till late in the afternoon.

Our casualties were:

Killed

Officers 2)   2 Lt. R.T. Shaw
             2 Lt. S.W.S. Child

Wounded

9)   Capt. E.F. Villiers
       Capt. de St Croix
       2 Lt. Fewtrell
         Lt. Dicker
       2 Lt. Miller
       2 Lt. Roberts
       2 Lt. Talbot
       2 Lt. Taylor
       2 Lt. Green

Missing

3)   Capt. R.F. Finke
       2 Lt. T.R. Juckes
       2 Lt. O. Austin

Other Ranks: Killed – 101 Wounded – 329 Missing – 118
Total: 14 Officers 548 Rank and File

Appendix 5

WAR DIARY: 2/2nd GURKHAS
Operations of 9 May, 1915

The orders issued were that at 5.32 am the assaulting companies, including the detachment of the 6th Jats, attached to this battalion, were to jump the parapet, occupy positions on the far side in column of platoons, and assault the German trenches at 5.39.

In order to facilitate the crossing of the stream in our immediate front the battalion scouts were sent out the night before to lay 17 bridges distributed at intervals along the front. The little wire existing was also cut.

In accordance with orders as above the assaulting companies on the right and the 6th Jats' detachment commenced to cross the parapet.

The company on the left was commencing to cross the parapet, when machine guns commenced to play on them. This, together with the fact that our own shells were falling close to our own parapet, necessitated the postponement of the assault till immediately before the conclusion of the bombardment of the enemy trenches. At 5.39, therefore, the left company crossed the parapet.

The whole line was immediately subjected to a very accurate machine-gun fire, and a number of casualties occurred.

The advance on the right continued, and the supporting company commenced to follow. On the left, however, the advance was arrested by the OC 4th Seaforths, who decided that it was impossible to advance further and ordered Captain Colenso, commander of the left company, to halt.

Meanwhile, I received a message that this had occurred, and the line was advised to halt. The OC 4th Seaforths came up and told me that it was quite impossible for his battalion to advance, and also that he had ordered my left company to halt. Captain Twiss arrived shortly afterwards and I told him what had occurred.

The OC 4th Seaforths then proceeded to Brigade Report Centre himself. While this was occurring, my reserve company was filing into the line trench with a view to getting ready to advance.

I noticed that we had already suffered a number of casualties, and the machine guns from about Point 59 were very active.

I was also informed that all British Officers who had crossed the parapet had been either killed or wounded.

Those men who had crossed the parapet were now lying down on both sides of the ditch in front.

Between 8 and 9 am I received another order to make another push. I issued all orders and was prepared to jump the parapet, when a signaller ran down to me from the signal station saying that I was to halt and come to the telephone at once. I was then ordered not to advance till further orders.

My order not to advance was too late to prevent part of my reserve company from crossing the parapet, led by Major Rooke. While at the telephone I was informed that Major Rooke had been killed.

Men of the reserve company carried forward the line, and some 8 or 10 men succeeded in getting within about 20 yards of the German trench. Two of these ultimately got into the trench.

It was noticed soon after this that the Germans were disorganized and could be seen retiring to their left.

I then went down to the OC 2/Welsh Regiment and asked him if he was game to storm the trenches with my battalion. He informed me that he had orders not to advance, and that his battalion was to be relieved by another one.

At some subsequent period (I regret that I cannot remember the time) I was asked to make another advance. I replied that I considered it essential for the battalion on my right to advance with me and asked whether these orders to attack were to stand good.

I was informed after a delay of ten minutes that the order had been cancelled.

Meantime, our machine guns and men lining the parapet were keeping up a heavy fire on the enemy and appeared to be doing some damage. About this time the German guns opened onto our parapets. The Germans then reinforced from the direction of the 'Keep' and opened up heavy rifle fire onto our parapets.

I may mention here that though our heavy guns had greatly damaged the enemy's parapet, a number of our own shells fell extremely near and some into our own trenches.

Orders were then received to consolidate the line. The trenches were cleared of casualties and repaired as far as possible.

About midday, I received orders that we were to be relieved by the Black Watch, and the battalion was to be withdrawn.

This was carried out without further casualties.

When the battalion was withdrawn there were between 200 and 250 men missing. About a hundred of these managed to get back during the course of the afternoon and night.

Major Commanding,
2nd Gurkhas
E.R.P. Boileau

Appendix 6

The table below shows the components of a division on the Western Front in April 1915 and their war establishment.

Infantry Division, April 1915

Divisional HQ
Infantry:

> 3 brigades, consisting of 12 Infantry battalions, with 4 machine guns each

Mounted Troops:

> 1 Cavalry squadron, 1 Cyclist company

Artillery:

> HQ, Divisional Artillery
> > 3 Field Artillery brigades (12 batteries – 18-pdr QF)
> > 1 Field Artillery brigade (4 batteries – 4.5-inch howitzer)
> > 1 Heavy battery (4x60-pdr BL)
> > 1 Divisional Ammunition Column

Engineers:

> HQ, Divisional Engineers
> > 3 Field companies

Signal Service:

> 1 Signal company

Pioneers:
        1 Pioneer battalions (4 machine guns)
        3 Field Ambulances
        1 Sanitary section
        1 Mobile Veterinary section
        1 Motor Ambulance Workshop
        1 Divisional Train

All Ranks	19,614
Horses and Mules	5818
Guns	68
18-pdr QF	48
4.5 Howitzer	16
60-pdr BL	4
Machine guns (Vickers)	52
Carts and Vehicles	958
Cycles	538
Motor Cycles	19
Motor Cars	11
Motor Lorries	4
Motor Ambulance Cars	21

Select Bibliography

Atkinson, C.T., *The Seventh Division 1914–1918*, John Murray, 1927

Beaverbrook, Lord, *Politicians and the War (1914–1916)*, Oldbourne Book Co. Ltd, 1960

Blunden, Edmund, *Undertones of War*, Richard Cobden-Sanderson, 1928

Boraston, J.H. and Bax, C.E.O., *The Eighth Division in War, 1914–1918*, The Medici Society, 1928

Charteris, Brigadier-General J. *Field Marshal Earl Haig*, Cassell, 1929

Clark, Alan, *The Donkeys*, Hutchinson, 1961

Edmonds, Sir J.E., *History of the Great War based on Official Documents, Military Operations. France and Belgium 1915, Vol. IV*, Macmillan, 1928

French, J.D.P., 1st Earl of Ypres, *1914*, Constable, 1919

Graves, Robert, *Goodbye To All That*, Cassell, 1927

George, D. Lloyd., *War Memoirs*, Nicholson and Watson, 1933–6

Holmes, Richard, *The Little Field Marshal, Sir John French*, Jonathan Cape, 1981

General Jack's Diary, ed. John Terraine, Eyre and Spottiswoode, 1964

Kearsey, Lieut.-Colonel A, *1915 Campaign in France*, Gale and Polden, 1929

Merewether, Lieut.-Colonel J.W.B. and Smith, Rt Hon. Sir Frederick, *The Indian Corps in France*, John Murray, 1917

Nash, D.B. *Imperial German Army Handbook*, Ian Allan, 1980

Terraine, John, *Douglas Haig: The Educated Soldier*, Hutchinson, 1963

Wauchope, A.G., *The Black Watch 1914–1919*, The Medici Society, 1925

Willcocks, General Sir James, *With The Indians in France*, Constable, 1920

Index